"Written by psychoanalytic scholars, researchers and clinicians, the publication presents a transformative multidimensional view of women's experience in a cultural context of a patriarchal society. In exploring dynamics of complex interactivity of biological, cultural and intropsychic factors, psychoanalytic theory is used to conceptualize the issues, as well as to offer novel ways to address them. By putting the inseparable link between the functioning female body and female psychological development at the center, the book takes the conversation on femininity and female development as primary to another level, towards true internal and external emancipation."

—**Eva D. Papiasvili, PhD, ABPP**, Co-Chair for North America of the International Psychoanalytical Association's Encyclopedic Dictionary of Psychoanalysis Task Force.

"This is a unique, important, and powerful book which has provided these authors with a unique platform from which to speak and be heard. The title calls our attention to and plays on Virginia Woolf's 1928 classic *A Room of One's Own*, which was a call to action for women writers to acknowledge and free themselves from the dominance of men in the literary world. As in this book, Woolf was critiquing the difference between the idealized position of women as objects and their experience of being silenced as subjects. This book takes Virginia Wolf's call for action to important new psychological levels, not centering the conversation in the usual abstract postmodern discourse, but speaking directly from women's bodies, their womb, their sexuality, and their ever present consciousness of rape as a crushing act of personal and political power. As a man, I did not feel talked down to but rather included in difficult and painful conversations including: choosing to become a mother or not; struggles with infertility; adoption; hooking up; and finding personal and communal voices through which to speak after being crushed and silenced by rape. I was quite moved by this book and began looking at women and their experience from a different, more truly egalitarian perspective. I enthusiastically recommend this book to women who will feel affirmed, recognized and empowered, and to men who will have a deeper appreciation for women as full subjects rather than simply as idealized mothers or fantasy sexual beings."

—**Joseph Newirth**, Derner Institute of Advanced Psychological Studies, Adelphi University and former Director, Postdoctoral Program in Psychoanalysis and Psychotherapy, NYU; author of *Between Emotion and Cognition: The Generative Unconscious*.

A WOMB OF HER OWN

Gender- and body-based distinctions continue to be a defining component of women's identities, both in psychoanalytic treatment and in life. Although females have made progress in many areas, their status within the human community has remained unstable and subject to societal whim. *A Womb of Her Own* brings together a distinguished group of contributors to explore, from a psychoanalytic perspective, the ways in which women's sexual and reproductive capabilities, and their bodies, are regarded as societal and patriarchal property, not as the possession of individual women. It further examines how women have been viewed as the "other" and thus become the focus of mistreatment such as rape, sexual slavery, restriction of reproduction rights, and ongoing societal repression.

Postmodern gender theories have greatly enhanced understanding of the fluidity of gender and freed women from repressive stereotypes, but attention has shifted prematurely from the power differential that continues to exist between men and women. Before the male/female binary is transcended, the limitations imposed upon women by the still prevailing patriarchal order must be addressed. To this end, *A Womb of Her Own* addresses issues such as the prevalence of rape culture and its historical roots; the relationship of the LGBTQ movement to feminism; current sexual practices such as sexting and tattooing and their meaning to women; reproductive issues including infertility, adoption, postpartum depression, and the actual experience of birthing—all from the perspectives of women. The book also explores the cultural definitions of motherhood, and how such definitions set exacting standards both for the acceptable face of motherhood and for women generally.

Though women's unique anatomy and biology have historically contributed to their oppression in a patriarchal society, it is the exploration and illumination of these capabilities from their own perspective that will allow women to claim and control them as their own. Covering a broad, topical range of contemporary subjects, *A Womb of Her Own* will appeal to psychoanalysts, psychoanalytic psychotherapists, as well as scholars and students of gender and women's studies.

Ellen L.K. Toronto is in private practice in Ann Arbor, Michigan. She is co-editor of *Psychoanalytic Reflections on a Gender-free Case: Into the Void* (Routledge, 2005), the author of *Family Entanglement* (CreateSpace, 2013), and writes a weekly parenting blog for PsychCentral.

JoAnn Ponder, PhD, is a psychologist and psychoanalyst in private practice in Austin, Texas.

Kristin Davisson, PsyD, is a clinical psychologist in private practice in Chicago, Illinois.

Maurine Kelber Kelly, PhD, FIPA, is a training and supervising analyst with the Contemporary Freudian Society and served as adjunct faculty member in the PsyD program at The George Washington University, Washington D.C.

A WOMB OF HER OWN

Women's Struggle for Sexual and Reproductive Autonomy

Edited by Ellen L.K. Toronto, JoAnn Ponder, Kristin Davisson, and Maurine Kelber Kelly

Routledge
Taylor & Francis Group

LONDON AND NEW YORK

First published 2017
by Routledge
2 Park Square, Milton Park, Abingdon, Oxon OX14 4RN

and by Routledge
711 Third Avenue, New York, NY 10017

Routledge is an imprint of the Taylor & Francis Group, an informa business

British Library Cataloguing-in-Publication Data
A catalogue record for this book is available from the British Library

Library of Congress Cataloging-in-Publication Data
Names: Toronto, Ellen L. K., editor. | Ponder, JoAnn, editor. |
    Davisson, Kristin, editor. | Maurine Kelber Kelly, editor.
Title: A womb of her own : women's struggle for sexual and reproductive
    autonomy / edited by Ellen Toronto, JoAnn Ponder, Kristin Davisson and
    Maurine Kelber Kelly.
Description: New York : Routledge, 2017. | Includes bibliographical
    references and index.
Identifiers: LCCN 2016033813 | ISBN 9781138194960
    (hardback : alk. paper) | ISBN 9781138194977 (pbk. : alk. paper) |
    ISBN 9781315532578 (e-book)
Subjects: LCSH: Sex (Psychology) | Gender identity—Psychological
    aspects. | Women and psychoanalysis. | Feminist therapy. | Motherhood.
Classification: LCC BF175.5.S48 W66 2017 | DDC 155.3/33—dc23
LC record available at https://lccn.loc.gov/2016033813

ISBN: 978-1-138-19496-0 (hbk)
ISBN: 978-1-138-19497-7 (pbk)
ISBN: 978-1-315-53257-8 (ebk)

Typeset in Bembo
by Apex CoVantage, LLC

Our book is dedicated to those women for whom anatomy has meant—not destiny—but unacknowledged grief and suffering. Our intent is to bring into public consciousness the experiences of oppression, rape and sexual assault, infertility, pregnancy loss, birthing, and postpartum depression in ways that fully acknowledge both women's suffering and their inner strength

"give her a room of her own and five hundred a year, let her speak her mind ...
and she will write a better book one of these days."

Virginia Woolf. *A Room of One's Own.*

CONTENTS

NOTES ON CONTRIBUTORS

Adi Avivi, PsyD, is a clinical psychologist in New York City where she has been working with disenfranchised populations in inpatient and outpatient hospital settings. She graduated from Long Island University—Post Campus's clinical psychology doctoral program, focusing her studies on severe mental illness, multiculturalism, and women's issues, including political and economic components influencing women's psyches and identities. Her dissertation examined internet communication among childfree women. After graduation, Dr. Avivi completed fellowships involving justice, leadership, and service disparity. She is a board member of NYSPA's Division of Culture, Race, and Ethnicity and mentors doctoral candidates at LIU Post.

Meredith Darcy, LCSW-R, is a licensed psychotherapist in private practice in New York City. She received her Master's Degree of Social Work from Columbia University and completed her psychoanalytic training at The William Alanson White Institute in Spring 2016. Darcy has specialized in working with patients with eating disorders, and with children and adolescents. Currently her practice focuses on women's issues, motherhood, somatic responses, and attachment. She has written and presented papers nationally at psychoanalytic conferences focusing on the therapist's affect, experience, and the body.

Kristin Davisson, PsyD, is a clinical psychologist in private practice in Chicago, IL, is current President of Section III of Division 39 (Women, Gender & Psychoanalysis), and is an Assistant Adjunct Professor at the Chicago School of Professional Psychology. She is the former recipient of Division 39, Section III's Dissertation Award and Division 39, Early Career Committee's Scholar Award and is a former fellow at the Chicago Center for Psychoanalysis. She has served on the Board of Section III since 2013 and is a member of the Early Career Committee of Division

39. Her areas of specialty include gendered experiences of trauma, childhood abuse, identity conflicts, multicultural issues, and self-image concerns among women. Kristindavissonpsyd.com

Katie Gentile, PhD, is Associate Professor of Counseling and Director of the Gender Studies Program at John Jay College of Criminal Justice (City University of New York). She is the author of *Creating Bodies: Eating Disorders as Self-Destructive Survival* and *The Business of Being Made: Integrating Cultural and Psychoanalytic Theories to Explore the Production of Temporalities in Assisted Reproductive Technologies*, both from Routledge. She is a co-editor of the journal *Studies in Gender and Sexuality* and on the editorial board of *Women's Studies Quarterly*. She has published numerous journal articles and book chapters on eating disorders and sexual and racial/cultural violence, intimate partner violence, participatory action research and collaborative methodologies, and the cultural and psychic production of temporalities around reproduction and fetal personhood. She is on the faculty of New York University's Postdoctoral Program in Psychotherapy and Psychoanalysis and in private practice in New York City.

Susan Kavaler-Adler, PhD, ABPP DLitt, NCPsyA, is a Psychologist-Psychoanalyst and a Training and Supervising Analyst in practice for 40 years. She is a Fellow of the American Board and Academy of Psychoanalysis and is Founder and Executive Director of the Object Relations Institute, a state chartered psychoanalytic institute in New York City. Dr. Kavaler-Adler is the author of five published books and sixty-five articles. She's won fifteen awards for her writing, including a Gradiva Award from NAAP in 2004 for *Mourning, Spirituality and Psychic Change: A New Object Relations View of Psychoanalysis* (Routledge, 2003). Dr. Kavaler-Adler integrates British and American theory for the most potent form of clinical work. Her latest Karnac books are *The Anatomy of Regret* (2013) and *The Klein–Winnicott Dialectic* (2014). She has monthly groups in meditation, mourning, therapy, roleplaying supervision, and in writing and creative process. www.kavaleradler.com; drkavaleradler@gmail.com

Maurine Kelber Kelly, PhD, FIPA, has, after earning a BA in History and an MS in English and teaching English in high schools and junior colleges, earned an MA and PhD at the University of Pennsylvania. Her first position as Assistant Dean and Assistant Professor offered painful lessons in gay male misogyny. She is a Training and Supervising Analyst with the Contemporary Freudian Society, served as adjunct faculty in the PsyD program at The George Washington University, and has presented at Division 39, APA, IPA, and at the Southeast Asia Psychological Association in Mumbai, India. Dr. Kelly was an editor of Section III's first book, *Into the Void*.

Marilyn Metzl, PhD, is a Psychologist/Psychoanalyst in independent practice in Kansas City, Missouri, treating adults, adolescents, children, couples, and families. Dr. Metzl, who is past president of the Missouri Psychological Association (MOPA), holds Diplomate status from the American Psychological Association (APA), and is a Fellow of APA (Division 39, Psychoanalysis). Dr. Metzl, who is former director of Kansas City Institute for Contemporary Psychoanalysis and is on the teaching faculty of the Greater Kansas City-Topeka Psychoanalytic Institute, has presented nationally and internationally on issues such as self-esteem, depression, men's issues, social competence, women's human rights, attention deficit, anxiety disorders, and narcissism. She is also on the teaching faculty of the Chinese-American Psychoanalytic Alliance. Dr. Metzl is Federal Advocacy Coordinator for Division 39 and represents governmental issues pertaining to psychoanalysis. In addition to her professional work, Dr. Metzl's interests include Pilates, snow skiing, and ballroom dancing.

JoAnn Ponder, PhD, is a psychologist/psychoanalyst in private practice in Austin, Texas. She completed postgraduate training in adult psychoanalysis and child psychotherapy at the Center for Psychoanalytic Studies in Houston, where she currently serves on the faculty. She also completed programs in object relational family/couples therapy, infant–parent Mental Health intervention, and psychoanalytic writing. Dr. Ponder is Past President of Section III. She has presented and published on topics such as race, trauma, domestic violence, parent loss, and adoption at psychoanalytic venues. In 2004, she was awarded the David A. Freedman Candidate Paper's Prize by the Houston Psychoanalytic Society.

Kristen A. Reale, LCSW, is a licensed psychotherapist in private practice in Manhattan. She received her BA with honors in cultural anthropology from the University of California Santa Cruz and her Master's degree with honors in clinical social work from the New York University Ehrenkranz School of Social Work. She works with adults, couples, and children, specializing in attachment and trauma. Alongside her private practice, she has worked as a social worker in many New York City inner city schools, and has taught in the masters' program at New York University, lecturing on infant attachment and human development. She has written and presented numerous professional papers at national psychoanalytic conferences focusing on the therapist's experience and the paramount role and process of supervision.

Richard Ruth, PhD, is Associate Professor of Clinical Psychology in the (psychodynamically oriented) PsyD program and on the core faculty of the interdisciplinary LGBT Health Policy and Practice graduate certificate program at The George Washington University. He is also on the steering committee, faculty, and supervisor with the Child and Adolescent Psychotherapy Program at the Washington School of Psychiatry. A clinical psychologist, a psychoanalyst, and a family therapist, his interests include cross-cultural clinical psychology, disability, trauma, and LGBT issues. He is proud to be among the first generation of legally married gay men.

Doris K. Silverman, PhD, is a faculty member and training psychoanalyst at IPTAR and the NYU Postdoctoral Program for Psychotherapy and Psychoanalysis. She has served on the editorial boards of various psychoanalytic journals, such as

Psychoanalytic Psychology, *Psychoanalytic Dialogues*, *International Journal of Psychoanalysis*, and the *Journal of the American Psychoanalytic Association*. In addition to co-authoring the book *Changing Conceptions of Psychoanalysis: The Legacy of Merton M. Gill*, Dr. Silverman has written more than fifty articles on a variety of topics including infant research and its relevance for psychoanalysis, female development and sexuality, the attachment system and the use of empirical data to augment therapeutic skills. She is the recipient of the 2007 Scientific Scholar Award from Division 39 of the American Psychological Association and has also received the Linda Newirth Memorial Prize.

Ellen L.K. Toronto, PhD, is a founding member and past President of the Michigan Psychoanalytic Council. She is currently past President of the Section on Women and Gender of the Division of Psychoanalysis of APA. She has published numerous articles on the topic of gender issues and non-verbal maternal communication. Dr. Toronto was first editor of the book *Into the Void: Psychoanalytic Perspectives on a Gender-Free Case* (Routledge, 2005) compiled by Section III Authors. Her recent book, *Family Entanglement: Unraveling the Knots and Finding Joy in the Parent-Child Journey*, uses psychoanalytic concepts, made accessible to a lay audience, to address difficult parenting issues. Dr. Toronto also writes a weekly blog on *PsychCentral* entitled *SeeSawParenting*.

Helena Vissing, PsyD, is a psychologist in Los Angeles, California. She earned an MS from University of Copenhagen and doctorate from Chicago School of Professional Psychology, Los Angeles. Her dissertation was a phenomenological and psychoanalytic study of the transition to motherhood. Dr. Vissing is a postgraduate trainee at Saturday Center for Psychotherapy and Training, Santa Monica, and serves on the Training and Research Committee of Maternal Mental Health NOW. She has presented and published on cultural representations of the post-pregnancy body and psychodynamics of motherhood. She is member-at-large for Section III and a Division 39 Graduate Student Scholarship recipient (2014–2015).

ACKNOWLEDGMENTS

The editors wish to acknowledge the support and contributions of Jessica Zucker, PhD, throughout this project.

INTRODUCTION

Ellen L. K. Toronto

While postmodern and feminist theory has carried us into a whole new view of gender as socially constructed and cautioned us, rightly so, to re-evaluate the traditional notions of male and female as binary opposites, women in a patriarchal society have not as yet been able to claim who they are as a function of their biology. The focus of our book is the exploration of the ways in which women's sexual and reproductive capabilities have been regarded as societal and patriarchal property and not as the possessions of the individual woman. To this end we will examine the centuries-old culture of oppression that women have suffered even as that suffering has been but a footnote to history. We will further endeavor to illuminate those uniquely female experiences, some of which have *remained virtually invisible*, as explained by those who live them.

We recognize the multitude of gender identities and experiences that have been historically masked by the dominant white heterosexual culture but it is women nevertheless who gestate the zygote and fetus and give birth. It is women who are predominantly the victims of rape throughout history and in every society. These experiences may differ as a function of culture and history, but they also possess irreducible factors that continue to affect the freedom and agency of women. Unless and until women claim their unique capabilities as their own, they will continue to be appropriated and controlled by a patriarchal society.

Before we can comfortably accept the socially constructed nature of gender we need to address as Lynne Layton (2004) states the area of discourse that arises "from the content of gender polarities created by gender inequality" (p. 35). Layton goes on to say that

> as long as power differentials continue to exist between masculinity and femininity, any theory that claims to transcend binaries or looks only at continuities between them keeps the power hierarchy intact. It is the power

difference between women and men (of all races) . . . that makes the male/ female binary . . . politically and personally meaningful.

It is a power differential that still exists and is not erased by the attention paid to the acknowledged fluidity of gender. It is this very ground that we wish to explore. McWilliams (2005, p. 114) confirms that "during our early development and . . . in the unconscious depths of our souls, we tend to be both categorical and binary." However intricate our new theories may be, we still live in a binary world and in a binary world women are in second place.

It is curious that we have begun to explore the fluidity of gender and dismantle its polarities before women have been able to explicate fully those capabilities contingent upon their biological sex. Attributes of female experience have typically been seen through the eyes of the dominant male culture and thus not fully defined from a female perspective. Irigaray has observed (Layton, 2004, p. 48), for example, that in a phallic order women have been unable to symbolize their relation to their genitals. Although women's breasts are often the subject of male fantasy, we have almost no representation of what it means to possess them. Would it be like the episode of *Friends* in which Joey covers himself with sand and fashions two female breasts for himself? It is clear that he enjoys having them but as objects of desire rather than as parts of his own body. Thus it is for a woman whose relationship to her own body remains in the vast expanse of unformulated thought (Stern, 1997).

Psychoanalytic writing has only begun to address these lacunae in our theories. Women as mothers are either vilified or held to impossible standards as the essential "socio-emotional environment" for positive human development. Schore's (1994) breath-taking compendium on affect regulation states as follows:

> A central thesis of this volume is that . . . the infant's transactions with the early socioemotional environment indelibly influence the evolution of brain structures responsible for the individual's socioemotional functioning for the rest of the life span. . . . To be attuned to the child's internal states and the changes in these states takes a significant amount of empathic attention and emotional involvement on the part of the primary caregiver.
>
> *(p. 540)*

Later in this discussion the author makes it clear that the "primary caregiver" should be the mother. Schore cites studies that indicate that nonmaternal care of even more than 20 hours per week presages untoward effects such as increased aggression and insecure attachment. No attention is paid to the effort required of women to accomplish this type of attunement.

It is as though our theories have skipped a step. Perhaps we really don't want to know. Is it possible that the subjective experiences of women who are mothers; women who give birth; women who are raped or who do not feel safe on a college campus or walking alone in the dark are too painful for us to contemplate? Are we collectively unable to look at what it is really like to care for small children on a daily basis without help or respite? Must we close our ears to the anguished cries of the rape of the Sabine women as they ring through the pages of history? Shall we remain ignorant of what is it like to be the subject of rape or its helpless witness? Can we comprehend the momentary "gut check" as to their safety that women experience as they walk through the neighborhood in the dark or admit a burly plumber or electrician to their homes?

Is it too much to imagine the wailing cry of a woman who has been told that the last efforts to achieve fertility have been expended? Must we protect our public discourse from the anguish of infertility, the hope of adoption, the often difficult decision to remain childless and the heart-wrenching experiences that they represent? Can we afford to bring out of the shadows the sorrow of a miscarriage or the wracking sobs that can accompany post-partum depression? On the other side are we aware of the experience of birth as a God-like connection with all of the universe? Can we finally elaborate the other half of the mother–child relationship—subtle, textured, infinitely diverse—but characterized in our texts as the "socio-emotional environment?"

Our purpose then in this volume is to address from a psychoanalytic perspective those "everyday miracles" that disproportionately affect women *as a function of their biology*. If it appears that we are going backward it is because we believe that women's stories from women's bodies have not been fully elaborated. Unless and until they can claim these experiences as their own, their power and their agency will remain compromised. From this viewpoint we are talking not about the self as the subject of discourse but rather about the psychic self or what Benjamin (1988) calls the "conflicted experiencing self." We are talking about women in a binary world, a patriarchal order "that sets up stringent binaries on the basis of anatomical sex differences and . . . does not allow for people to deviate from that binary without suffering grave consequences" (Davisson, personal communication).

Our book is divided into four sections each of which is designed to explicate the lived experience of women in a patriarchal society. We move from the societal and cultural influences, a cultural third as it were, that have defined women as sexual objects to the psychic and individual as women continue to represent their uniquely female bodies and their experiences of motherhood. The first section explores the sexual subjugation of women as it exists in a rape culture, rape being a universal in all societies. It then examines as a case in point, that is, the current "war against women" in the United States in which the gains of the last 30 years are being challenged in backlash legislation against affirmative action, abortion rights, and gay marriage. The section then addresses the so-called sexual freedom as it continues to exploit women and finally the LGBTQ movement as it has ironically drawn from the feminist movement and yet rejected the feminine as inferior. The question, hovering over all of these topics, asks what our discipline has to contribute to an understanding of the tenacity of a rape culture or the continuing view of women as inferior.

In the second section we focus on women's experience of sexual trauma, as evidenced first in the problem of date rape and the intra-psychic development of women that predisposes them to become its victims. We address the often over-looked effects of secondary sexual trauma and the lived experiences of the women who are its previously silent witnesses. Finally, we consider the problem of campus sexual assault and the introduction of a bystander as a third party, similar in function to a psychoanalytic third, as a model of prevention.

The latter two sections of the book focus on topics related to the work of mothering, which, as we know, has been given short shrift in the psychoanalytic lexicon. Women as baby carriers and nurturers are highly significant but their sub-jective experiences as mother or not-mother are unimportant. Rothman (2000) has pointed out that, ironically enough, patriarchy and liberal feminism have converged in giving short shrift to the physical and correspondingly emotional processes of gestation, labor, delivery, and lactation. Both ideologies have discounted and deval-ued pregnancy and the challenging work of mothering infants and young children.

Yet it is still women who give birth and who mother and, in the absence of opportunities to share these experiences, women continue to suffer narcissistic wounds in that these vital contributions are not identified or venerated in any ongoing manner. Our textbooks abound with what children need for healthy development but little attention is paid to the exhausting work of providing that experience. We have little to say about what it means to be a "socio-emotional environment."

In the third section we consider issues of motherhood, again not from the per-spective of the child, but from the subjective experience of the mother as she makes decisions about adoption and remaining childfree. We also consider the recent Birth Rights Movement that glorifies and idealizes the birthing experience in a way that once again duplicates a controlling approach toward female reproduction. In the final section we have included some very personal narratives as viewed through a psycho-analytic lens. We consider issues of maternity leave, the actual birth experience and post-partum depression as they affect the woman both as a person and as a therapist. These accounts bring us face to face with what Vissing terms "experiences of losing control, not succeeding in actively taking charge of the task, and feeling violated by interventions, whether medicalized or not . . . likely experienced as major defeats of the self" and burdened with "potential for psychic restructuring" (p. 179, this volume). All of the above issues have been given but a passing nod in psychoanalytic discourse.

References

Benjamin, J. (1988). *The Bonds of Love*. New York, NY: Pantheon Books.

Layton, L. (2004). *Who's That Girl? Who's That Boy?* Hillsdale, NJ: The Analytic Press.

McWilliams, N. (2005). Mothering and fathering in the psychoanalytic art. In E.L.K. Toronto, G. Ainslie, M. Donovan, M. Kelly, C.C. Kieffer, & N. McWilliams (Eds.), *Psychoanalytic Reflections on a Gender-free Case: Into the Void* (pp. 154–170). London: Routledge.

Rothman, B.K. (2000). *Recreating Motherhood*. New Brunswick, NJ: Rutgers University Press.

Schore, A.N. (1994). *Affect Regulation and the Origin of the Self: The Neurobiology of Emotional Development*. Hillsdale, NJ: Lawrence Erlbaum Associates.

Stern, D.B. (1997). *Unformulated Experience: From Dissociation to Imagination in Psychoanalysis*. Hillsdale, NJ: The Analytic Press.

SECTION I
A culture of oppression

COMMENTARY ON SECTION I

A culture of oppression

Maurine Kelber Kelly

Dr. Ellen L.K. Toronto's introduction and first chapter provide a most impressive account of the world's oldest prejudice: misogyny, and a tour de force of the history of sex and gender through the ages.

As Dr. Toronto explores the impact of a patriarchal society on cultures in many parts of the world, during war, in literature, in both the Old and New Testaments of the Bible, we could not possibly deny the terrible cost to all societies that perpetuate male dominance of females through family structures, the workforce, and in every aspect of life throughout history. Dr. Toronto addresses the psychoanalytic foundations for this dominance of over half the human population and offers many approaches to overcoming practices so detrimental to all members of society. Among important questions addressed are: "What is the meaning of living in a gendered body?" and "How can women bring into conscious awareness the full extent of their experiences both as victims of oppression and as owners and agents of their remarkable capability?"

So much of Dr. Toronto's introduction took me back to my days at the University of Pennsylvania where as a mother of two young children I first encountered Consciousness Raising Groups at local Haverford College. I immersed myself in questioning my own female role(s) and in the writings of many radical feminists. In my dissertation I addressed these topics and issues so important to my own life, especially when I became pregnant with my third child. I feared I would lose my scholarship and be considered unfit to become a PhD psychologist if I didn't show 100 percent devotion to my studies as the male students were more likely to do.

Dr. Toronto and all of the authors in this section compel us to look at our own internal contributions to the perpetuation of sexism in our lives and in society at large. Dr. Toronto concludes "that as long as women are not in control of their sexuality or their reproductive capabilities the male–female power differential will remain." She appropriately stresses the importance of understanding the anatomical and biological differences between the sexes. Dr. Toronto brilliantly uses Biblical references to illustrate the misogyny in both Testaments. She points to the origin of the female's definition as a part-object as traced to the story of Adam and Eve.

Dr. Doris K. Silverman's chapter begins with a summary of the ideas promulgated by French feminist Cixous four decades ago—ideas that ring as true today. Under a patriarchal society women are reduced to a subsidiary role, marginalized by the central androcentric culture. Cixous called for women to demonstrate their unique voices, to write their experiences, and to honor their bodies. Dr. Silverman's sharing of her own experiences during the 1970s when women researchers began to focus on both sex and gender again resonated with my own. I was told in my senior year at Northwestern University, having been encouraged to apply for a Woodrow Wilson in History, that the only reason I didn't win it was that I was a woman. In 1962, it never occurred to me that that was unfair; I decided I would get graduate training in English where my competition would more likely be other women.

Dr. Silverman's analysis of sexism in society today begins with her discussion of advertising, particularly ads for Cialis in which happily married heterosexual couples dramatically exhibit benevolent sexism. One could say the media greatly contribute to the perpetuation of our investment in patriarchy. As Dr. Silverman moves on to discuss the films *The Little Mermaid* (1989) and *Frozen* (2013), she continues to illustrate both progressive and regressive pulls. Then in her discussion of sexting and hooking up, Dr. Silverman illustrates positive features in terms of females owning their bodies and gaining a sense of agency and an affirmation of their sensual–sexual selves. However, she also cites research claiming that "seventy-eight percent of unwanted intercourse takes place in hooking up."

Dr. Richard Ruth's personal history of growing up gay and his very positive identification with the women's movement, Feminist Liberation, was both very moving and also typical of many gay men. These men gathered courage from "Women's Lib" to come out of the closet and to fight for equal treatment of homosexuals, another demeaned and oppressed population. Dr. Ruth's thorough knowledge of the literature on the history of male homosexuality in the US and around the world is most impressive. With the AIDS epidemic, the gay movement turned away from politics of liberation to narrower politics of civil rights. Dr. Ruth's 4-year treatment of two fathers and their teenage son is illustrative of the internalized homophobia of homosexual males, and the resulting misogyny as they project all that they despise in themselves onto women. Dr. Ruth cites many excellent sources in his exploration of reasons gay men lack interest in supporting women's right to choose in the face of today's serious threats to women's health and reproductive rights. In the case illustration as in many male couples who pursue parenting, the disparagement of women poses a serious detriment to the psychological and emotional development of their children and in their own relationship with their children. I recall the first time I met a woman who proudly proclaimed that her daughter was conceived with the assistance of a sperm bank. She was very outspoken about her determination never to tell her daughter anything about the child's biological father. My fantasy is that the daughter of that woman, like the son of the two fathers presented by Dr. Ruth, would bring her mother to therapy seeking help for her own academic and social adjustment. When parents disparage all members of the opposite sex, most likely they are projecting unwanted and hated aspects of themselves.

Dr. Marilyn Metzl, in her section response, offers us innumerable examples of the disparagement and degradation of women: violated and oppressed from the home, to the work place, to all facets of society in our country today. Although we are able to point to evidence of progress for women in their quest for equality, we most certainly have not won the battle and truly must dedicate ourselves to fighting in our schools, communities, and in our local and national government before women attain that goal.

This section offers well-written and thoroughly researched chapters, compelling both in their clinical relevance and in their relevance to today's increasing threat to women's reproductive rights and struggle for equality in the home, in the work place, in our government, indeed in every aspect of life.

1

GENDER INEQUALITY IN A (STILL) BINARY WORLD

Ellen L. K. Toronto

The focus on the socially constructed nature of gender has allowed us to see beyond the limiting characteristics of gender stereotypes but, as Layton (2004) states, it has kept the power hierarchy intact. The ideology of patriarchy permeates all of society. Barbara Rothman (1994) states that "the ideology . . . goes much deeper than male dominance. . . . The ideology of patriarchy is a basic worldview, and, in a patriarchal system, that view permeates all of our thinking" (p. 143). It views women as carriers of genetic material, an essential activity to the preservation of the male line. Rothman states "it is women's motherhood that men must control to maintain patriarchy" (p. 141). My perspective in this argument is that as long as women are not in control of their sexuality or their reproductive capabilities, the male–female power differential will remain. For women to wrest control of their unique capabilities we/they must bring into conscious awareness the full extent of their experiences—both as victims of oppression and as owners and agents of their remarkable capability.

As theorists and clinicians, we are attempting to understand the multiplicity of gender identities, but the women and men who enter our consulting rooms may be struggling to consolidate any sort of cohesive identity. They may be processing heavily inflicted wounds that have resulted from living within a body that is anatomically either male or female. Females in every culture still remain the focus of oppression in the form of rape, sexual slavery, restriction of reproductive rights, and ongoing societal oppression. Within the intimate context of men and women, the very real anatomical differences have become the culturally sanctioned focus of male obsession, hostility, and control. The male perspective, insofar as it is shaped by the culture, has been predisposed to regard women as objects either to possess, despise, or discard. This chapter will explore the lived experience of women within patriarchy insofar as it has been historically and universally circumscribed by biology and dictated by cultural norms. Using clinical examples, it will address the ways in which cultural and biological imperatives are woven into the issues and concerns of individual people. Finally, it will present possibilities for reimagining the prescriptions of patriarchy.

An intimate enemy

Among groups that are ostracized or subjugated women are unique. They are a majority of the population. Their numbers cut across all races, ethnicities, religions, and socio-economic groups such that the dictates of religious or ethnic cleansing do not apply. They are essential as child-bearers, sexual partners, and mothers. They do not live in segregated towns or villages. They are in intimate contact with men on a daily basis. As Simone de Beauvoir (2009) has stated, men and women are viewed as a fundamental biological unity, one that men for a multitude of reasons have been predisposed to dominate. Women are seen not as separate subjective beings but as appendages of men through which male sexual and reproductive needs are gratified. Nevertheless, they still may be unconsciously construed as despised objects on which the powerful members of society project disavowed feelings. They are susceptible to the same forces that fuel the bitter hostility between competing factions. Thus at deepest levels women represent a threat, a danger to the religious, political, and economic order. The real equality of men and women would represent a universal seismic shift, the ramifications of which are difficult to comprehend.

The cultural history of women confirms that, although they have achieved significant progress in the economic and social world over the last 100 years, their roles as real or potential mothers and as sexual objects, partners, or wives have undergone only superficial alterations. Women are still in many circumstances as de Beauvoir (2009) has said "the victim of the species" (p. 23). Kestenberg (1982) states that "from time to time there occurs a shift in emphasis from one . . . of these . . . tasks and they take on different forms as the standards for motherhood, woman's work and her role in relation to man change" (p. 81). I would add that for the majority of the world's women, maternity and sexuality are still the defining factors of life.

Why has progress in these areas has been so scant? Why is it that women in many parts of the world have no political rights or that thousands of women in the United States, *even in Ann Arbor, Michigan*, exist in sexual slavery? For many centuries men have held political power over women and, as with other political or ethnic minorities, have viewed them as "other," without acknowledgement or regard for their separateness and difference. What will it require for civilization to accord women equality, equality anchored in their reproductive and sexual autonomy, which then allows them the freedom to explore the multitude of shapes that gender may inhabit? Again, as with the discipline of psychoanalysis, I am approaching this argument from within a Western Judeo-Christian tradition. I believe that the answers lie within a complex inter-weaving of biological, political, cultural, and intra-psychic factors that psychoanalysis is uniquely prepared to explore.

It may be argued that the patriarchal order plays out differently as a function of race, ethnicity, or socio-economic status, and that is undoubtedly correct. Women inhabit mothering in vastly different ways as a function of many factors. The circumstances surrounding birth may also be different, but it is still females who do it. It is still females who produce the heirs to the male line. Moreover, it is difficult to imagine how the experience of rape would be other than a humiliating and degrading assault upon the physical and psychic space of another human being. But as with psychoanalysis itself that emerged out of Western Judeo-Christian culture we can apply our insights across a diverse range of cultures.

Biological factors

Biology is a harsh task master for women. Menstruation, child-bearing, not child-bearing, child-rearing, and menopause loom large in the middle 40 years of women's lives. A number of writers have suggested that parturition rather than coitus is the culmination of the sex act for women. Helen Block Lewis (1987) states that women's attitude toward sex is embedded in the framework of maternity and thus organized around her impregnation, which she may or may not desire. Anxiety about impregnation reduces her chances for orgasm. The focus on the vagina would then be only a part of female sexuality. Rather it would be a complex whole-body response, difficult to verbalize or even identify. The vagina itself, as Barnett (1966) has stated, possesses elements that lend themselves to its repression. She mentions that because the orifice lacks voluntary muscle control, there is a continual threat to body integrity. A second factor is that, unlike the mouth or anus, it has no contents that could be viewed as a part of the self. Kestenberg (1982) has pointed out that feminine modalities such as nurturing and receptivity are far less noticeable than are male aggression and intrusion. Important aspects of the female sexual experience are internal. A full discussion of the biological factors as they permeate the cultural and intra-psychic experiences of women is well beyond the scope of this project. But I concur with Rosemary Balsam (2012) who states that "we cannot sustain any cogent theory of mind . . . without establishing the location of the body in our theories . . . and that the functional female body needs to be as central to any useful psychoanalytic theory as the male body traditionally has been . . . " (p. 4).

When the medical is political

From a societal perspective woman has remained, as first described by Simone de Beauvoir (2009), "embedded within the species," and the decisions about her sexual and reproductive health have been in the service of a patriarchal civilization—a male possession. Far too often those decisions have resulted in violence and exploitation in many forms. As long as women are barred from decision-making bodies that legislate female sexuality, that will continue to be the case, no matter what their gains may be in other areas. Our task then as psychoanalysts is to look closely at the ways in which the culture has taught us that woman's sexuality is not her own.

Historically, proscriptions about child-bearing have been determined by cultural norms prescribed by men. Decisions about reproduction are made by men with the fallacious assumption that they speak accurately for women. For example, women, of necessity, were the ones to produce a male heir, that all-important individual who would inherit the wealth, sit on the throne, or carry on the name. A woman who didn't produce a male heir was easily replaced or discarded by her husband or the ruling male. Patriarchal society has also dictated whether or not birth control will be available. Legislatures determine when or if a woman may terminate a pregnancy. Governments decree a one-child-per-family law. Women are excluded from the decision-making process even when it is, quite literally, they who do the "heavy lifting."

A male-dominated medical profession has functioned to divorce women from their bodies and has usurped, insofar as possible, the child-bearing experience with mind- and body-numbing anesthetics. In *Witches, Midwives and Nurses*, Ehrenreich and English (1973) have reported the early prevalence of women as midwives and healers and their exclusion until recent years from the medical profession. Women's knowledge, experience, and skill were viewed as a threat to the medieval Catholic Church, tragically culminating in the persecution of people, primarily women, who were accused of witchcraft. Witches were accused of many things, but their most significant so-called crimes centered on issues of sexuality. Lust in either men or women was blamed on the female. Ehrenreich and English (1973) cite the *Malleus Maleficarum*, considered the best source for the day-to-day operations of the witch-hunts and for insights into the mentality of the witch-hunter. It describes witches who were mostly women as having the power to provoke uncontrollable passion in men, change them into beasts, destroy the procreative power of both men and women, obtain abortions, and give children to the devil. Women's sexuality has long been regarded as a fearsome force and one that cannot be left to their individual control.

Culture and the unconscious

Much as we might wish to claim the unique and individual nature of our world view, we are inevitably shaped by the culture that surrounds us. A huge body of work, including visual art, literature, myth, music, and religious text, has informed our thinking as to the nature of the relationship between men and women. Culture imposes a powerful influence upon the unconscious through the complex interaction and influence of its many manifestations in our daily lives. The unconscious, as the site of primary mental processes, dreams, fantasies, and wishes, makes its presence known in disguise, displacement, and condensation. Escaping the repression and censorship of everyday discourse and disrupting the conventional ways of being, it operates outside the rules of logic. Culture, art, religion, and myth can wreak havoc within that lawless region. Rustin (2007) pointed out that creative artists dating back to the Greek tragedians have illuminated those unruly thoughts, desires, and connections well before their psychoanalytic discovery. Our experiences with reading and re-reading literature, for example, become in Caruth's (1996) terms an encounter, both moral and epistemological, of that which we cannot know in conscious thought. Through artistic symbolization this exposure creates within us responses to the human condition that are wider than our own individual world view. The relative immortality and permanence of great art gives its insights respectability and stature that validates our own resonate musings even as it sends our disclaimers scuttling for cover. Thankfully the cross-disciplinary movement in the humanities of the last 30 years has allowed us a far more sophisticated view of the complex structure of patriarchal mores and the insidious ways in which it perpetuates female subordination. In this section I want to focus in particular on women's sexuality and reproductive capability and the ways in which societal norms, as they are conveyed in and through the culture, have appropriated those unique capacities.

Religion and myth have been highly influential carriers of culture since antiquity. Religious texts make clear from the very beginning that the female is scarcely a person in her own right but rather one who is defined by her reproductive capabilities and whose very existence is dependent upon the male. In Genesis we read that after God had created the earth and all living creatures including man, it was discovered that man did not have a partner, a help meet. The Lord caused a sleep to fall upon Adam and took out one of his ribs. He made from it a woman and took it to Adam. Adam then affirmed that this creature would be a part of him: "bone of my bones and flesh of my flesh" (Genesis 2:23, King James Version). He named her "woman" because she was taken out of man. In a compelling moment that rings down through the ages, the female is defined as a part-object of the male. In *Sex and the Superego: Psychic War in Men and Women*, Lewis (1987) writes that the text from Genesis not only denies the importance of the womb but is a fusion of thoughts about the penis in the vagina. The rib is a symbolic equivalent of the penis. Eve was created from the rib of Adam. We are given the image of a woman created from a male body part when the actual gestation of humans takes place within the womb. Making matters bad for men, but worse for women, God tells Adam and Eve that they will be under a curse: Adam will labor by the sweat of his brow but Eve will be forever ruled by her husband. Parenthetically one might ask whether in the Garden of Eden the sexes would have been equal. But after they are expelled from the Garden, it is certain that this will not be the case. Her task moreover will be to bear children. Throughout the biblical narrative women are mentioned infrequently and most often in relation to their capacity for having children, specifically sons.

The New Testament, a kinder, gentler text, is nevertheless specific in defining the role of women. In 1 Timothy 2:15 it states, "But I suffer not a woman to teach, nor to use authority over the man: but to be in silence." Tinkle (2010) points out that a number of influential writers of the medieval era including Augustine, Jerome, Chrysostom, and Chaucer have affirmed that women must remain silent since even the act of speaking is sexual and seductive, threatening men's self-control. The female body is sexualized—"intellectually unthreatening if overwhelmingly seductive" (p. 31). Tinkle states that the story of Eve prevails and women's words and actions are irrelevant except as sexual temptations. Thus they are encouraged to accept blame for men's sexual excesses, a view that has prevailed into the twentieth century in which accusations of rape have initiated an intense scrutiny of the victim's sexual history. In other scriptural references, in which men attempt to appropriate and control women's reproductive capabilities, male priests, who speak for God, can guide a supplicant to be born again. Though women undeniably possess the power to create life within their bodies, men, and men only, can elevate human beings to a higher level of purity and righteousness once they accept the tenets of their religion in a way that allows them to be born into new life. Symbolic baptism, typically orchestrated by males, re-creates the mother's womb and provides spiritual cleansing and re-birth.

Like religion, early myths provide a particularly powerful message because they are not evidence-based but founded in the undefinable realm of spirit, imagination, and belief. In *The Power of Myth*, Joseph Campbell (1988) tells us that because women give birth or give life they are associated with the earth that also sustains life. Woman is also the nearer parent for most of us. The man is distant or maybe even dead or gone. Mythical stories abound in which sons go off in search of their fathers. Telemachus goes off in search of his father Odysseus. In modern myth Luke Skywalker expresses his desire to know who his father is. The mother quest is usually unnecessary. Mother is there—giving birth, nursing, and caring until a child is old enough to go in search of his father. Mother becomes like the air we breathe or in Kantian terms a *form of sensibility*. She is the surround within which we move and have our being. Ships are named after women as are nations, like Mother Russia. She is Lady Liberty or Charity or Wisdom. She is essential—giving and nurturing life and/or representing its best qualities. But her power is abstract, idealized, and lacking in individual or collective political clout that would give her control over her own affairs or her individual destiny. She is important, essential even, not as an individual or a subjective presence but rather as an appendage—an indefinable but undeniable part of our being.

Rape as a cultural crime

Nowhere is the evidence of women's lack of separateness and subjectivity more striking than it is in the history of rape as both an individual and a cultural act. The origins of the word rape are found in the ancient Greek—meaning to steal. Until recent history the rape of women has been viewed as a property crime directed against the "owner" of the victim—her husband or father. In the Hamarabic code women were seen as equally liable for the crime and both the victim and perpetrator were punishable by death. During the middle ages Jewish women won the right to pursue legal action against the perpetrators. During the reign of Henry II women could file suit against their rapists as long as they weren't married to them.

Beginning with the battles and bodies littered throughout the Old Testament, women, or rather their bodies, i.e. their sexuality, are regarded as the spoils of war, trophies over which the wars are often waged. It is clear early on that it is men who are dishonored when women are defiled. In Genesis 34:27 we read: "The sons of Jacob came upon the slain, and spoiled the city, because they had defiled their sister." The Old Testament describes the rape of women of conquered tribes as an accepted routine. Lamentations 5:11 states "They ravished the women in Zion, and the maids in the cities of Judah." When an army conquers an enemy the women who have known men are slain while virgins are kept alive. In Numbers 31:17–18 it states: "Now therefore kill every male among the little ones, and kill every woman that hath know man by lying with him. But all the women children, that have not known a man by lying with him, keep alive for yourselves." This is Moses speaking, and he was one of the good guys.

From earliest civilization the crime of rape has also been considered a crime against the state. At present it is considered a war crime by the Geneva Convention. Though this modification represents a significant step forward, it still fails to address the experience of the victim and her long-term health and well-being. Maya Angelou describes it in the following manner:

> and then there is the pain. A breaking and entering when even the senses are torn apart. The act of rape on an eight-year-old body is the matter of the needle giving because the camel can't. The child gives because the body can, and the mind of the violator cannot.
>
> *(as cited in Brown, 2003, p. 6)*

Nancy Rabinowitz (2011) addresses the question of the ambiguity of rape among the ancient Greeks. That is, did the women go with the men because they wanted to or because they were in love? Once they became a conquered people, did the women who became sexual slaves fall in love with their captors? Rabinowitz points out the fact that Greek women were given in marriage by their fathers but without their consent. Once married, they were denied both the ability to consent and the ability to withhold consent. If they were in marriage without their consent, did marital sex constitute rape?

Rabinowitz cites Aeschylus' story of the fifty daughters of Danaus who attempt to avoid marriage with the fifty sons of Aegyptus, their father's brother. The men claim to want marriage but the women resist—describing the men as violent and prideful. The women resist marriage and take their case to the gods including Zeus whose reputation is far from sterling. That is, they depend upon men to save them from men. In other such tales Creusa is raped by the god Apollo but her ambivalence is clear. She describes him as beautiful with his shimmering golden hair. Is it possible to be attracted to someone and yet resist penetration as Creusa did when she called out to her mother? Did Helen go willingly with Paris? Can a woman fall in love with her captor after years of sexual slavery? Can a relationship that begins with rape and slavery become a marriage? The question arises in modern times when female slaves in the American south were taken as sexual partners and became mistresses or virtual wives. Rabinowitz successfully points out the ambiguities inherent in the sexual relationship in which violence and force merge into desire and normative sexual relations. The problem for women who have long been regarded as the property of men is in identifying and fostering their own desire and emboldening the agency with which to pursue it.

Twentieth-century literature

Beginning again in biblical time rape was seen as a reward to the victors. Foreign women were kidnapped in times of war and the insult was against the defeated. Women were taken and became the property of the winners and in modern times rape continues to be used as an intentional tactic of terror. Sadly enough, the view of women as property is one that still prevails in modern times. The cultural message, i.e. that women's sexuality is not her own, continues in some of the best-loved literature of the twentieth century. In E.M. Forster's *A Passage to India* (1924), set in India at the height of the British colonial era, racial tension underscores every aspect of life. When a British visitor, Adela Quested, comes to Chandrapore and then ventures out into the Indian countryside, she claims to have been "insulted" by Dr. Aziz, an Indian native, in one of the Marabar Caves. A trial ensues and the issue readily becomes one of racial hatred between the British and the colonials. Women's honor must be defended but as a symbol of all that is most precious—not as the subjective possession of an actual woman. The combatants begin speaking of "women and children"—a phrase that conjures up all that is best about home and family and those brave men who must defend them. The identity of the individual woman and her suffering is lost.

Tensions at the trial run high with the natives assuming for good reason that their colleague, Dr. Aziz, will inevitably be found guilty. The attitude of the prosecutor is that everyone knows that the accused is guilty. The defense attorney asks that the court room be cleared of Europeans so as not to intimidate native witnesses on behalf of the defendant. It is an all-out racial war.

When Miss Quested finally takes the stand, however, she recants. She says that she has made a mistake and that the accused never followed her into the cave. Miss Quested has reversed her testimony and the courtroom erupts. One side erupts in cheers of victory while the other accepts ignominious defeat. Miss Quested is now invisible and it becomes clear that the war and the victory are not about her as a person. It is entirely about the man who honored or insulted her sexuality and the society he represents.

In the beloved twentieth-century classic *To Kill a Mockingbird* we hear a similar tale in which a white woman again falsely accuses an African American man of raping her. We are justifiably outraged at the inequities of the trial and the sentencing that ultimately leads to the death of Tom Robinson. Atticus Finch is surely one of the most admired heroes in the American literary canon. But the plight of Mayella Ewell goes largely unnoticed. We know that Mayella Ewell is beaten by her father and probably sexually assaulted as well. Tom Robinson is kind to Mayella Ewell, but she knows that if her father finds him in her yard, he will beat her as he has many times before. So she makes up a tale of Tom assaulting her. Her story ignites the town and battle lines are drawn. Atticus has the uncommon courage to defend Tom even though he knows that it is unlikely that he will get a fair trial. While the text compels us to applaud Atticus' courage and weep for Tom, Mayella Ewell is largely ignored. She brought this on herself, right? But we know that she didn't, that forces beyond her control made her as much a victim as Tom. Her sexuality and its ownership became a celebrated cause but the real woman will go on, suffering poverty, disrespect, and abuse until the end of her days.

The history of rape as a normative act within our culture is long and strong. It continues into the present day in the egregious accounts of sexual assaults on college campuses and in the military. It remains a continuing struggle to prosecute the crimes in courts of law rather than as infractions best kept silent behind the closed doors of institutions. Though many men may be horrified by the act of rape and feel certain that they would never force a woman sexually, they find it difficult to identify with the woman and the pain and humiliation that she feels. Women understand among themselves that they are vulnerable at all times to rape, but it doesn't rise to a level of cultural consciousness. That is, it remains a secret shared among females and somehow not communicated to males. In *The Peach Keeper* by Sarah Addison Allen (2011) a telling scene beautifully describes the plight of a woman who is outnumbered, helpless, or incapacitated by drink. All women share a universal knowledge of the danger of her situation even if it has never happened to them personally. It is a part of a woman's collective unconscious. It is the subjective experience of rape or the potential for rape that has yet to rise to a level of cultural awareness.

Cultural scripts in clinical settings

Women and men share a cultural history retold in a multitude of ways including literature, politics, myth, and religious text, which define women as beings whose fertility and sexuality are controlled by men through their legislative, economic, and religious power. Women produce heirs who inherit property. Women's potential infidelity introduces the possibility of property passing to persons who are not biologically related. Female sexuality has historically been viewed as the property of male relatives and its exploitation has become an avenue for dishonoring men defeated in battle. Men and women are to this day steeped in sociopolitical forces that inevitably infiltrate their inner lives. Muriel Dimen (2011) writes: "it made sense to consider psychoanalysis' conventional subject—interior life—as steeped in sociopolitical forces, that psychic life is made equally of inner and outer worlds . . ." (p. 3). Dimen goes on to state that "[c]ulture saturates subjective experience. Indeed, it is the business of psychoanalytic practice to document this approach to treatment" (p. 4.). The following clinical vignettes illustrate the powerful scripts that shape women's and men's views of female sexuality and reproductive autonomy.

The first illustration involves a woman now in her early 40s who I have seen for over 10 years. She first came into treatment because she was dating a married man and had been advised by another therapist and a woman's support group to stop seeing him. He was separated from his wife but was unwilling to divorce her. My patient, whom I shall call Michelle, did not want to terminate her relationship, but she did want her partner to divorce his wife and move in with her. A major focus of the first years of treatment was that of providing support for Michelle, to insist that her partner divorce his wife and eventually marry her.   '

The power imbalance between Michelle and her partner was striking. My patient was a beautiful young woman of ethnic background. Her partner, whom I shall call Jake, was 10 years older—rich and powerful—with three children from his first marriage. In order to establish a secure place in the relationship, Michelle was required to jump through hoops. For example, she had to "prove" that she could get along with her partner's children, and she expended great effort to do so. She cooked for them, made them gifts, bathed and cared for the younger ones when they were visiting, and included them in her creative activities.

From the outset it appeared to me that this was not going to be a viable relationship for my patient. However, she did not want to leave and though she was ambivalent she enjoyed the benefits of a wealthy lifestyle. She was able to quit her job and spend most of her time caring for Jake and his children. She made special food for him when he was trying to lose weight. She planned parties and took care of all household repairs and services. He, in turn, showered her with lavish gifts at birthdays and Christmas and brought her on expensive cruises. Though she disagreed with his child-rearing practices, including extravagant presents and virtually no rules or limits in their household, she largely kept silent.

We were barely able to touch on the factors from Michelle's childhood that predisposed her to stay in such a relationship. Her biological father left when she was very young and her mother had to support Michelle and her older brother on her own. Their poverty was dire until a stepfather appeared on the scene. He was physically abusive to her mother and brother and occasionally to the patient. She recalls a trip to the "woodshed" on a day that she had skipped school and hid. Her mother finally threw the stepfather out after he broke her arm. Michelle is still in contact with her mother, whom she describes as an eccentric hoarder, but she is estranged from her brother, an angry and bitter man whom Michelle once adored. Michelle's beauty and talent have won her many boyfriends, but she has not been able to sustain the long-term relationship that she consciously desires.

Through the lengthy treatment we have focused on enabling Michelle to become more assertive in her relationship with Jake. She was eventually able to insist that they marry despite his reservations. Early on she talked with Jake about the possibility of having a child. Though he was clearly reluctant, he never said a firm "No." She had begged him to get his vasectomy reversed, and he continued to avoid any decisive action. The years went by and Michelle realized that her window of fertility was coming to a close. She became more and more invested in having a child, in part because she had become interested in her own ethnic background, a positive development in enhancing her self-esteem.

Michelle became extremely preoccupied with becoming pregnant. She joined a support group and underwent medical procedures to facilitate the process. She began dieting strictly, eating only those foods which would contribute to fertilization. After extensive testing it became apparent that her eggs were only marginally viable. It also became clear that Jake was not going to have his vasectomy reversed. He continued to be evasive and avoid appointments where the procedure would be discussed. Their only chance would be in vitro fertilization. As Jake became increasingly reluctant to participate, Michelle considered other options including a sperm bank and an egg donor though she wanted somehow to preserve their own genetic material. The relationship with her husband was becoming increasingly contentious over this issue.

Finally, Jake was persuaded to donate his sperm so that they could proceed with IVF. Michelle went with him and later described to me the look on his face after the procedure. It was some indecipherable combination of horror, anger, and disgust—a look she had never seen before. Shortly after that he announced that he was moving out and stated that the donated sperm would no longer be available to her. The patient was devastated and begged him to stay, promising to give up the quest to have a child.

Viewed from a cultural perspective this excerpt highlights important issues regarding women's reproductive autonomy and the threat it poses to the male establishment. Michelle's partner and husband possessed many of the accoutrements of white male power. He was financially successful and had influential friends from many walks of life. He was an executive with access to expensive cars, trips, and homes. He attempted to maintain contact with the children from his previous marriage but apparently did so by providing them a lavish lifestyle rather than with his time and genuine interest. He was accustomed to having his needs met, often without even asking.

My patient obliged him, functioning as his unpaid secretary, housekeeper, and sexual partner. From her perspective she asked little of him until her biological clock began to implode. At that point she became a "tiger mother" with all of her considerable energy and determination going toward having a child. She became powerful within the relationship in ways that she never had before. Given her background of abuse and abandonment by the men in her life, it is not surprising that she was unable to pull together a more assertive stand vis-à-vis her husband. Yet somehow when she decided that she wanted a child, her power kicked in and she was not going to be deterred. Her husband had manifest reasons for not wanting another child including his age and the opinions of his nearly adult children. He also carried the reminder of his own father who had left his mother for a much younger woman and then subsequently had a child who was never assimilated into the family.

There were I believe latent reasons at work as well. My patient was asserting her power in ways that she never had before. She was calling the shots. Fertility treatments of necessity center on the female and her cycles. Jake would be required to re-schedule business trips to accommodate the time frame. As far as he was concerned adoption was out of the question. If, God forbid, my patient had gone to a sperm bank, he implied that he would not even raise the child. This apparently narcissistic man wanted no part of raising a child that was not his idea and on his terms. He could not tolerate a relationship in which his wife had autonomy that he could not control. In terms described by Dimen and Goldner (2002) Jake had become a "subject-as-object," a sperm donor, now taking the despised role of "other" in relation to his wife. He became the object of desire, not as a sexual partner but as a biological necessity that would complete her wishes to have a child.

In the ensuing months Michelle has been dealing with Jake's rejection of her as well as the knowledge that her fertile years are over, spent in a relationship with a man who, despite his equivocation, never intended to have a child with her. As never before we have been able to look at the patterns in her relationships in which she chooses men who will ultimately abandon her. We are able to explore her choices as repetitions of the abuse and abandonment that she suffered as a child.

The second vignette involves a man who entered treatment after breaking up with a woman for whom he cared deeply. The break-up involved in part the fact that she was in a higher socio-economic class and held ambitions for him that he could not meet. The patient, Charlie, began treatment in his early 50s. He had been married twice previously and had a daughter who he was trying to help. She had five children and no partner. Charlie also had a chronic inherited medical condition that required careful and frequent monitoring. Though he followed protocol he was in denial about the serious nature of his illness and pushed himself physically beyond realistic limits.

Initially the treatment focused on helping Charlie to acknowledge the vital need to take better care of himself physically, to manage his finances more effectively and to assess and modify his avoidant behavior both in the sessions and in running his life. Initially he talked in a scattered fashion, bouncing from one topic to another in a way that was difficult to follow and nearly impossible to address in a meaningful way. Still he was very motivated to understand himself and the effects of the chaotic working-class background in which he had been raised.

He described his mother as overly invested in him in a way that was not overtly sexual but too close for comfort. She sacrificed to send him to a private religious school when neither of his two younger siblings was sent there. His mother ultimately had an affair with a co-worker and that broke up the parents' contentious marriage. His father died when the patient was in his 20s of the same genetic disease that the patient carries.

Both parents abused alcohol and held wild parties in which numerous relatives came to drink. The men in the family, his father's brothers, were much worse than his father—drinking and hitting their wives. They were known to be cheating on them as well. The patient witnessed all of this even as he attended a private school where he was admonished to avoid any impropriety, sexual or otherwise. He dated a girl through high school and was afraid even to kiss her because of the teachings of the church and school.

Throughout a lengthy treatment the patient has progressed in many ways. He is better able to manage his medical issues and his finances. He is able to set limits with his daughter and yet provide much-needed help to her. His confidence at the non-profit agency where he works has improved, and he reports accolades for his accomplishments there. Yet he continues to pursue activities that he had mentioned as a problem from the beginning of treatment. That is, he persists in searching out prostitutes and spends inordinate amounts of time and money on pornographic sites. He keeps this activity secret from everyone including the woman who was his romantic partner and is now his housemate.

He is, however, aware of the problems that these activities pose, both in terms of safety and his lack of integrity in regard to his partner. We have explored the roots of this behavior in relation to his upbringing and the activities that he witnessed as well as the hypocrisy that so angered him in the form of teachings at his religious school. Yet it is only as I have been able to listen to detailed accounts of his exploits—cruising for women, visiting them in seedy apartments owned by pimps and drug lords, hearing about the needs of their neglected children and vivid accounts of the sexual acts they pursue—that we have begun to break through the defenses and compartmentalization that he has constructed. I have expressed my physical and emotional discomfort in listening to the material. He is now in the presence of a living, breathing woman, one whom he finds helpful and trustworthy. He is able to see first-hand that women are human beings with feelings and not merely a collection of body parts.

Charlie prides himself on treating women as equals at work and in other relationships. He doesn't decline, for example, to do "women's work" in the home. But in the sexual arena he views them differently. His motivations are a complex interaction of internal fantasies, family background, and cultural messages that inform his view of women as objects—not human beings—there for his exploitation. For the purposes of this argument we will focus on the cultural messages he was given—that women are not to be treated with dignity but as sexual objects, part objects that only serve to complete him as a person.

Discussion

The treatments of Michelle and Charlie present each in different ways the cultural scripts for the roles that men and women play out in our society. In the case of Michelle a very traditional picture emerges in which the male is the more powerful in terms of money and prestige and the woman subordinate. Her role is to please her man, accommodate his wishes, and shore up his self-esteem—very much the comfort woman. But when Michelle decides that she wants to have a child and her time is running out, the balance of power threatens to change. She is calling the shots—compelling him to have his sperm count checked, directing him toward a diet that might enhance fertility, scheduling doctor appointments to accommodate her schedule, not his. The ultimate threat is that she might use another man's sperm to have a baby. Her husband has excuses that seem reasonable—he is too old; he already has children; it would change their relationship. Among their friends the patient indicated that men were more sympathetic to her husband and women to her. Each had points of view that seemed reasonable to their own sex.

How then should it be decided if one partner wants a child and the other does not, as in the case of my patient, Michelle? Her husband, Jake, could not tolerate leaving the decision in her hands. With another female patient the choices were reversed: her husband had hidden her birth control pills. She was threatening to leave him and he wanted to tie her to him by having another child with her. What if she had become pregnant? Who should decide the fate of the pregnancy? What happens in those countries where there are limits to the number of children a family may have? Are there women involved in making those laws or regulating the exceptions? Can we even imagine a world where women are the deciders about birth control, abortion, pregnancy, number of children? Women would emerge from the shadows as the powerful beings that they are—essential and, in many ways, in charge of our survival as a species. As it is, however, they are far too often the unwilling victims of their biology, codified within the prevailing system that is patriarchy.

My patient Charlie, though in many ways a good, caring, and generous person, acts out another familiar cultural script. In some part of his makeup he views women as sexual objects, lacking in humanity or subjective presence. When he seeks out prostitutes he loses contact with his humanity. He is meeting a need and the woman becomes a thing, an object whose function is to satisfy his need. Charlie is able to encapsulate his feelings so that he doesn't have to imagine what it is like for the women he sees. He tells himself that he is kind. He doesn't beat them or perform sadistic acts. He talks with them and hopes they will talk with him. But he is unable to empathize or view them as real in important ways. It does not register that, though the woman is not technically forced to perform these services and receives pay for them, her situation in society is such that she doesn't have a choice. She may need money to support a child. She may be forced by a pimp who acquired her when she was a child. Perhaps she is using the money to better herself, but the wounds to her being will never be healed.

With these two patients we see the complex interplay between the cultural and the intra-psychic. The culture becomes the carrier, the enforcer, if you will, of biological differences between the sexes, and the messages, insinuated into the psyche, are enacted willy-nilly in the lives of men and women. My clients, Michelle and Charlie, are thoughtful people—well able to undertake the intellectual rigors of psychoanalytic treatment. They are able to focus on and comprehend layers of meaning that propel human behavior. Yet the biological imperatives, clothed in the robes of culture, to which each are subject—having a child before time runs out, or satisfying sexual urges—hit like a Mack truck and undermine purer, more self-actualizing intentions. In the grip of these motivations their action takes on a fire and urgency that destabilizes everything in its path.

Am I suggesting that we are all really at the mercy of our biological urges or that we may rely on evolutionary biology as an explanatory concept? I am not. I am proposing that we have not as yet fully untangled the multitude of ways that patriarchy has organized and encoded sexual differences. I am stating that women as bearers of the species have not as yet had their say and that we do not have a fully explicated narrative as to the horrors of rape, the humiliation attendant upon sexual slavery, the pain of infertility, the mandate to multiply and replenish, or the unforgiving tedium of childcare. At this point in human history we have the female narrative *as it is determined by biology* largely from a patriarchal perspective. The task we have assigned ourselves is to extricate the lived subjective female experience from its grip.

I believe that if we are to transcend the dictates of biology, it will be through the reasoned transformation of the culture that defines it. I concur with the famed Prince of Denmark who so eloquently transcended biology when he said:

> What a piece of work is a man! How noble in reason, how infinite in faculty! In form and moving how express and admirable! In action how like an Angel! In apprehension how like a god! The beauty of the world!
>
> *(Shakespeare's* Hamlet, Prince of Denmark, *Act II, Scene 2)*

I would only add, "What a piece of work is a woman!" As human beings we are well able to choreograph a world view that encompasses both men and women as actors in charge of their own destinies.

A cultural transformation

I have presented a brief glimpse of the problems that women subject to men have endured over the centuries of human civilization. They have been routinely viewed as property and sex objects—the spoils of war with barely a nod given to their suffering. Their role as bearers and nurturers of children is codified in law and religion so that individual decision-making is taken out of their hands. The cultural and psychic tropes that maintain the status quo are daunting indeed. Can we go beyond the patriarchal order as the only way of organizing the relationships between men and women? Are women as child-bearers and child-nurturers destined to remain "the victim of the species" (de Beauvoir, 2009, p. 23)? Are these questions important? Why are we still asking them in the present day? Can we even imagine a different world view? Does the deconstruction of gender make such a project impossible or irrelevant? Does it circumvent the problem of women's exploitation and oppression? Layton (2004) points out that in any discussion that categorizes masculinity and femininity, a hierarchy is established in which the masculine is in a superior cultural position. Layton goes on to state that some postmodern feminists have "found it difficult to defend their deconstruction of gender identity while maintaining an allegiance to women's political struggles" (p. 301). Is hierarchy an inevitability in a binary world or can we obliterate the problems of patriarchy by redefining the outlines of gender? It will, most definitely, require a significant shift in our perspective if we as a civilization are to see women as fully human, entitled to be safe and free.

The shift will be enormous and its implications far-reaching because women are not a minority. They are not a subgroup. They represent half of the human family. In revolutions of the past, rebellious subgroups were a minority, and if they attained some measure of equality, it did not affect the hierarchy within the home. Men were still accorded dominance and women were the "other," a close and familiar repository of weakness, irrationality, and vulnerability—the weaker sex. If women take their place as separate subjective beings with political and legal control of their reproductive capabilities, it will demand new responses from all of us. It will require a seismic shift for all of the human family. It will not simply mean changes in the abstract but rather changes in behavior on a daily basis. It will alter the traditional hierarchies within the home and within organized religion. It will alter the culturally accepted catcalls that women endure when they walk down the street. It will modify acceptable practices within the classroom, the office, the board room, and the halls of government.

Of necessity we will face the possibility that the radical view described by Juliet Mitchell (1973) as "primary oppression" is accurate. In *Women's Estate* she declares that the most extreme perspective is not that women's oppression arises within an economically exploitive society but rather that is an oppression that is separate from any historical context. It is out of a need for power that men must dominate women. This perspective assumes that we are in a war, unnamed but pervasive, in which men as a group feel compelled to dominate the other half of humanity and have attempted to do so since the beginning of time. The sexualization of women in the media, the statistics on the universality of rape, the existence of human trafficking throughout the world, the status of women in many parts of the world, and the evidence in the United States for a "war on women," as described by Metzl in this volume, are all factors that support that view.

We will, in addition, need to untangle our belief from earliest history that women are a subcategory of men—Adam's rib. Simone de Beauvoir (2009) writes about the category of "other" being as primal as consciousness itself. Men and women are seen as a totality, united by a biological bond. If the couple is a fundamental unity with the two halves riveted together, the cleavage of society along the lines of sex becomes impossible. "Every individual concerned to justify his existence involves an undefined need to transcend himself, which he does in part through domination of the 'other'" (p. 58). Males nurtured and raised by females have related to women, beginning with their mothers, as self-objects. The female body, perceived as available from infancy through adulthood to satisfy men's needs, has been viewed not as belonging to a separate person but as an appendage that men may control at will.

Silverman (1996) elaborates upon the idea that men respond to women as an extension of the self and that their view of women is idiopathic. Woman is viewed as an object or possession, lacking separate human qualities that would necessitate empathy or recognition of important differences. The idiopathic approach may be familiar to us as a kind of cultural narcissism in which only those traits that mirror and reinforce the self-image of the subject are acknowledged. From this perspective women's experience has not registered in a cohesive world view as proscribed by law, religion, or morality. Men as dominant have been shaped by countless cultural prescriptions to acknowledge women only as they support and strengthen their dominance.

The heteropathic perspective (Silverman, 1996), a perspective that acknowledges the separateness of the other, does not presuppose an imaginary unity and is able to assimilate important differences. But it has been difficult to embrace in the relationship between men and women. It is as if men at the cultural level possess disorders of the self so that the essential self is either chronically depleted of self-esteem or unrealistically heightened in self-acceptance. Dependence on women as love objects prevents fragmentation. If women were to act independently as agents of their sexuality and reproductive capabilities, the illusion of merger would be dismantled.

A characteristic of many oppressed groups and one that is certainly true of women is they cannot assist in their own defense. Women have suffered what might be called "cultural trauma" (Aaron Toronto, personal communication, 2014). They are thus impaired by the symptoms that we all recognize in a person who has suffered post-traumatic stress disorder. Individual women may be extremely well-balanced, enhanced, and empowered, but as a group one can readily identify symptoms associated with ongoing trauma.

Marilyn Charles (2011) calls this phenomenon "structural trauma" and describes it as follows:

> Prejudice, intolerance and stigma are endemic in human interactions, and yet they can be relatively invisible. These "structural traumas" are often obscured by social convention such that environmental difficulties are experienced as internal deficits. When basic human functions become gendered, disrespect for the more primary ways of knowing associated with feminine sensibilities become internalized. The internalized disrespect threatens to leave us disconnected from sensory aspects of awareness, including the affective signals that are crucial to social development.
>
> *(p. 337)*

The Psychodynamic Diagnostic Manual (2006) lists as common subjective experiences of PTSD that of feeling overwhelmed, loss of a sense of security, fears of injury and death, and a "profound emotional numbness" (p. 101). Recurring traumatic experiences may disrupt mental capacities and disturb the capacity for symbolization. Judgment and reality testing may be impaired. Sufferers may experience grief, guilt about anger, destructive impulses, and shame about feeling helpless. They may feel, like my patient Michelle, dissociation of affect with an inability to connect negative feelings with the events that gave rise to the trauma. All of these factors in an individual would make it difficult for her to assist in her own defense. An abused woman may identify with the power of her abuser and vociferously defend him. There are, in fact, large cohorts of women who argue for the status quo and the continuance of women's suppression. Yet it is the entire group, the half of humanity, that must come together to fight for freedom in all aspects of life—beginning with reproductive autonomy.

The barriers toward equality and mutuality between the men and women abound, not the least being the pervasive effects of women as nurturers of children.

In her well-known treatise, *The Bonds of Love*, Jessica Benjamin (1988) states that "domination and submission result from a breakdown of the necessary tension between self-assertion and mutual recognition that allow self and other to meet as sovereign equals" (p. 12). The mother–child dyad that would serve ideally as a template for mutuality all too often fails. Unable to be so attuned with each other as to maintain the constant tension of mutuality, the subjectivity of the mother is sacrificed to the well-being of the child. His (and I mean *his*) needs become paramount in the eyes of the world and in the cultural scripts that mothers have internalized. The female child in identification with the mother forsakes her subjectivity and becomes the submissive partner in relationships to come.

Resolution: Some possibilities

Our understanding of the nature of mutuality in relationships tells us that in order for women and men to be autonomous beings, each must stand alone with a narrative, a lived experience that each has authored. Only from a vantage point that each has created can human beings hold both the unity of merging and the duality of separateness. In ways yet to be discovered males and females will merge, re-emerge and merge again while retaining an autonomous psychic wholeness. My patient, Michelle, who has been drawn again and again to powerful men who exploit her and then leave, will allow herself to be powerful in her own right. Charlie will be able to explore the dissociated aspects of himself that view women as not human—objects to satisfy his desires.

Yet mutuality—a union of equals—remains elusive between the sexes. There are practical actions that can and must be taken. Education and financing directed toward women in undeveloped countries are certainly essential. Political representation by and for women in every country is indispensable. Birth control, reproductive choice, maternal and prenatal care, as well as basic necessities of food and shelter must be available to all. But the modifications and improvement will shift and change with the cultural and political climate unless we address the formidable forces that drive the human male to own and control women's sexuality. That particular need has shaped law and religion, war and peace, art and philosophy—virtually all of the underpinnings of culture since time began. Women must take up the call to tell the story and weave it into a world view—one that acknowledges in public ways the horrors of rape and sexual exploitation, the joy and sorrow that is childbirth, and the gift to civilization that mothering represents.

History tells us that when any oppressed group is fighting for freedom, they must, if they want to succeed, have help from the members of the ruling class. Women cannot win this fight alone. In the US battle against slavery, the abolitionists were of the ruling class, and yet they cared and empathized with the plight of the slaves and lent enormous political and financial support on behalf of the cause. In women's battle for real freedom, men, many men, will be required to take up the campaign of full equality, again, beginning with reproductive autonomy. It will require the support of men like Charlie—"nice" men who say that they respect women but who carry in their rucksack of secrets a place in which women are "things," objects to be exploited in order to shore up their own self-esteem. It will mean that they identify with women and what they are experiencing when they are raped or abused or denied access to appropriate health care. It will not be enough for them to be horrified at what other men do but to search within themselves to evaluate whether they could or would do it as well.

Eve Ensler (2001) in her ground-breaking play *The Vagina Monologues* creates a marvelous image that I believe captures the magnitude of the change that will be required for women to be truly free. In her introduction, she states: "We have not cracked the tectonic plate at the center of the human psyche that is more terrifying to love than to kill. . . . It is the culture that has to change—the beliefs, the underlying story, and the behavior of the culture" (p. xx). Patriarchal culture is based on a need for conquest, power, and aggression. It depends upon a bond, either spoken or unspoken, between the rulers and the oppressed. Equality among all persons, and in particular between the sexes, demands mutuality and the possibility of love. For women to participate they must become agents and arbiters of their sexual and reproductive lives.

References

Allen, S.A. (2011). *The peach keeper.* New York, NY: Bantam.

Alliance of Psychoanalytic Organizations. (2006). *Psychodynamic diagnostic manual.* Silver Spring, MD: Author.

Balsam, R.M. (2012). *Women's bodies in psychoanalysis.* New York, NY: Routledge.

Barnett, M. (1966). Vaginal awareness in the infancy and childhood of girls. *Journal of the American Psychoanalytic Association, 14*, 129–141.

Benjamin, J. (1988). *The bonds of love.* New York, NY: Random House.

Brown, S. (2003, Spring/Summer). *Feminist history of rape.* Olympia, WA: Washington Coalition of Sexual Assault Programs.

Campbell, J. (1988). *The power of myth.* New York, NY: Anchor.

Caruth, C. (1996). *Unclaimed experience: Trauma, narrative and history.* Baltimore, MD: Johns Hopkins University Press.

Charles, M. (2011). What does a woman want? *Psychoanalysis, Culture and Society, 16*(4), 337–353.

de Beauvoir, S. (2009). *The second sex* (C. Borde & S. Malovany-Chevallier, Trans.). New York, NY: Vintage.

Dimen, M. (2011). *With culture in mind.* New York, NY: Routledge.

Dimen, M., & Goldner, V. (2002). *Gender in psychoanalytic space.* New York, NY: Other Press.

Ehrenreich, B., & English, D. (1973). *Witches, midwives and nurses.* New York, NY: The Feminist Press.

Ensler, E. (2001). *The vagina monologues.* New York, NY: Villard.

Forster, E.M. (1924). *A passage to India.* New York, NY: Harcourt.

Kestenberg, J. (1982). The inner-genital phase—Prephallic and preoedipal. In D. Mendell (Ed.), *Early female development* (pp. 81–125). New York, NY: Spectrum.

Layton, L. (2004). *Who's that girl? Who's that boy? Clinical practice meets postmodern gender theory.* London: The Analytic Press.

Lee, H. (1960). *To kill a mockingbird.* New York, NY: Harper and Row.

Lewis, H.B. (1987). *Sex and the superego: Psychic war in men and women.* London: Lawrence Erlbaum Associates.

Mitchell, J. (1973). *Women's estate.* New York, NY: Norton.

Rabinowitz, N. (2011). Greek tragedy: A rape culture? *EuGeStA, 1,* 1–21.

Rothman, B. (1994). *Beyond mothers and fathers: Ideology in a patriarchal society.* New York, NY: Routledge.

Rustin, M. (2007). Introduction. In C. Bainbridge, S. Radstone, M. Rustin, & C. Yates (Eds.), *Culture and the unconscious* (pp. 1–4). New York, NY: Palgrave.

Shakespeare, W. (1988). *The complete works.* New York, NY: Dorset Press.

Silverman, K. (1996). *The threshold of the visible world.* New York, NY: Routledge.

Tinkle, T. (2010). *Gender and power in Medieval exegesis.* New York, NY: Palgrave MacMillan.

2

FEMINISM

A revolutionary call about female sexuality

Doris K. Silverman

Four decades ago, Cixous (1976), a strong, well-regarded French feminist, issued a call to arms for women. She maintained that women suffered under the restraints of a patriarchal society, that they were reduced to a subsidiary role. She wanted females to demonstrate their unique voices, to write their experiences, to own and honor their bodies and their unique singularities. Yes, women were marginalized by the dominant androcentric culture. However, as Cixous argued, there were narrow passageways, disorienting marginalia, wherein women could alter and resist the center dominated by the male hierarchy.

A personal example of my recognition of phallocentricity and its consequences occurred when I was a graduate student at The Research Center for Mental Health, part of the doctoral program at NYU. It was a hot-bed of empirical research. I slowly realized that all the experiments conducted then had only male subjects. When I questioned this issue, I was told that "females mess up the data," and so they were omitted from research. Marginalized! This led to my support of experimental research on females: my professional focus and published work dealt frequently with sex, gender, and developmental issues for females, and I maintained an affiliation with Division 35.

Feminists, including psychoanalysts, responded to Cixous's call. Views about female sexuality were initially the only focus. The relevance of the concept of gender wasn't entertained until the feminists in the 1970s began making distinctions between sex and gender. Women researchers began studying and writing about the female experience; their research reflected the domains of both sex and gender. We seemed to be on a revolutionary road.

Many decades have passed. How have we fared?

Major advances for women are always being touted even though we continue to be fewer in number in many important positions. Nonetheless, there are now more female executives, heads of universities, deans, department heads, and professors even at Ivy League universities. More women are now in Congress. We have two serious Presidential contenders. Women function as anchors on TV, and we maintain important voices on radio. Our own field has changed dramatically, and it is filled with smart, competent females who are role models. We no longer are an almost exclusive female audience with males dominating the lectern at professional meetings. Recently I finished a 12-year term as head of the Rapaport-Klein Study group. This was a group centered on the work of David Rapaport, a brilliant theoretician of psychoanalysis, who had enormous influence on his male students and colleagues. It was initially an all-male power-house of intellectual brilliance, and it was maintained that way for a considerable period of time. A female broke that intellectual barrier.

Significant gains have definitely been made but if we look more closely at the various ways in which the culture reflects the prevailing views of women, I believe a different picture emerges. I will first briefly explore advertising and the media as highly significant barometers of the societal views of women. I will then consider the new sexual mores exemplified in tattooing, sexting, and hooking up that reflect contemporary societal views and more relevant feminist views.

Advertising and the media

Items from advertising and movies capture both the regressive and progressive pulls for women. Consider ads for Cialis, a product that deals with male erectile dysfunction. What is noticeable in the interactions of heterosexual couples in the ads are the marked hierarchical differences in the couple. For example, one ad depicts a woman who enjoys hopping on one foot as she enters the room where her husband sees her. She is caught by surprise, apparently because she did not anticipate his presence. The "understanding" husband sees her hopping as a cute, quirky feature and she shyly enjoys his response. A second ad shows a couple playing checkers. The woman jumps a checker and looks up at her husband and beams while the man follows by jumping two checkers. He is the much smarter and better player, but he enjoys her adorable qualities. A third ad illustrates a women cheating at golf. Her man catches her but finds it endearing. These ads apparently serve to preserve the power and competence of males, especially since use of Cialis represents a loss of virility.

One way of safeguarding phallocentric behavior and men's esteem, while hiding their narcissistic vulnerability, is by minimizing females—depicting them as shallow, silly, and feckless. Not all ads are like this; they are slowly changing. Yet it is important to recognize that it is still with us. The women in the Cialis ads are depicted as younger and less mature; they are not equal to their older male partners. It maintains what Glick and Fiske (1997) have labeled benevolent sexism. Benevolent sexism is a subtle view of the interactive relationship. It is defined by the authors as "characterizing women as pure creatures who ought to be protected, supported and adored and whose love is necessary to make a man complete" (Glick & Fiske, 1997, p. 119). Men demonstrate idealization of the woman in their benevolent sexism attitude and, according to these authors, men view this role as "cherishing" of women. Nevertheless, it continues a hierarchical relationship in which women are seen as unequal and less competent, thereby needing and accepting male superiority and protection. Many women experience benevolent sexism as comforting and satisfying and are willing to be in a subordinate position; they appreciate and foster such arrangements. Culturally, such a position is sanctioned. It reflects what Glick and Fiske label as the "good woman." It is a conventional view of women as selfless caregivers, ones who focus on the needs of others whether it is a spouse's, children's, parents', or friends'. Such a stance resists Cixous's interest in overturning traditional views and writing a unique story of individuality and competence.

Switching to film I want to compare the 1989 *The Little Mermaid* (Clements & Musker) with the 2013 film *Frozen* (Buck & Lee), which presents a new and distinctly different version of a woman and her love object. Since my own children are grown I'm no longer accustomed to visiting Disney movies. However, I was told about *Frozen* by my 5-year-old grandson in great detail who encouraged me to see it.

The Little Mermaid seems a typical fairy tale story of a princess yearning for the love of a handsome, strong prince. The mermaid initially defies her father, Neptune, the king of the seas, because she is curious about the world. She finds items from the human world that interest her, above all the attractive, young sailor prince with whom she falls in love. Her father forbids her to pursue anything human; after all, she is a mermaid. She risks hazards and the depths of hell to contact an evil sorceress. She wishes to become human so she can be with her gorgeous guy. As is typical there is great testing for both characters. There are storms, turmoil, near-death experiences, and finally romance and the uniting of the mermaid as human with her beloved prince. Even Neptune accepts that his daughter is in love and nothing can be done to sunder this love match. However, forgoing her mermaid-hood and becoming human, she gives up her voice and now is a silent woman, the ancient role of females subservient to their men.

Almost two and a half decades later, the film *Frozen* arrives. This is the story of two sisters and their love for each other. The older daughter, Elsa, is cursed with unusual power. She can turn everything to ice. During the course of growing up she secluded herself in her room, fearful of her great power because when she was young she accidently hurt her younger sister. A troll healed the younger sister, Anna, and made her forget her sister's powers. When the parents, the king and queen, die, Elsa is to become the next queen. She and her sister fight because Anna has made an unfortunate, hasty decision to marry a deceptive, evil, but handsome duke. Elsa knows this and refuses to grant her sister permission to marry. They fight and Elsa unleashes her power creating a cold, icy winter. She is after all the Snow Queen, of an old Hans Christian Andersen tale. Everyone in her kingdom is unhappy to live in a frozen, congealed winter prison. Elsa realizes she cannot royally manage the kingdom and she departs and builds herself a remote ice castle removed from civilization.

Alone, climbing to her icy aerie, she sings a powerful song about not having to live the life of a perfect, well-behaved girl who conceals her consuming emotions. She sings the hit song from the movie, "Let It Go," while simultaneously throwing shards of ice through the air, stamping her feet to produce marvelous geometric ice shapes, her arms offering artfully floating curlicues of snow, her body movements transforming the landscape with kaleidoscopic and voluminous crystal formations. With a sense of abundant, robust freedom she sings of her newfound isolation where she can let loose all that she can't keep inside any longer. In the song she recalls past directives to suppress her emotions and hide her true nature. These are juxtaposed with an inability or unwillingness to live up to them anymore. The song speaks of exploring her potential, and throughout there is an overall sense of triumph. And while a written description can't do the song justice, perhaps my 5-year-old grandson's rendition would as he unabashedly belts it out, imitating all her movements and casting icy fractals into the air—a marvelous sight. The appeal of this movie includes both boys and girls.

Although I will present many of the features that demonstrate an enhanced thematic characterization of female roles in a current Disney picture, there is also a stereotypic reliance on old sexist notions about beauty and appearance for women. As Elsa sings her song of independence, she increasingly takes on characteristics of a Barbie doll. She flings her hair about so that it is long and loosened, not the more prim appearance when we first see her. As queen she wears a modest dress that completely covers her body. In her song of freedom, she wears a sexy off-the-shoulder dress with an erotically revealing skirt. The outfit highlights her idealized small waist and curvaceous figure. This new look is that of the typically enticing sexy woman that she is supposed to have given up in her quest for isolation. Here is the more familiar and traditional objectification of females based on their bodily appearance that the Disney movie highlights.

In the progressive features of *Frozen*, there is a new female anthem of freedom, no longer the silent women, but rather one of power, liberty, and selfhood. Elsa is willing to tolerate and even endorse isolation, rather than fulfill an insistent need to offer up her independence and confidence to achieve security under the protection of a husband.

Elsa's willingness to remove herself from the world is, of course, the opposite of the Little Mermaid who makes a great self-sacrifice to be part of the human world, the goal of which is a significant love relationship.

There are a number of dynamic issues that converge on understanding Elsa's isolation. Elsa, the older sister, had to tolerate the arrival of her younger sibling. Anna is full of energy and naïve, lighthearted love. She is the direct, impulsive one, full of frolicking fun and engagement with what she experiences as a loving world. She is not the thoughtful, careful, controlled future queen. When they were younger, Elsa's ambivalence resulted in severely damaging her sister. It was the temporary enactment of her hostile impulse toward her younger, care-free sister. She punished herself by abandoning all human contact. Her removal to a remote citadel is in part her guilt over the harm she has caused her sister and her need for atonement. Elsa contains strong emotions as reflected in the theme song "Let It Go." Her song demonstrates a frenzied storm within her; the lyrics reflect her rage-filled embattlement that becomes more intense and gale-like as she proceeds up to her ice fortress. The eruption raging within is matched by the ice-cold winter without.

Yet, there is another feature of this isolation. Elsa is an artist, capable of producing sculptures of icy beauty. They are large, magnificent structures, dizzying swirls of curlicues, gorgeous geometric patterns, icicles that float and lift to the sky. She has filled her world and it is a gratifyingly aesthetic one to behold. Like many artists, she needed to remove herself from civilization, to maintain a hermit-like existence to produce beauty (think of Virginia Woolf who needed *"A Room of One's Own"* to depart and be alone to be generative [Gillian Silverman, personal communication, 2015]). Elsa's isolating herself can be thought of as a retribution for her aggression as well as a transformational sublimation for her creative life.

The second important feature of this postmodern fairy tale is the love of two sisters and the enduring trial of Anna to reach and restore their love for one another. This is the unusual point of this tale. The movie also has an unusual ending. Typically, the female protagonist needs the kiss of the strong, handsome prince who loves her and has endured trials which free her from her imprisonment and allow her to marry. True love in *Frozen* does not come from a man but from a sister who wants to restore their loving relationship. The turn is toward another woman rather than a man, a really unusual finality, suggesting all kinds of new partnering that can offer love and caring friendship. I see this as an important revolutionary turn.

Tattooing

I am at the gym. Women surrounding me are pumping iron and engaging in athletic feats that once were thought the sole ability of men. Adorning many female bodies are exotic, sometimes elaborate, tattoos. Increasingly more adolescents and young women are tattooing parts of their anatomy. In fact, now tattooing is more common among females than males (Hawkes *et al.*, 2004). Tattooing, even more than temporary body adornment, suggests a powerful, personal form of narrative. This is body painting that communicates a unique message for each individual. Sanders (1991), offering a history of tattooing, commented that tattooing was frequent among the aristocracy in the nineteenth century. By the early twentieth century in our own country, women frequently engaged in cosmetic tattooing (eyes, eyebrows, lips, cheeks). However, such painted ladies were condemned in newsprint and tattooing developed negative associations. It was gradually linked to disreputable types such as criminals, prostitutes, and biker chicks (Sanders, 1991, p. 150). Tattooing was considered the province of loose, rootless, transgressive females.

Currently, women engaged in tattooing come from a wide range of sociocultural backgrounds. They tend to paint different parts of their bodies than was typical in earlier times. Now tattoos are placed on the breast, back of the shoulder, the hips, pubic area, and lower abdomen. (On her celebration of her 40th birthday, the Barbie doll was given a visible tattoo of a butterfly [Mifflin, 2013].) Because there is individual selection of tattooing, it can give expression to a variety of symbolic meanings—from fearsome to benign. Biker chicks, associated with a more rebellious sub-culture of females, tend toward more disruptive tattoos such as skulls, frightening masks, scary spiders, and vipers. More typically, today's females are inclined to select benign symbols such as floral pieces, butterflies, gentle mythical beasts (unicorns), and colorful birds (Sanders, 1991). Breast cancer mastectomies are now replaced by tattoos for some, rather than prostheses or breast reconstructions. Such an act can be considered artistic as well as constructive. Such tattoos are covered by insurance as stipulated in The Breast Cancer Recovery Act. Some tattoos are on public display and others hidden, which undoubtedly are different forms of coded communications to the larger society.

In spite of it being more widespread, there is still negative commentary on females who tattoo. It is considered inappropriate and outside the norm of acceptable behavior (Forbes, 2001). Women who tattoo are typically deemed less attractive, sexually promiscuous, with a tendency for high consumption of alcohol (Swami & Furnham, 2007; Koch *et al.*, 2005; Hawkes *et al.*, 2004). Among college students there is greater risk taking and use of drugs among those who tattoo (Forbes, 2001).

Whereas some studies indicate negative features about tattooing, its "edginess" lends tattooing its important symbolic value for the avant garde. For example, in the October issue of American *Vogue* magazine (2015), there is a full-page presentation of an androgynous figure facing away from the reader. The figure has a large feral animal covering a major section of the upper back. The animal is somewhat mystical and somewhat terrifying, yet beautifully executed. The rest of the figure's body and arms are covered with smaller more delicate tattoos (Native-American and Japanese symbols) that contrast with the one that mostly covers the back of the figure. Here is cutting-edge fashion display. It is stylish and in (V)vogue. It is artistically done and it captures the imagination. There is ferocity and power along with delicacy and finesse. Women may like the connection with the fierceness and in-your-face assertions of difference in identification with biker chicks.

For many, permanent body painting is an important expression of their lived experience (Mifflin, 2013). Others feel it is part of their self-expression, a unique stamp. Some discuss their sense of empowerment. Permanent body paint can be a form of artistic expression, using the body as a canvas. Rather than traditional symbols of flowers and butterflies, now many take to designing their own tattoo reflecting personal meaning such as the *Vogue* depiction (Mifflin, 2013). It can enhance a sense of cultural resistance to conformity by attacking stereotyped norms of feminine adornment and behavior. It can mark a sense of belonging to a particular sub-group. It can ritualize a transition in one's life. For example, a young woman can be proclaiming she is no longer a child, and she can use her body to express her new identity. It has some consistency with Cixous's idea of writing what is distinctive for a particular woman and thus it reflects, for marginalized females, her typical narrative written on her body.

Sexting

A phenomenon undreamed of when the feminist revolution began is the practice of sexting, which is now quite common. Stasko and Geller (2015) reported that 80 percent of people surveyed on-line from ages 18 to 82 (more than half of whom were female) sexted. Many females sexted as part of a committed relationship, and more than 40 percent sexted as part of a casual relationship. The number of girls and teens sexting is not clear. What is typically reported is that a majority of teens are sexting. When girls, as well as teens, are calculated, the percentage appears to vary from 50 to 80 percent. (The latter figure is offered by Gadson *et al.*, 2014.) Sexting appears to increase with age.

The Atlantic (Rosin, 2014) did an in-depth study of this topic. Sexting refers to sexual messages delivered, and now, often accompanied by photos. Girls send nude photographs of themselves because, in most instances, they are pressured to do so by boys, sometimes friends, sometimes boyfriends. Her article covers sexting in middle school (6th through 9th grade) and through high school. In most cases, nothing untoward occurs for these young females. However, for some young girls who feel coerced to sext by a boy, they discover that their picture is then shared with many other males without their consent. A small number of these girls are so humiliated that they commit suicide (Rosin, 2014, p. 74; see also Bauman, 2015). The humiliation is understandable in that when photos are shared, the girl is often labeled a slut or ho (whore) or a thot (that ho over there). Boys, by contrast, do not experience any aftermath of criticism or shame whether they sext or not. For example, Hasinoff (2015) reported on a case of two cheerleaders who were suspended from school for sexting. The recipients of these photos distributed them without permission and they received no punishment. Despite the serious violation of these young girls' privacy, no penalty was exacted from the perpetrators. A double standard for the sexes still exists.

In the male pursuit of nude photos, there is an implicit objectification of females. As contemporary research reports, "To sexually objectify women is to mentally divide her body and mind in order to focus on her sexual body parts. Her body parts and their functions are no longer associated with her personality and emotions but are seen as instruments to be used by others (Bartky, 1990)" (as cited in Ramsey & Hoyt, 2015, p. 151; Weiner, 2015). Objectification appears to be ubiquitous in our culture without the recognition of the subtle, insidious effects it can produce in females (Fredrickson & Roberts, 1997; Ramsey & Hoyt, 2015). Objectification can have a demeaning, overly self-conscious, and shame-inducing effect on susceptible young women's ideas about their bodies.

Some data support the idea that it is the more vulnerable girls who respond to sexting pressure (Bauman, 2015; Drouin & Tobin, 2014; Drouin *et al.*, 2015; Reyns *et al.*, 2014). Middle school girls who are sexting are more likely to be engaging in sexual activity, a bit surprising for this age group (Houck *et al.*, 2014; Rice *et al.*, 2014). Older teenagers who sext may do so because they have problems with substance abuse and other personal issues, which lead to high risk behavior (e.g., unprotected sex) (Crimmins & Seigfried-Spellar, 2014; Drouin & Tobin, 2014; Temple *et al.*, 2014).

The positive feature of sexting is that it appears, for many girls, to be a normal feature of sexual experimentation and young women are actively taking advantage of exploration. They are pleased with their bodies and are willing to exhibit them.

There is also a sense of freedom and independence and resistance of conventional norms. Characteristic of this teenage position, one young girl commented, "This is my life and my body and I can do whatever I want with it. I don't see any problem with it. I am proud of my body" (Rosin, 2014, p. 67).

My summarizing of the literature on sexting suggests a complex picture of sexting. Middle school girls appear to be more troubled by sexting. They experience shame, especially when their photos are dispersed without their consent. Reputations can be seriously blemished with negative name labeling associated with girls who sext. Age appears to be a relevant consideration. Some studies report that female college students sext more frequently and have serious mental issues such as impulsivity, drug and alcohol use, insecure attachment relationships, and poor self-image. Although there may be an increased use of drugs and alcohol consumption, for many students, it is accomplished in the social context of a sanctioned college environment. As Hasinoff (2015) has opined, sexting is a form of "interpersonal intimacy and communication" (p. 1). She maintains that teens need protection from "malicious peers and overzealous prosecutors" and there is need for recognition of girls' agency and choices when there is consensual sexting (p. 2).

Hooking up

Before I present issues involved in the practice of hooking up, I need to mention that for many it is a vague term with different meanings for each of the sexes. The Online College Social Life Survey, which is a collaborative endeavor among a number of colleges, interviewed both sexes about hooking up. It covers a multitude of behaviors including: "kissing and non genital touching (34%), oral sex but not intercourse (15%), manual stimulation of the genitals (19%) and intercourse (35–40%). It can mean going all the way or everything but" (Kimmel, 2008, p. 195).

A narrative

I am reading a Sunday Style section article from the *New York Times* called "Modern Love" by Ali Rachel Pearl (October 18, 2015). The author is in her mid-20s—a working woman. In part of her story, she described a sexual experience she had with a man she had met 8 days before. She explained that he is a "stranger." She did not know him and thus to have sex with a stranger, she needed to drink a half-bottle of bourbon before they met.

Although she did not label their interaction, she was hooking up. She found the experience quite pleasurable. She described it in detail, including their spontaneity and lack of hesitation. It was "fun, invigorating and kind." Their first sexual experience on that eventful evening took place on a "wooden swing near a river in the trees behind the barn," and the second time occurred that same evening within the barn. They were both pleased with the experience and she described it as "romance and a whirlwind; It was sweat and sweet" on a humid summer evening. What is relevant is her willingness to describe her hook-up experience. She is open and direct about her sexual proclivities; that is, when she finds herself abstaining from sexual intimacy and when she is free to engage in it.

Sufficient cultural change has occurred so that there is acceptance of a woman offering her private confidences and intimacies in a public forum. What may have been once seen as a moral code of confidentiality, even secrecy about one's sexual intimacy with a stranger, is now brazenly overturned. It has much in common with sexting. Hook-ups can be considered an extension of sexting but it involves more than just the visual. The increased frequency of both experiences appears to be a function of a number of factors: the more relaxed sexual attitudes of the past half century, the feminist movement, accessibility of pornography, the media, and technology all probably contributed to their development.

As with the practice of sexting, there are positive features about hooking up and the personal narratives they give rise to. The sense of stimulation and excitement; the freedom in the moment of decision; the pleasure in the sexual act, and even for some, temporary romance can be part of hook-ups as it appears to be for Ali Rachel Pearl.

Casual carnal sex has been with us for a long time, although not necessarily communally supported. For many women, hook-up experiences provide a sense of self-assertion and exploration, a positive expression of their own sexual vitality and femininity, an affirmative feeling of their sensual-sexual selves that they wish to freely exhibit and communicate along with their appreciation of men's responsiveness to them. It expresses, as well, women's own equally lustful feelings toward another with the possibility of a hook-up leading to a relationship. Those who view themselves as affectionate and warm, uninhibited and direct about sex, are also likely to engage in hook-ups (Manthos et al., 2014). Hook-ups have certainly increased and are fairly wide-spread among college students (I will report on one high school commentary). It is the college age group that is typically investigated by researchers (England et al., 2007; Manthos et al., 2014; Kimmel, 2008).

What disturbs the picture presented above are the results of certain research. A portion of the research literature offers a different narrative for many young women. The sociological background of this phenomenon offers increased clarity that suggests a more complex view of hooking up. It starts with the double standard for the sexes, which, though reduced, still exists and reflects the lack of equality and the greater need for more progress. Kimmel (2008), whose research involves extensive surveys of students at college campuses, maintains that hooking up is really about male culture and their desires. Females accommodate to this culture. Thus, he claims, "When a guy says he hooked up with someone he may or may not have sex with her, but he is certainly hoping that his friends think he has. A woman, on the other hand, is more likely to hope they think she hadn't" (Kimmel, 2008, p. 197).

"The stereotype that males chase sex and are driven by lust but that females chase relationships and are driven by love" still has current valence (Reid et al., 2011, p. 548; see also Bogle, 2008). This leads to the idea that young women can have sex within relationships but young men are free to pursue sex indiscriminately. Thus, the hidden message for women seems to be the encouragement of being sexually attractive, thus inducing male's desire, but not the active pursuit of their own desire. (This is the view of passive females whom Freud wrote about in the early twentieth century.) If females desire sex, they are easily considered bad girls, sluts, and hos (Armstrong *et al.*, 2010). Thus, a study demonstrates that high school females' popularity decreases with more partners, even when some of these interactions become established relationships (Reid *et al.*, 2011). High school males, by contrast, experience an increase in popularity (Kreager & Staff, 2009). In college such men are called "studs" and "players" (Kreager & Staff, 2009). Women are not given favorable labels. In college hook-ups, it is clear that females have to delimit their desire to guarantee their status as viable for future relationships.

It is also relevant to illuminate the cultural and psychosocial factors that engage males during the period of high school, college, and somewhat beyond. Male attitudes and behavior contribute to a negative impact on women's sexual experience. Investigation of males between the ages of sixteen and twenty-six illuminates their development and the pressures they experience (Kimmel, 2008). This author maintains that these young boys and men continue to live out the Peter Pan syndrome. They never quite grow up. They are plagued by group and family demands to be "manly," and this idea is accommodated with its fantasy distortion of what it means to be manly. They drink, focus on sex and conquests, watch pornography, play video games, concentrate on sports, and see violent shoot-em-up movies. If not following these rules, they can readily be labeled "faggots" (Corbett, 2001) and suffer the physical and psychological abuse that follows this label.

Heterosexual males of college age appear less interested in relationships with females. Their buddy connections appear far more important, hence the expressions, "hanging out with their bros" and "bros before hoes." These expressions mean that nothing should interfere with their relationship to the guys in their group, especially not girlfriends or females in general. What is important to them are such questions as how each man stands in the pecking order; how manly or studly he is; how frequently he "scores." He wants to be seen as a cool, virile guy by his male friends or, as a patient offered, a "big dick guy."

Such male standards, especially characteristic of the college fraternity experience, lead to the need for sexual conquest. In particular, as Swope (2012, p. 27) states, "Research has suggested that hyper-masculine attitudes can be encouraged by fraternities or other peer groups characterized by competition, athleticism, heavy drinking, sexual domination of women, and sexism among members (Boeringer, 1999; Martin & Hummer, 1989; Schwartz & DeKeseredy, 1997)." Thus, there is the increased report of sexual coercion, rape, or attempted rape on college campuses.

Almost 28 percent of "college women have reported unwanted sex that met the legal definition of rape or attempted rape" (Koss *et al.*, 1997; Flack *et al.*, 2007). A survey reported that almost 13 percent of completed rapes, 35 percent of attempted rapes, and 23 percent of threatened rapes took place on a date (Kimmel, 2008, p. 273). Seventy-eight percent of unwanted intercourse takes place in the context of hooking up (Fisher *et al.*, 2000; reported by Kimmel, 2008). This is a compelling statistic; yet, newspaper reports typically indicate that in most instances the experience of rape goes unreported.

There are complex reasons for unwanted intercourse occurring, but high on the list is high alcohol consumption (Flack *et al.*, 2007). A huge amount of alcohol is consumed by both males and females when partying on campus. In addition, drugs are used. Males supply the "date rape drugs." Power inequality and sexual abuse frequently dominate with the use of alcohol and drugs. Research demonstrates that there is considerable male coercion of females. For example, a third of sexually active college males admitted to coercive and manipulative responses to get a disinclined female to have sex with them (Ramsey & Hoyt, 2015).

Females report that even when in relationships that are not hook-ups, these relationships threaten female academic achievement. They contribute as well to females feeling, or actually being, controlled and manipulated in ways that interfere with their friendships, often inducing jealousy in their male partners. In some instances the control by male partners escalates into stalking behavior (Armstrong *et al.*, 2010, p. 26).

Given the need to "score," it is important to seduce an attractive, sexy female. Male focus tends to be on the stereotyped physical attributes of females; that is, the objectification of female bodies mentioned earlier (Kozak *et al.*, 2009; Strelan & Hargreaves, 2005). The problem for females is that they, too, highlight their body parts and then believe that their desirability is based on their physical attributes. Their self-scrutiny and physical health can be in jeopardy (anorexia or binge eating and vomiting). Not only are females self-objectifying but, more important, they are less likely to concentrate on their own needs and desires and instead focus on those physical attributes that may be pleasing to males. It minimizes the likelihood of freedom to choose one's own sexual path.

For some females, hook-ups are a way of coping with stress. They can lose themselves in the abandonment of drugs, alcohol, and sex. Others need an attachment and even a brief encounter can feel salubrious. For a distinct group of students, there is significant evidence of alcohol abuse, depressive symptoms, feelings of loneliness, and low levels of religiosity for those engaging in hook-ups (Manthos *et al.*, 2014). Nevertheless, many females engage in hook-ups because they realize it is an important way of finding and establishing a relationship (Bogle, 2008).

Summing up

Starting with the sexual revolution, much change has taken place in the area of gender equality. Some believe a transformation has taken place in that women are succeeding in so many areas of life that previously were unavailable to them (Rosin, 2010; Kindlon, 2007). The movie *Frozen* is an example of a female assuming a new independent role, displaying her anguish as well as her strength, and upturning traditional norms about intimate desires. Sexting and hook-ups reflect women's body-affirming spirit and mettle; tattooing displays their personal narratives. Females today are more assertive and ambitious and less concerned about demonstrating it.

They are far more expansive in their thinking about the skills they possess or can acquire. They seek academic excellence and often exceed men in many graduate school placements and accomplishments. They are entering fields that were heretofore unavailable to them.

Yet, this is clearly not the whole picture. Heterosexual relationships are still quite fraught. We know this by the divorce rate. Women still undertake the greater amount of childcare and household work while holding down full-time jobs, often leading to conflict in relationships (Schiebinger & Gilmartin, 2010). Such disparities may be influenced by the idea that it takes some men a long time after college to give up their commitment to their buddies and the wish for sex rather than intimacy and relationships of care and genuine equality (Kimmel, 2008).

Currently there are both engagement and significant difference of views between two female authors who are in the public sphere of influence, Sandberg (2013) and Slaughter (2012, 2015). They discuss the problems of professional work lives of women. Sandberg exhorts women not to be subservient. Strong women in powerful positions are necessary and they need to give voice to their significant concerns. Women need to be assertive in both the domestic and the work sphere. They need to "lean in." They need to persevere until they reach the top. They, of course, also need to select an appropriate husband that can allow for a woman's high executive achievement. Slaughter, on the other hand, has left just such a high-powered political position because her adolescent child needed her during a difficult period for him. She felt, she said, "I'd been part, albeit unwittingly, of making millions of women feel that they are to blame if they cannot manage to rise up the ladder as fast as men and also have a family and an active home life (and be thin and beautiful to boot)." Given the current economic business demands and its culture, Slaughter does not believe "women can have it all." Not in the current climate where there is inflexibility in the workplace and women are penalized when they need time off for pregnancy, childcare, or eldercare. (This is, of course, even more the case for poor or single women where color and class distinctions are particularly relevant.)

In addition, Faludi (2013) points out that public policy contributes to sexism and discrimination. While mentioned by Sandberg, it is clear that this is not Sandberg's focus. Instead, she wants individual women to work harder (as though they are not doing more than that already). The clashing reality of family and demanding work lives takes a major toll on women. Their unavailability and increased stress for high-functioning women places great strains on intimacy and sexuality. It creates tension between husbands and wives and often, because of long work hours, leads to the neglect of childcare needs. One choice for some professional women is to drop out of the workplace and obsessively concentrate as a chief executive of their children's lives (Martin, 2015). Another choice some women make is to forego child-bearing and rearing (Daum, 2015). Today, almost a fifth of women in their mid-40s do not have children (Bolick, 2015). In this instance, smart, strong, empowered professional women know that time out for bearing and raising children means "catch up," which is difficult to accomplish and hampers careers. They opt out of bearing and bringing up children.

In addition to various forms of gender discrimination, there is still much stereotypical behavior discussed in this chapter and some women contribute to it by their tolerance and pleasure in their experience of benevolent sexism. Women's acquiescence to much in our androcentric culture continues to maintain their marginality. For Faludi (2013), women need to lean in individually but also join collectively to alter the many forms of inequality that continue to exist. Faludi's position contrasts Cixous's in that the latter's emphasis is on challenging sexism through individual narratives, not strong collective and supportive endeavors. A fair estimate of our current situation is what Schiebinger and Gilmartin (2010) have stressed: that we have won "half a revolution." We need to recognize that much has changed and much needs change. There is still the need for attention and hard work before true equality exists in the multiple spheres of women's lives.

References

Armstrong, E.A., Hamilton, L., & England, P. (2010). Is hooking up bad for young women? *Contexts, 9*(3), 22–27.

Bartky, S.L. (1990). *Femininity and dominance: Studies in the phenomenology of oppression.* New York, NY: Routledge.

Bauman, S. (2015). Cyberbullying and sexting: School mental health concerns. In R.H. Witte & G.S. Mosley-Howard (Eds.), *Mental health practice in today's schools: Issues and interventions* (pp. 241–263). New York, NY: Springer.

Boeringer, S. (1999). Associations of rape-supportive attitudes with fraternal and athletic participation. *Violence Against Women, 5*, 81–90.

Bogle, L. (2008). *Hooking up: Sex, dating and relationships on campus.* New York, NY: New York University Press.

Bolick, K. (2015, April 6). Selfish, shallow, and self-absorbed. Book review section. *The New York Times.*

Buck, C., & Lee, L. (Directors). (2013). *Frozen* [Animated film]. United States: Walt Disney Pictures.

Cixous, H. (1976). The laugh of the Medusa. *Signs, 1*, 875–891.

Clements, R., & Musker, J. (Directors). (1989). *The little mermaid* [Animated film]. United States: Walt Disney Pictures.

Corbett, K. (2001). Faggot = Loser. *Studies in Gender and Sexuality, 2*, 3–28.

Crimmins, D.M., & Seigfried-Spellar, K.C. (2014). Peer attachment, sexual experiences, and risky online behaviors as predictors of sexting behaviors among undergraduate students. *Computers in Human Behavior, 32*, 268–275.

Daum, M. (2015). *Selfish, shallow, and self-absorbed: Sixteen writers on the decision not to have kids.* New York, NY: Picador.

Drouin, M., Ross, J., & Tobin, E. (2015). Sexting: A new digital vehicle for intimate partner aggression? *Computers in Human Behavior, 50*, 197–204.

Drouin, M., & Tobin, E. (2014). Unwanted but consensual sexting among young adults: Relations with attachment and sexual motivations. *Computers in Human Behavior, 31*, 412–418.

England, P.E., Schafer, E., & Fogarty, A.C.T. (2007). Hooking up and forming relationships in today's college campuses. In M. Kimmel (Ed.), *The gendered society reader.* New York, NY: Oxford University Press.

Faludi, S. (2013). Facebook feminism: Like it or not. *Baffler, 23*. Retrieved from http://the-baffler.com/salvos/facebook-feminism-like-it-or-not

Fisher, B.S., Cullen, F.T., & Turner, M.G. (2000). *The sexual victimization of college women.* Retrieved from the National Institute of Justice Research Report website: http://www.ojp.usdoj.gov

Flack, Jr., W.F., Daubman, K.A., Caron, M.C., Asadorian, J.A., D'Aureli, N.R., Gigliotti, S.N. . . . Stine, E.R. (2007). Risk factors and consequences of unwanted sex among university students: Hooking up, alcohol, and stress responses. *Journal of Interpersonal Violence, 22*, 139–157.

Forbes, G.B. (2001). College students with tattooing and piercing: Motives, family experiences, personality factors, and perception by others. *Psychological Reports, 89*, 774–786.

Fredrickson, B.L., & Roberts, T.A. (1997). Objectification theory: Understanding women's lived experience and mental health risks. *Psychology of Women Quarterly, 21*, 173–206.

Gadson, C.A., Griggs, T.L., & Duan, M.G. (2014). Developing a taxonomy of negative sexting experiences: A qualitative and exploratory study. *American Psychological Association Convention Presentation.*

Glick, P., & Fiske, S.T. (1997). Hostile and benevolent sexism. *Psychology of Women Quarterly, 21*, 119–135.

Hasinoff, A.A. (2015). *Sexting panic: Rethinking criminalization, privacy and consent.* Urbana, IL: University of Illinois Press.

Hawkes, D., Senn, C.Y., & Thorn, C. (2004). Factors that influence attitudes toward women with tattoos. *Sex Roles, 50*, 593–604.

Houck, C.D., Barker, D., Rizzo, C., Hancock, E., Norton, E., & Brown, L.K. (2014). Sexting and sexual behavior in at-risk adolescents. *Pediatrics, 133*, 276–282.

Kimmel, M. (2008). *Guyland: The perilous world where boys become men.* New York, NY: HarperCollins.

Kindlon, D. (2007). *Alpha girls: Understanding the new American girl and how she is changing the world.* New York, NY: Rodale Press.

Koch, J.R., Roberts, A.E., Armstrong, M.L., & Owen, D.C. (2005). College students, tattoos, and sexual activity. *Psychological Reports, 111*, 97–106.

Koss, M.P., Gidyez, C.A., & Wisniewski, N. (1997). The scope of rape: Incidence and prevalence of sexual aggression and victimization in a national sample of higher education students. *Journal of Consulting and Clinical Psychology, 55*, 162–170.

Kozak, M., Frankenhauser, H., & Roberts, T. (2009). Objects of desire: Objectification as a function of male sexual orientation. *Psychology of Men and Masculinity, 10*, 225–230.

Kreager, D., & Staff, J. (2009). The sexual double standard and adolescent peer acceptance. *Social Psychology Quarterly, 72*, 143–164.

Manthos, M., Owen, J., & Fincham, F.D. (2014). A new perspective on hooking up among college students: Sexual behavior as a function of distinctive groups. *Journal of Social and Personal Relationships, 31*, 815–829.

Martin, P.Y., & Hummer, R.A. (1989). Fraternities and rape on campus. *Gender and Society, 3*, 457–473.

Martin, W. (2015, May 17). Poor little rich women. *The New York Times.*

Mifflin, M. (2013). *Bodies of subversion? A secret history of women and tattoo.* Brooklyn, NY: Powerhouse.

Pearl, A.R. (2015, October 18). Modern love. *The New York Times.*

Ramsey, L.R., & Hoyt, T. (2015). The object of desire: How being objectified creates sexual pressure for women in heterosexual relationships. *Psychology of Women Quarterly, 39*, 151–170.

Reid, J.A., Elliot, S., & Webber, G.R. (2011). Casual hookups to formal dates: Refining the boundaries of the sexual double standard. *Gender and Society, 25*, 545–568.

Reyns, B.W., Henson, B., & Fisher, B.S. (2014). Digital deviance: Low self-control and opportunity as explanations of sexting among college students. *Sociological Spectrum, 34*, 273–292.

Rice, E., Gibbs, J., Winetrobe, H., Rhoades, H., Plant, A., Montoya, J., & Kordic, T. (2014). Sexting and sexual behavior among middle school students. *Pediatrics, 134*, 21–28.

Rosin, H. (2014, November). Why kids sext. *The Atlantic Monthly*, 64–77.

Rosin, H. (2010, July/August). The end of men. *The Atlantic Monthly*.

Sandberg, S. (2013). *Lean in: Women, work, and the will to lead*. New York, NY: Knopf Doubleday.

Sanders, C.R. (1991, Winter). Memorial decoration: Women, tattooing, and the meaning of body alteration. *Michigan Quarterly Review, 30*, 146–156.

Schiebinger, L., & Gilmartin, S.K. (2010). Housework is an academic issue: How to keep talented women scientists in the lab where they belong. American Association of University Professors. Retrieved from http://www.aaup.org/article/housework-academic-issue#. Via7EsvD85s.

Schwartz, M.D., & DeKeseredy, W.S. (1997). *Sexual assault on the college campus. The role of male peer support*. Thousand Oaks, CA: Sage Press.

Slaughter, A.-M. (2012). Why women can't have it all. *The Atlantic Magazine*, July–August.

Slaughter, A.-M. (2015). *Unfinished business: Women, men, work, family*. New York, NY: Random House.

Stasko, E., & Geller, P. (2015). How common is sexting? Reframing sexting as a positive relationship behavior. Retrieved from http://commonhealth.wbur.org/2015/08/sexting-adults-relationships

Strelan, P., & Hargreaves, D. (2005). Women who objectify other women: The vicious cycle of objectification. *Sex Roles, 52*, 707–712.

Swami, V., & Furnham, A. (2007). Unattractive, promiscuous and heavy drinkers: Perceptions of women with tattoos. *Body Image, 4*, 343–352.

Swope, K.H. (2012). Rape myth acceptance: An exploration of influential factors among college students. Theses and Dissertations, Indiana University of Pennsylvania, Indiana, PA.

Temple, J.R., Le, V.D., van den Berg, P., Ling, Y., Paul, J.A., & Temple, B.W. (2014). Brief report: Teen sexting and psychosocial health. *Journal of Adolescence, 37*, 33–36.

Vogue (2015). American edition. October.

Weiner, J. (2015, May 30). The pressure to look good. Contributing Op-Ed Writer Sunday Review. *The New York Times*.

Woolf, V. (1929). *A room of one's own*. Raleigh, NC: Lulu Press.

3

"WE'RE (NOT) PREGNANT"

Gay men and women's reproductive rights

Richard Ruth

Gay men's lives are shaped by the oppression we experience in a still decidedly homophobic society. Homophobia often makes its most pointed attacks when gay men assert our right to control our bodies—how we move, how we express our desires, how we protect ourselves—with self-determination and pride (Plummer, 1999). We should therefore be the natural allies of women's demand for reproductive rights, which is, at its core, about the right of women to control their bodies.

But the reality is that we are not. At a time when women's reproductive rights are under renewed legal, political, psychological, and often physical assault (Ernst *et al.*, 2003/4), gay men, collectively, have not taken a pro-women, pro-feminist stand for women's reproductive rights (Miller, 2000). To the contrary, some currents in the—progressive and welcome—move toward gay male couples parenting are starkly misogynist.

This disturbing, and dangerous, emerging reality is all the more critical to understand at the current historical juncture. Backlash against advances in the rights and safety of gay men (Bronski, 2000) and backlash against advances in women's rights and safety, especially the right to unencumbered reproductive freedom (Faludi, 2009), are both on the rise. Hard-won gains are eroding, and at heightened risk of eroding further—most especially, women's right to reproductive freedom (Greenhouse & Siegel, 2011).

This chapter aspires to contribute to turning this situation around by examining how the disjuncture between feminism and gay men—and the gay civil rights movement—has developed since the launch of the gay movement in the US following Stonewall (Duberman, 2013) and by examining some threads of misogyny in the move toward gay parenting as they uniquely become visible through the lens of a psychoanalytic case.

Gay men and feminism: A historical perspective on beginnings

The focus of the women's liberation movement, as it was called in the 1960s and 1970s (Evans, 1979) and is now called second-wave feminism (Baxandall & Gordon, 2002), was women's rights and freedom in a society then even more rigidly and oppressively patriarchal than US society is now. There was nothing subtle about it; the status of women's oppression was not a matter principally of attitudes but rooted in the objective denial of women's legal and economic rights, violence against women, and patriarchal power. (There are distinct intersections of women's oppression and racial/ethnic oppression that now lead many to speak of feminisms, rather than feminism; for examples of these analyses, which lie largely outside the scope of this paper, see Chow [1987]; Collins [2000]; García [1997]; Hooks [1981]; Hull *et al.* [2003]; Smith [2005]; Thompson [2002]. Similarly, this chapter will focus mostly on developments in the United States.)

Yet, from the beginning, second-wave feminism recognized, and taught the broader society and its social movements, about the intimate ways that oppression reaches deeply into subjective experience and personal, emotional realities. This was captured in the insight that "the personal is political" (Hanisch, 1969/2006) and in the methodology of consciousness-raising groups (Larson, 2014) that the women's movement of the time practiced and spread widely.

In 1969, gay men and lesbians in the US were inspired by the example of the women's movement, and other social movements of the time, to take a public stand for our right to live in freedom, and with pride. (Although the gay movement included both gay men and lesbians, the alliances were loose, with more differences in focus than a common trajectory [Johnston, 1973]. Similarly, the distinct narratives and experiences of gay men of color [Beam, 1986; Brown, 2014; Hemphill, 1991; Leong, 2014; Marsiglia, 1998; Rodríguez, 2006] deserve separate treatment.) Beginning with a violent protest against police harassment at the Stonewall bar in New York, led by drag queens (Duberman, 2013), a movement that called itself the gay liberation movement arose (Cruikshank, 1992; Kissack, 1995; Thompson, 1994; Valocchi, 1999a). The movement named itself in parallel to the women's liberation movement, and other radical social movements of the time in the US and the Third World, and framed itself intentionally not as a narrowly focused movement for civil rights but as a movement with an ambitious broader scope—in its own conceptualization, liberation, with both personal and political dimensions (Valocchi, 2001).

The movement of gay men that began at Stonewall adopted the use of consciousness-raising groups from the women's movement (Jay & Young, 1992). Across the US, and in other countries in Europe and Latin America, small, intimate groups of gay men met to share our experiences, learning that our shame, inhibitions, and experiences of internalized homophobia were not private or unique experiences, but rather were the psychological expression of a collective oppression (Larson, 2014). The movement intentionally melded consciousness raising with other forms of political activity, following the vision and successful trajectory of the women's movement of the time (Jay & Young, 1992; Teal, 1971).

Placing myself in history

Feminist scholarship (Fonow & Cook, 1991) critiques other trends in contemporary social and behavioral science and advocates that we not just insert but locate our studies in our personal experience. I bring that perspective to this chapter.

I grew up male, with an incipient awareness that I was gay, before the women's movement of the 1960s and 1970s introduced not just women but men to the notion that male lives could be lived in different ways—less oppressive to women and less constricting and thus less oppressive to men (Kaufman, 1994, has written theoretically about this phenomenon)—from what had been envisioned in the years after the suppression of first-wave feminism (Banks, 1986).

Like many, if not most, gay males of my 1960s generation, I internalized early in life that my failure to embrace or live up to (heterosexual) male ideals meant that I was destined to rejection, loneliness, sometimes physically violent bullying, and misery. Though I did not know, at the time, that pre-feminist US psychoanalytic theorizing held that male homosexuality is the product of an overinvolved mother, a distant father, and, therefore, developmental arrest (Drescher, 2008), I knew that the playground was dangerous and adolescent social life was hell. My fantasies of personal and sexual fulfillment took proscribed forms; "successful" male socialization, I knew well, would occur, to the extent it did, at the price of the death of my soul. One of the first things I learned about my emerging sexual identity was that, in most parts of the Western world, it was illegal at the time and therefore dangerous (Johnson, 2009).

Before Stonewall, it was the women's liberation movement that gave me a sense of possibility. I hungrily consumed Friedan's *The Feminine Mystique* (1963/2010) as a teenager and Hanisch's "The Personal is Political" (1969/2006) when it first appeared, transcribing the texts from a female to a gay male idiom. Feminism gave me vision and empowerment to come out short years after Stonewall.

One of my first actions after coming out was to join a consciousness-raising group. We shared painful experiences of oppression, awkward first steps in being out, and dreams of a different future, and we saw each other through for three crucially transformative years. We did not take each other on about the equal reality of gay men having male privilege, a gap I realized only in hindsight.

I went through graduate school, and then psychoanalytic training, as an out gay man, something not common in the 1970s. I feel very fortunate to have had the support of feminist women in my personal life, and my emerging professional life, from the beginning of my journey to become a clinical psychologist and a psychoanalyst. This bolstered my courage and perseverance, though I was painfully aware that, as I encountered some colleagues' overt homophobic dismissal, I had no role models ready at hand. None of my graduate school professors, analytic institute instructors, or supervisors was gay; as in an earlier phase of my development, I felt tolerated, at times warmly tolerated, but alone. I learned important insights about who I was in my consciousness-raising group that felt impossible to extend into my seminars and training analysis. Contextualizing my early professional development, I lived through the first stages of the divergence that came to divide the women's movement from the gay movement, not aware at the time of what was happening, where it came from, or its implications.

Feminism and gay men: History and politics in the post-Stonewall years

Like many radical movements, the gay liberation movement faced the challenges of surviving oppression's assaults, maintaining its momentum, broadening its appeal beyond narrow circles, and avoiding cooptation (Jay & Young, 1992; Power, 1995; Sears, 2005; Thompson, 1994; Valocchi, 2001). The dynamics and implications of this shift are complex and largely lie beyond the scope of this chapter. However, the largely white and relatively affluent nature of the early gay movement (Barrett & Pollack, 2005; Bernstein, 2002; D'Emilio, 1997, 2000, 2002, 2014; Richardson, 2005; Valocchi, 1999b); the fear-inducing impact of government repression against the social movements of the 1960s and 1970s (Churchill & Vander Wall, 2002); and conformist pressures in gay culture (Connell, 1992; Milton & MacDonald, 1984; Taywaditep, 2002) have been implicated in the early moves away from a more expansive view—closer to the feminism that had given rise to the gay liberation movement—of gay male possibilities.

Political and ideological tensions in gay communities and the gay movement were refracted, in the early 1980s, through the devastating effects of the coming of AIDS (Armstrong, 2002; Herek, 1999; Herek & Greene, 1995; Jonsen & Stryker, 1993). Thousands became fatally ill—not only gay men, but largely gay men—with a disease whose causes were unknown. The medical establishment was slow to mobilize desperately needed research efforts (Herek & Glunt, 1988) and reluctant or unwilling to provide needed health care (Grmek, 1993). The intense homophobia that shaped early reactions to AIDS is difficult but important to remember. Evangelical Christian voices welcomed AIDS as God's way of ridding society of gay men (Fetner, 2008), and voices in the gay movement felt the epidemic must have arisen as a product of a government conspiracy against gay men (Ross *et al.*, 2006). Anti-gay hatred and fear-fueled danger had its impact.

Activist organizations, such as the Aids Coalition To Unleash Power (ACT UP) (Gould, 2002), and community-built and -run organizations in which gay men and our allies cared for people with AIDS (Kayal, 1993) necessarily became the focus of organizing efforts in gay men's communities. A largely untold aspect of this period involves the many feminist women who helped take care of gay men when the gay male community's resources were taxed by the political and human demands of the early phases of the epidemic. I received my first HIV test from one such lesbian feminist woman who helped me overcome my terror. I do not know her name, but I owe her my life.

The discovery of protease inhibitors was a direct result of AIDS activists confronting the political and scientific establishments and insisting on new research directions and access to health care, and mental health and social services, to combat AIDS (Gould, 2002). With this and related discoveries, AIDS is now, for those with access to care, a chronic, manageable disease (Fee & Fox, 1992).

These welcome advances were, in significant part, the result of efforts of radical elements of the 1980s gay movement. But AIDS before protease inhibitors also brought with it the loss of thousands of the first gay male activists. The impacts—social, political, and psychological (Jonsen & Stryker, 1993; Morin *et al.*, 1984)—have been heavy. For a time, the politics of survival overcame the politics of possibility, and such changes, once established, are difficult to shift.

Currently, the gay liberation movement has largely given way to a gay civil rights movement (D'Emilio, 1997, 2000, 2002, 2014; D'Emilio *et al.*, 2000; Marcus, 1992; Mohr, 1995; Vaid, 1995; Valocchi, 2001; Wolfson, 1993). This has led to important advances, such as the elimination of anti-sodomy laws, the widespread (though still not universal) enactment of anti-discrimination laws for gay men and lesbians (and, to a lesser extent, for transgender persons), election of gay men to public office, the elimination of *de jure* bars to gay men serving in the military, changes in cultural values, and, increasingly, the right to gay marriage.

But, in the context of the focus of this chapter, here's the rub: The gay civil rights movement (as it now frames itself) largely turns away from the feminist critique of marriage as an institution (Auchmuty, 2004; Echols, 1989; Josephson, 2005) as well as feminist thought and the feminist agenda more broadly. An emerging literature critiques what has been lost in the gay movement's turn away from the politics of liberation toward a narrower, and differently oriented, politics of civil rights (Bersani, 1995; Crimp, 2002; D'Emilio, 1997, 2014; Muñoz, 2009; Warner, 1999). Yet much of this critique looks inwardly, toward dynamics and politics within gay communities and movements, and concerns itself less with gay men's interactions with other communities and social currents. It does not take up the broader problem of the gay movement's divergence from feminism (Halberstam, 2008; Weed & Schor, 1997) and the implications of this turn at the current juncture.

I first got in touch with this disturbingly pervasive and insidious trend when a colleague convinced me to watch an NBC series *The New Normal* (Murphy, 2012–2013). Its main protagonists were two white gay men (an obstetrician and a television producer) living privileged lives in an opulent California home. The show intermixed humorous moments, moving flashbacks to the protagonists' childhood rejection, depictions of their on-going family-of-origin tensions, and narration of the main characters' class and male privilege. A meandering plot line traced the two gay male protagonists' decisions to have a child by a surrogate and to marry. The protagonists often voiced the happy line, in common parlance among gay men today preparing to become fathers by surrogacy, "We're pregnant!" But they were not pregnant; their child's birth-mother-by-surrogacy was. The protagonists' playful dismissal of the surrogate mother's role was rooted in misogyny—treated playfully, but unmistakable. Over time, they came to develop some respect and fondness for the woman who was giving birth to the child they intended to raise, but they originally cast and treated her as an inconvenient means to their desired ends, and their dismissive, insensitive, and often hostile attitudes toward women kept breaking through.

That such a product of popular culture could so explicitly mark the turn in gay men's perspectives away from feminism, and any sense of collective alliance between gay men and women's rights to reproductive freedom, got me thinking. In the ways of psychoanalysts who see possible clues to broader social phenomena in themes that arise in our clinical work (Craib, 1990; Danto, 2005; Gaztambide, 2012; Layton *et al.*, 2006; Nguyen, 2012; Stake, 1978/2000), I began reflecting on my clinical experiences with gay men and what they might reveal.

Misogyny in gay male parenting: A case vignette

The men I will call Tom and Rick, a gay male couple in their thirties, originally sought couple and family therapy for help with their adolescent son, whom I will call Mike. They described Mike as defiant at home and achieving poorly in school. Tom and Rick had been together 9 years when our work together began.

Tom became Mike's father in a previous heterosexual marriage. He entered into the marriage though he knew he was "mostly gay" at the time. He told me he had spoken about this with the woman—who, by the time of the therapy, was his ex-wife—before they married, but I learned that they had never explored the implications deeply.

Tom assumed sole parental responsibility for Mike, his only child, with the consensual dissolution of the marriage and with the formal and legal agreement—again, not deeply considered together—of his ex-wife, who had a history of psychiatric problems. Tom spoke about his ex-wife in disparaging terms and overtly misogynist cast, referring to her as "crazy," "dysfunctional," and "hysterical," sourcing these traits in her femaleness. In our early sessions, he never narrated how he had come to care for her and to marry her, nor how it had come to be that he had made no overtures toward including her in parenting decisions and the parenting process with Mike, either at the time of the divorce or in the subsequent years.

Tom showed signs of bipolar disorder, though this had not been diagnosed at the time the couple began their 4 years of work with me. He equated his inattentiveness, periods of elevated mood, forgetfulness, and rejection of others' social expectations of him with the degrees of freedom from conventionality he assumed as an out gay man. Tom was out to the members of his working-class family of origin, who lived in another state and with whom he wished, and had, little contact. He also was out to his co-workers and preferred to socialize almost exclusively with other gay men.

Rick became sexually active with other males as a teenager, but he did not begin identifying as gay until after he had been with Tom, his first and only committed partner, for 2 years. Unlike Tom, he was from a middle-class family and had a college education. He described himself as "out to himself" and to a few close friends but not to his co-workers or to his family of origin. He liked going to gay bars, sometimes with Tom and sometimes on his own, and participated in social organizations in the gay community. In his personal manner, and in his behavior in sessions, however, I found him anxious, introverted, and quite shy.

In their initial meetings with me, Tom and Rick assumed that the gay solidarity they correctly perceived to be present among us would leave important questions and assumptions unexplored. They wanted help with Mike's "problem behaviors"; they did not want to explore their early histories, their inner lives, their dynamics as a couple, or their relationships with Mike's mother or with anyone else. I negotiated with them, indicating that these explorations were necessary to meaningful psychotherapy, and they warily and grudgingly agreed, ceding me authority as "the doctor"—which I experienced as investing me with an element of male heteronormative privilege. (That they knew I was gay did not seem to be an obstacle to the unfolding of this process, which I understood as a kind of projective identification.)

Rooted again in their perception of what they felt gay solidarity with me brought with it, in early sessions Tom and Rick would make "humorous" comments that put down Mike's mother and other women and assumed I would share their bemusement. I let them know they were welcome to speak freely with me but that I did not share their perspectives on women and hoped they would explore with me how they had come to hold their attitudes toward women. I told them these attitudes might be more relevant than they thought to their difficulties with Mike. They were skeptical.

The successful working out of these negotiations early in the treatment—that our shared and positively affirmed identity as gay men did not preclude the need to uncover and explore their couple and family dynamics and did not imply an alliance against women—remained essential to our work throughout the treatment. I worked with Tom, Rick, and Mike for 4 years.

Telescoping for purposes of this chapter, Tom and Rick's parenting was loving but lacked predictability and structure, which—as Mike came, in time, to articulate—had long left him hurt, angry, needy, and at loose ends. Mike loved his fathers and was not homophobic. Compounding the family dynamics, however, Tom and Rick both perceived Mike—comfortable in his male, securely heterosexual identity—as overly feminine. They saw Mike as "soft" and too expressive of his emotions. They themselves, like a sizable number of gay men (Nardi, 1999), emphasized if not overemphasized their masculinity. I hypothesized with them that their unstructured and unpredictable parenting along with their view of Mike as feminine were linked and essential for us to explore. They dismissed my speculation, but, again grudgingly, were willing to consider and explore it when I said I thought this would be productive.

In my meetings with Mike, I found him reflective and likable. His values were positive and prosocial; he aspired to become a high school teacher. His transference to me was positive. He saw me as a gay male object who, unlike his fathers, understood him, empathized with him, and did not reject him. He spoke openly about his frustrations and anger with his fathers. He described feeling too chronically upset with his home situation to focus fully at school and frequently provoked by criticisms from his fathers that—to use the words he used—he "acted like a faggot, like a girl." He wanted more contact with his mother but was afraid that voicing the request would escalate his fathers' belittling and emotional aggression.

As we explored the roots and workings of the family and—initially at my insistence—couple dynamics, Tom and Rick both increasingly came to vent overt and considerable misogyny. They expressed belittling views of their own mothers, whom they described as too preoccupied with their own needs (both worked outside the home and were in marriages where it was assumed they would do all the housework and childcare) to be, as they saw it, sufficiently attentive to Tom and Rick during their developmental years. They felt their mothers should have intuited their emerging sexual identities and attendant needs for understanding and support, though, when I asked about this, both admitted they had dated heterosexually as adolescents and had assiduously hidden any trace of expression of gay interests or emerging identities. They projected their subjective feelings toward their mothers into a broader, and deeply entrenched, contempt for women and for any characteristics they perceived as female (Holland, 2006). Their attraction to each other, it emerged over time, had initially been driven by a desire for refuge from the women in their lives.

This in turn, we learned together, stemmed from internalized homophobia that took the form of hatred of aspects of themselves they perceived as feminine. Their macho presentations served a defensive function; we uncovered powerful fears that any divergence from traditionally male interests and behavior would place them at risk of homophobic disparagement, rejection, and assault (Kimmel, 2004).

This insight was upsetting and disruptive to Tom and Rick, and it took considerable work together for the upset to yield. What helped, beyond time to process, reflect, and integrate, was their emerging awareness that they had adopted a philosophy of parenting that emphasized eradication of anything that could be construed as tenderness or mothering toward Mike and that this lay at the root of what had left Mike enraged, unhappy, and distanced. They had projected their fear of a rejecting heterosexual, male society into Mike, and, in ways subtle and overt, they had attacked him for being both a heteronormatively privileged male, as they were not, and at the same time, in their projective identification, overly feminine. As these ways of seeing and treating Mike began to yield, Mike's behavior, and emotional well-being, improved.

The contempt Tom and Rick held for Mike's mother, however, did not yield readily and remained only partially resolved at the end of the therapy. They encapsulated their understanding of their misogynist attitudes and their misogynistically driven behaviors within their relationship with Mike. They could not see the ways in which their construction of Mike's mother as Other—psychiatrically ill (as Tom continued to deny he was), unreliable, needy, weak—tracked with elements of their own self-constructions; once again, a projective process seemed at work.

As happens too often in therapy, when symptoms improved, will and motivation to do the hard, disruptive work of therapy waned. This was particularly so in a psychoanalytically informed couple/family therapy where the principal improvement was in Mike as the identified patient. Sometimes, when the identified patient improves, other disruptions emerge in the family system and some of its members; at other times, the family comes together to preserve the coherence of their patterns of functioning (Dell, 1982).

I saw the decision of Tom and Rick to leave therapy as having a sociopolitical dimension, as well as psychodynamic and family-systems dimensions. As I have argued elsewhere (Ruth, 2008), it can be the case that psychotherapists cannot expect to take our patients beyond parameters that exist in the broader society. The pervasive misogyny in US society (Holland, 2006), and its particular expression among gay men (Connell, 1992; Halberstam, 2008; Plummer, 1999; Weed & Schor, 1997), were not something Tom or Rick could get more fully beyond in our years of work together. A key lesson learned through the history of the gay movement (as well as the feminist movement and other movements for social change) is that changes in self-constructed subjective experience sometimes hinge on the progress of social movements, and on activist involvement in social movements (Layton *et al.*, 2006; Stryker *et al.*, 2000).

Still, my work with Tom, Rick, and Mike was not superficial. The shifts to which it gave rise took place primarily on tectonic levels. To my thinking, tracing these shifts evinces the deadening effects of misogyny on gay men in our times. The changes Tom and Rick achieved in therapy were also reflective of constraints on gay male development—individual and collective (the issues Tom and Mike presented were not the result of individual or family aberrations, so much of their development had commonalities with the personal trajectories of gay men in a homophobic US society)—that our collective turning away from feminist lessons and insights leaves us unable to overcome.

Concluding thoughts: Toward transformative action

As *The New Normal* portrayed in sharp focus, many gay men who parent through adoption or surrogacy do so while not informed by a feminist appreciation of the complexity of women's reproductive lives. Perhaps understandably, studies of gay male parenting have tended to focus on children's positive psychological development in households headed by gay men (Martin, 1993; Patterson, 1992), not on how gay men's parenting affects women who act as surrogates or whose children are placed in foster or adoptive care. The charged question of how gay male adoption or parenting through surrogacy affects birth mothers' already complex experience (Hushon *et al.*, 2006; Wadia-Ellis, 1995) has not yet entered the research agenda or general psychological and psychoanalytic discourse.

But it needs to do so. Perhaps the failure, to date, to analyze how gay men's parenting affects women, and women's reproductive rights, is among the implications of the disjuncture that has arisen between the contemporary gay movement and feminism. As long as this goes unchallenged, therapists working with gay male parents or potential parents have a stark choice: leave our gay male patients' foundational misogynist beliefs and choices unexplored or embrace a model of therapy (necessarily informed by feminist notions of psychoanalytic psychotherapy [Benjamin, 2013; Eichenbaum & Orbach, 1983; Mitchell, 1974; Prozan, 1992]) that takes our gay male patients' covert and overt misogyny on.

Several implications flow from this. One is that much theoretical and clinical work needs to be done to better understand the intertwining between internalized homophobia and misogyny in gay men. Though we have more than two decades of theoretical, clinical, and empirical work on the deleterious effects of homophobia on gay men (Greene & Herek, 1994; Plummer, 1999), we do not, as yet, have extensive psychological and psychoanalytic understandings of the links between internalized homophobia and gay men's misogynist views of women—as were evidenced to play key roles in the case of Tom and Rick. We need to have a better understanding of misogyny in gay men, both to help our individual gay male patients as well as those with whom they interact if they assume parental roles, and to help the contemporary gay movement move past its overly narrow agenda and recover more of its original vision of liberation.

A corollary is that exploratory, and not just affirmative/psychoeducational/supportive, directions are needed in therapeutic work with gay men who are coupling, marrying, and parenting in new ways. This involves working with our gay male patients to understand, with deep roots in feminist theory and practice, the ways coupling and parenting can be and are being re-conceptualized in our times (Goldner, 1985; Jackson & Scott, 2004; O'Reilly, 2008; Silverstein & Goodrich, 2003). Not to weave in the necessary lines of therapeutic work would imply failing to recognize that gay men have male privilege, and often attendant misogynist values, that have potential to misshape the marital relationships, and other forms of relationships, we choose to enter (Brod & Kaufman, 1994; Wolfson, 1993, 2007) as well as how we approach the vicissitudes of parenting (Goldberg, 2010).

A farther shore is that clinical work along the lines proposed here has lessons that need to inform social and political debates. Gay men embracing marriage and parenting have a historical debt to pay. Once we deepen our appreciation of feminism's essential role in the birth of the gay liberation movement and today's emergent gay possibilities, gay male couples seeking to parent—and gay communities collectively—need to take responsibility not to be a safety valve for the currently precarious reproductive rights of women. We must remain responsibly aware of the still-damaging impact on women's parenting through ongoing patriarchal social and economic discrimination. We need to take action as women's staunch allies in the protection of women's rights to reproductive freedom, now under mounting attack (Faludi, 2009).

Gay men's desire to parent must ground itself in feminist thought and feminist practice. If that takes us from the nurseries to consulting rooms, the courts, and the streets, then that is where we need to be. It's as simple, and as urgent, as that.

References

Armstrong, E.A. (2002). *Forging gay identities: Organizing sexuality in San Francisco, 1950–1994.* Chicago, IL: University of Chicago Press.

Auchmuty, R. (2004). Same-sex marriage revived: Feminist critique and legal strategy. *Feminism & Psychology, 14,* 101–126.

Banks, O. (1986). *Becoming a feminist: The social origins of "first wave" feminism.* Brighton, UK: Wheatsheaf Books.

Barrett, D.C., & Pollack, L.M. (2005). Whose gay community? Social class, sexual self-expression, and gay community involvement. *The Sociological Quarterly, 46,* 437–456.

Baxandall, R., & Gordon, L. (2002). Second-wave feminism. In N.A. Hewitt (Ed.), *A companion to American women's history* (pp. 414–432). Malden, MA: Blackwell.

Beam, J. (1986). *In the life: A black gay anthology.* Boston, MA: Alyson Publications.

Benjamin, J. (2013). *The bonds of love: Psychoanalysis, feminism, & the problem of domination.* New York, NY: Pantheon.

Bernstein, M. (2002). Identities and politics: Toward a historical understanding of the lesbian and gay movement. *Social Science History, 26,* 531–581.

Bersani, L. (1995). *Homos.* Cambridge, MA: Harvard University Press.

Brod, H., & Kaufman, M. (Eds.). (1994). *Theorizing masculinities.* Thousand Oaks, CA: Sage.

Bronski, M. (2000). *The pleasure principle: Sex, backlash, and the struggle for gay freedom.* New York, NY: Macmillan.

Brown, L.B. (2014). *Two spirit people: American Indian lesbian women and gay men.* New York, NY: Routledge.

Chow, E.N.L. (1987). The development of feminist consciousness among Asian American women. *Gender & Society, 1,* 284–299.

Churchill, W., & Vander Wall, J. (2002). *The COINTELPRO papers: Documents from the FBI's secret wars against dissent in the United States.* Cambridge, MA: South End Press.

Collins, P.H. (2000). *Black feminist thought: Knowledge, consciousness, and the politics of empowerment* (2nd ed.). New York, NY: Routledge.

Connell, R.W. (1992). A very straight gay: Masculinity, homosexual experience, and the dynamics of gender. *American Sociological Review, 57,* 735–751.

Craib, I. (1990). *Psychoanalysis and social theory.* Amherst, MA: University of Massachusetts Press.

Crimp, D. (2002). *Melancholia and moralism: Essays on AIDS and queer politics.* Cambridge, MA: MIT Press.

Cruikshank, M. (1992). *The gay and lesbian liberation movement.* New York, NY: Psychology Press.

Danto, E.A. (2005). *Freud's free clinics: Psychoanalysis and social justice, 1918–1938.* New York, NY: Columbia University Press.

Dell, P.F. (1982). Beyond homeostasis: Toward a concept of coherence. *Family Process, 21,* 21–41.

D'Emilio, J. (1997). Capitalism and gay identity. In R.N. Lancaster & M. DiLeonardo (Eds.), *The gender/sexuality reader: Culture, history, political economy* (pp. 169–193). New York, NY: Psychology Press.

D'Emilio, J. (2000). Cycles of change, questions of strategy: They gay and lesbian movement after fifty years. In C.D. Rimmerman, K.D. Vald, & C. Wilcox (Eds.), *The politics of gay rights* (pp. 31–53). Chicago, IL: University of Chicago Press.

D'Emilio, J. (2002). *The world turned: Essays on gay history, politics, and culture.* Durham, NC: Duke University Press.

D'Emilio, J. (2014). *Making trouble: Essays on gay history, politics, and the university.* New York, NY: Routledge.

D'Emilio, J., Turner, W.B., & Vaid, U. (Eds.). (2000). *Creating change: Sexuality, public policy, and civil rights.* New York, NY: St. Martin's Press.

Drescher, J. (2008). A history of homosexuality and organized psychoanalysis. *Journal of the American Academy of Psychoanalysis and Dynamic Psychiatry, 36,* 443–460.

Duberman, M. (2013). *Stonewall.* New York, NY: Open Road Media.

Echols, A. (1989). *Daring to be bad: Radical feminism in America, 1967–1975*. Minneapolis, MN: University of Minnesota Press.

Eichenbaum, L., & Orbach, S. (1983). *Understanding women: A feminist psychoanalytic approach*. New York, NY: Basic Books.

Ernst, J.L., Katzive, L., & Smock, E. (2003/4). The global pattern of U.S. initiatives curtailing women's reproductive rights: A perspective on the increasingly anti-choice mosaic. *University of Pennsylvania Journal of Constitutional Law, 6*, 752–795.

Evans, S.M. (1979). *Personal politics: The roots of women's liberation in the civil rights movement and the new left*. New York, NY: Vintage.

Faludi, S. (2009). *Backlash: The undeclared war against American women*. New York, NY: Broadway Books.

Fee, E., & Fox, D.M. (Eds.). (1992). *AIDS: The making of a chronic disease*. Berkeley, CA: University of California Press.

Fetner, T. (2008). *How the religious right shaped lesbian and gay activism*. Minneapolis, MN: University of Minnesota Press.

Fonow, M.M., & Cook, J.A. (Eds.). (1991). *Beyond methodology: Feminist scholarship as lived research*. Bloomington, IN: Indiana University Press.

Friedan, B. (2010). *The feminine mystique*. New York, NY: Norton. (Original work published 1963.)

García, A.M. (Ed.). (1997). *Chicana feminist thought: The basic historical writings*. New York, NY: Psychology Press.

Gaztambide, D. (2012). "A psychotherapy for the people": Freud, Ferenczi, and psychoanalytic work with the underprivileged. *Contemporary Psychoanalysis, 48*, 141–165.

Goldberg, A.E. (2010). *Lesbian and gay parents and their children: Research on the family life cycle*. Washington, DC: American Psychological Association.

Goldner, V. (1985). Feminism and family therapy. *Family Process, 24*, 31–47.

Gould, D.B. (2002). Life during wartime: Emotions and the development of ACT UP. *Mobilization: An International Quarterly, 7*, 177–200.

Greene, B., & Herek, G.M. (Eds.). (1994). *Lesbian and gay psychology: Theory, research, and clinical applications* (Vol. 1). Thousand Oaks, CA: Sage.

Greenhouse, L., & Siegel, R.B. (2011). Before (and after) *Roe v. Wade*: New questions about backlash. *The Yale Law Journal, 120*, 2028–2087.

Grmek, M.D. (1993). *History of AIDS: Emergence and origin of a modern pandemic*. Princeton, NJ: Princeton University Press.

Halberstam, J. (2008). The anti-social turn in queer studies. *Graduate Journal of Social Science, 5*, 140–156.

Hanisch, C. (2006). The personal is political. Retrieved from http://www.carolhanisch.org/CHwritings/PIP.html (Original work published 1969)

Hemphill, E. (Ed.). (1991). *Brother to brother: New writings by black gay men*. Boston, MA: Alyson Publications.

Herek, G.M. (1999). AIDS and stigma. *American Behavioral Scientist, 42*, 1106–1116.

Herek, G.M., & Glunt, E.K. (1988). An epidemic of stigma: Public reactions to AIDS. *American Psychologist, 43*, 886–891.

Herek, G.M., & Greene, B. (Eds.). (1995). *AIDS, identity, and community: The HIV epidemic and lesbians and gay men*. Thousand Oaks, CA: Sage.

Holland, J. (2006). *Misogyny: The world's oldest prejudice*. New York, NY: Carroll & Graf.

Hooks, B. (1981). *Ain't I a woman: Black women and feminism*. Boston, MA: South End Press.

Hull, G.T., Scott, P.B., & Smith, B. (Eds.). (2003). *But some of us are brave: All the women are white, all the blacks are men—Black women's studies*. New York, NY: Feminist Press at CUNY.

Hushon, K., Sherman, S.B., & Siskind, D. (2006). *Understanding adoption: Clinical work with adults, children, and parents*. Lanham, MD: Jason Aronson.

Jackson, S., & Scott, S. (2004). The personal is still political: Heterosexuality, feminism and monogamy. *Feminism & Psychology, 14*, 151–157.

Jay, K., & Young, A. (Eds.). (1992). *Out of the closets: Voices of gay liberation* (2nd ed.). New York, NY: NYU Press.

Johnson, D.K. (2009). *The lavender scare: The cold war persecution of gays and lesbians in the federal government.* Chicago, IL: University of Chicago Press.

Johnston, J. (1973). *Lesbian nation.* New York, NY: Simon and Schuster.

Jonsen, A.R., & Stryker, J.E. (1993). *The social impact of AIDS in the United States.* Washington, DC: National Academy Press.

Josephson, J. (2005). Citizenship, same-sex marriage, and feminist critiques of marriage. *Perspectives on Politics, 3*, 269–284.

Kaufman, M. (1994). Men, feminism, and men's contradictory experiences of power. In H. Brod & M. Kaufman (Eds.), *Theorizing masculinities* (pp. 142–164). Thousand Oaks, CA: Sage.

Kayal, P.M. (1993). *Bearing witness: Gay men's health crisis and the politics of AIDS.* Boulder, CO: Westview Press.

Kimmel, M. (2004). Masculinity as homophobia: Fear, shame, and silence in the construction of gender identity. In P.S. Rothenberg (Ed.), *Race, class, and gender in the United States: An integrated study* (6th ed.; pp. 81–93). New York, NY: Worth.

Kissack, T. (1995). Freaking fag revolutionaries: New York's gay liberation front, 1969–1971. *Radical History Review, 4*, 105–134.

Larson, P. (2014). Consciousness-raising groups. In T. Teo (Ed.), *Encyclopedia of critical psychology* (pp. 308–311). New York, NY: Springer.

Layton, L., Hollander, N.C., & Gutwill, S. (Eds.). (2006). *Psychoanalysis, class and politics: Encounters in the clinical setting.* New York, NY: Routledge.

Leong, R. (Ed.). (2014). *Asian American sexualities: Dimensions of the gay and lesbian experience.* New York, NY: Routledge.

Marcus, E. (1992). *Making history: The struggle for gay and lesbian equal rights, 1945–1990: An oral history.* New York, NY: HarperCollins.

Marsiglia, F.F. (1998). Homosexuality and Latinos/as: Towards an integration of identities. *Journal of Gay & Lesbian Social Services, 8*, 113–125.

Martin, A. (1993). *The lesbian and gay parenting handbook: Creating and raising our families.* New York, NY: HarperPerennial.

Miller, A.M. (2000). Sexual but not reproductive: Exploring the junction and disjunction of sexual and reproductive rights. *Health and Human Rights, 4*(2), 68–109.

Milton, H.L., & MacDonald, G.J. (1984). Homosexual identity formation as a developmental process. *Journal of Homosexuality, 9*, 91–104.

Mitchell, J. (1974). *Psychoanalysis and feminism.* New York, NY: Pantheon.

Mohr, R.D. (1995). *A more perfect union: Why straight America must stand up for gay rights.* Boston, MA: Beacon Press.

Morin, S.F., Charles, K.A., & Malyon, A.K. (1984). The psychological impact of AIDS on gay men. *American Psychologist, 39*, 1288–1293.

Muñoz, J.E. (2009). *Cruising utopia: The then and there of queer futurity.* New York, NY: NYU Press.

Murphy, R. (2012–2013). *The New Normal: The complete series.* [Television series] New York, NY: NBC. Retrieved from http://www.amazon.com

Nardi, P.M. (1999). *Gay masculinities.* Thousand Oaks, CA: Sage.

Nguyen, L. (2012). Psychoanalytic activism: Finding the human, staying human. *Psychoanalytic Psychology, 29*, 308–317.

O'Reilly, A. (Ed.). (2008). *Feminist mothering.* Albany, NY: SUNY Press.

Patterson, C.J. (1992). Children of lesbian and gay parents. *Child Development, 63*, 1025–1042.

Plummer, D. (1999). *One of the boys: Masculinity, homophobia, and modern manhood.* New York, NY: Routledge.

Power, L. (1995). *No bath but plenty of bubbles: An oral history of the Gay Liberation Front, 1970–1973.* London: Cassell.

Prozan, C.K. (1992). *Feminist psychoanalytic psychotherapy.* Lanham, MD: Jason Aronson.

Richardson, D. (2005). Desiring sameness? The rise of a neoliberal politics of normalisation. *Antipode, 37,* 515–535.

Rodríguez, R.T. (2006). Queering the homeboy aesthetic. *Aztlán: A Journal of Chicano Studies, 31*(2), 127–137.

Ross, M.W., Essien, E.J., & Torres, I. (2006). Conspiracy beliefs about the origin of HIV/AIDS in four racial/ethnic groups. *Journal of Acquired Immune Deficiency Syndromes, 41,* 342–344.

Ruth, R. (2008). The teacher of music: Therapy with a transgender person. Paper presented at the Spring Meeting of the Division of Psychoanalysis of the American Psychological Association.

Sears, A. (2005). Queer anti-capitalism: What's left of lesbian and gay liberation? *Science & Society, 69,* 92–112.

Silverstein, L.B., & Goodrich, T.J. (Eds.). (2003). *Feminist family therapy: Empowerment in social context.* Washington, DC: American Psychological Association.

Smith, A. (2005). Native American feminism, sovereignty, and social change. *Feminist Studies, 31,* 116–132.

Stake, R.E. (2000). The case study method in social inquiry. In R. Gomm, M. Hammersley, & P. Foster (Eds.), *Case study method* (pp. 19–26). Thousand Oaks, CA: Sage. (Original work published 1978)

Stryker, S., Owens, T.J., & White, R.W. (Eds.). (2000). *Self, identity, and social movements.* Minneapolis, MN: University of Minnesota Press.

Taywaditep, K.J. (2002). Marginalization among the marginalized: Gay men's anti-effeminacy attitudes. *Journal of Homosexuality, 42,* 1–28.

Teal, D. (1971). *The gay militants.* New York, NY: Stein and Day.

Thompson, B. (2002). Multiracial feminism: Recasting the chronology of second wave feminism. *Feminist Studies, 28,* 337–360.

Thompson, M. (Ed.). (1994). *Long road to freedom: The* Advocate *history of the gay and lesbian movement.* New York, NY: St. Martin's Press.

Vaid, U. (1995). *Virtual equality: The mainstreaming of gay and lesbian liberation.* New York, NY: Anchor Books.

Valocchi, S. (1999a). Riding the crest of a protest wave? Collective action frames in the gay liberation movement, 1969–1973. *Mobilization: An International Quarterly, 4,* 59–73.

Valocchi, S. (1999b). The class-inflected nature of gay identity. *Social Problems, 46,* 207–224.

Valocchi, S. (2001). Individual identities, collective identities, and organizational structure: The relationship of the political left and gay liberation in the United States. *Sociological Perspectives, 44,* 445–467.

Wadia-Ellis, S. (1995). *The adoption reader: Birth mothers, adoptive mothers, and adopted daughters tell their stories.* Seattle, WA: Seal Press.

Warner, M. (1999). *The trouble with normal: Sex, politics, and the ethics of queer life.* New York, NY: Free Press.

Weed, E., & Schor, N. (Eds.). (1997). *Feminism meets queer theory.* Bloomington, IN: Indiana University Press.

Wolfson, E. (1993). Crossing the threshold: Equal marriage rights for lesbians and gay men and the intra-community critique. *NYU Review of Law & Social Change, 21,* 567 et seq.

Wolfson, E. (2007). *Why marriage matters: America, equality, and gay people's right to marry.* New York, NY: Simon and Schuster.

RESPONSE TO SECTION I

A culture of oppression

Marilyn Metzl

The articles in Section I provide a mixed picture of the gains that women have achieved over the past decades. Dr. Silverman quotes Schiebinger and Gilmartin (2010) who state that we have won "half a revolution." The rhetoric of war is a common approach in tales of epic cultural change. Thus although women have achieved significant advances in the last decades, here in the United States right-wing politicians appear to be turning the clock backward in what some have called a "war against women." In an article called "U.S. Culture War With Women at Its Center" *The New York Times* (April 3, 2012) has pointed out that recent political campaigns have focused again on limiting women's rights in the areas of abortion, access to health care, equal pay, and domestic violence.

In the *Washington Post* of 2010 Jessica Valenti states as follows: "We're currently under the mass delusion that women in America have achieved equality. Despite the immeasurable rights gained over the past decades, women are still being raped, trafficked, violated and discriminated." International organizations are joining together to eliminate and attempt to end the abuse and oppression of women and girls worldwide. Women have remained the hated "other" and a disdained minority. Can these disquieting developments be called a war on women? That is a topic for political discourse but that changes are occurring in a regressive direction are indisputable.

It is important to face the misogyny at our doorstep and to spotlight the methodical gender oppression that is still very much a part of our society. Although the war is led by the right, leaders on all sides are guilty. What are the weapons in this devastating and unjust war? How does it restrict and harm women? Can we mediate a cease-fire and restore and increase women's civil and personal rights? At the heart of the matter is the question of why they are discriminated against. It remains one of the more perplexing questions of our time.

We must first be able to recognize that a war is taking place. While the wars waged by the United States Armed Forces receive rigorous visibility and heated national discussions, the war on women is often hushed and invisible, secretly plotted and waged by reigning conservative government officials. The right wing's insidious and intensifying "war on women" has been stealthily yet steadily gaining ground.

According to the ACLU (American Civil Liberties Union), the War on Women describes

> the increasing aggressive legislative and rhetorical attacks on women and women's rights taking place across the nation. It includes a wide-range of policy efforts designed to place restrictions on women's health care and erode protections for women and their families.
>
> *(ACLU [n.d.], War on Women).*

The ACLU cites examples that include "restricting contraception; mandating medically unnecessary ultrasounds; abortion taxes; forcing women to tell their employers why they want birth control, and prohibiting insurance companies from including abortion coverage in their policies."

American women reportedly are the envy of women in other cultures, having progressed over the past decades in domestic, economic, and political arenas. Yet while international organizations are cooperating on laws that advance gender equality and end the oppression of women and girls worldwide, a growing group of US right-wing politicians and governmental officials have been doggedly fighting to reverse the gains women have achieved over the past decades.

On December 3, 2015, Defense Secretary Ash Carter announced that women in the US military could now serve in combat posts (*The New York Times*, 2015). Some may consider this a victory of equality for women—this announcement that officially authorizes women to fully participate in war. Yet for years, women have been forced into an escalating guerrilla war waged by conservative and right-wing politicians. Women have been thrust onto battlegrounds vaster than the Syrian Desert and more treacherous than the terrorist-riddled mountains of northern Afghanistan. Without the benefits of arms or armor, women have been relentlessly attacked in their most vulnerable arenas.

Of the four areas mentioned above in which women's rights are being restricted, reproductive rights have been a key target. On the grounds that it was channeling taxpayer money to facilitate abortions, conservatives in 2014 began a move to cut off US government aid to Planned Parenthood. The Congressional Budget Office found the 1-year defunding would produce about $235 million in federal savings. But Michael Hiltzik (*Los Angeles Times*, 2015) states that that amount is barely a rounding error, "but that the real costs would be borne by low-income and rural women." Hiltzik writes that as many as 650,000 women, chiefly in low-income neighborhoods or communities without access to other health care clinics, would lose at least some access to care. The measure would limit Planned Parenthood's ability to provide much-needed services for low-income women and, as a result, thousands of unwanted pregnancies might occur—exactly the opposite result of what was intended.

These lapses in humane medical treatment for women go beyond denying normal preventive health measures. If veterinarians ignored clients' reports of their pets yelping in pain, the uproar would be significant and predictable. Yet women's pain and symptoms are routinely ignored and undertreated. In their research study, Diane E. Hoffmann and Anita J. Tarzian (1995) concluded that women experience and report more frequent and greater pain than men and yet are less likely to be treated. Through greater awareness and education health care providers must readjust their preoccupation with objective factors and embrace alternative approaches to ensure that women's voices regarding understanding and treatment of their pain are heard.

A report from the Guttmacher Institute (2012) details the extent of 2011's war on women's reproductive rights. The report states:

> By almost any measure, issues related to reproductive health and rights at the state level received unprecedented attention in 2011. In the 50 states combined, legislators introduced more than 1,100 reproductive health and rights-related provisions, a sharp increase from the 950 introduced in 2010. By year's end, 135 of these provisions had been enacted in 36 states, an increase from the 89 enacted in 2010 and the 77 enacted in 2009. Fully 68% of these new provisions—92 in 24 states—-restrict access to abortion services, a striking increase from last year, when 26% of new provisions restricted abortion. The 92 new abortion restrictions enacted in 2011 shattered the previous record of 34 adopted in 2005. Abortion restrictions took many forms: bans (6 states), waiting periods (3 states), ultrasound (5 states), and insurance coverage (3 states joined the existing 5 with such restrictions), clinic regulations (4 states), medication abortion (7 states).

Domestic violence continues to be an area in which women's safety remains an area of disagreement. Every 15 seconds, a woman is beaten by her husband or partner (Uniform Crime Reports, Federal Bureau of Investigation, 1991). Three to four million women in the United States are beaten in their homes each year by their husbands, ex-husbands, or male lovers (1990, Senate Hearing 101–939). Rep. Gwen Moore, a Wisconsin Democrat, expressed indignation after revealing that she had been the victim of domestic violence and sexual assault. She stated in her interview in *The Daily Beast* (2012) that "violence against women everywhere knows no ethnicity and no socio-economic boundary." Grassroots efforts and the growing awareness of the severity of the problem have finally contributed to the passage of a more comprehensive bill, passed by Congress in February of 2013 (https://www.fas.org/'sgp/crs/misc/R42499.pdf).

Any war inevitably turns on economics. The availability of secure financial resources confers power and power wins wars. According to the National Women's

Law Center, a woman makes only 78 cents for every dollar a man earns (National Women's Law Center Fact Sheet, 2015). For women of color, the pay gap is even more pronounced. Working-class women frequently have low-paying jobs with little flexibility. One in three American women—42 million women, plus 28 million children—either live in poverty or are on the brink of it and about 3.7 million women work two or more jobs (Tahmincioglu, 2010).

Female managers and executives face their own struggles. According to Kathy Caprino (2013, *Forbes*) corporate America remains male-dominated at the leadership levels. The differences in women's style, approach, communication, decision making, leadership values, focus and energy, are not understood or valued. Women's choices and styles may clash with the dominant culture and they are then overlooked for management positions. Many women leaders place emphasis on connection, empathy, emotional cue-taking, consensus-building, risk-taking, mutuality, and questioning, traits that are often perceived as embodying a less-than-leadership style.

An effective war machine must be able to disseminate propaganda. The media are remarkably effective at manipulating perceptions and fostering bias. While 80 percent of all purchasing decisions are made by women (Sachs, 2014) only 3 percent of significant positions in the mainstream media—telecommunications, entertainment, publishing, and advertising—are held by women. Only 3 percent of creative directors within ad agencies are women (Rolfe, 2011).

Television is a highly influential method of propaganda. Many smart and confident female characters have paraded onto the small screen over the past few years. But the more astute and capable the character, the more likely she is also emotionally disturbed. Women are not necessarily portrayed as complicated, difficult, thorny or complex, but rather as volcanoes that could blow at any minute. Worse, the very abilities and skills that make them singular and interesting come coupled with some hideous deficiency. Many shows suggest that a female character's flaws are inextricably linked to her strengths.

But why the war? Why are women still the hated minority? The answer may lie in part with the history of our country. It is the world's oldest democracy but the embrace of democratic ideals belies a record of oppression based on race, gender, and ethnicity. The United States of America was founded by men whose desire for power and control compelled them to oppress and subdue groups or classes. In 1870 black men gained the right to vote under the 15th Amendment. Since those voters' rights were established, political leaders and institutions established laws and regulations designed to oppress African Americans and deter their development as full citizens. Legal maneuvering included literacy tests, poll taxes, elaborate registration systems, and unreasonable Voter ID requirement (Omi & Winant, 2015). For example, in 2011, South Carolina passed a restrictive Voter ID law that kept more than 180,000 African Americans from casting a ballot. This systematic oppression fueled a myth that African Americans were inferior.

A similar process fuels the ongoing oppression of women. The foundation of American democracy seems rooted in the concept of white male domination. Even though the right of suffrage was granted women in 1920, a multitude of subtle biases and perceptions have contributed to women's subjugation in the twenty-first century. There are many faces to the ongoing oppression of women. The first explanation is simple sex discrimination. Women entering the workforce are met with overt hostility. Women who are more assertive and dominant in their areas of expertise are not seen as brilliant or knowledgeable but as bossy and annoying. Either a woman is barely heard or she is too aggressive. This may not be hostility towards women but instead preference for men and their interpersonal style, which is more familiar.

Erik Erikson (1959) hypothesized that each human group became convinced it was the sole possessor of the true human identity. Thus, each group also became a pseudo-species, adopting an attitude of superiority over others. He called the process *pseudo-specialization*. Historically, Erikson postulated, each group developed a distinct sense of identity wearing skins and feathers like armor to protect them from other groups who wore different kinds of skins. For many males, this attitude persists. Women, viewed as the "other," are often met with overt hostility when they enter the workplace. Assertive businesswomen are not seen as brilliant or knowledgeable, but as bossy and annoying. The current male-driven culture makes it difficult for strong women to succeed.

Other psychoanalytic theorists have attempted to explain women's status as the "other," a disdained minority. From the earliest relationship with their mothers, males both fear and desire women. Men's earliest human experience is with the mother. According to Elise (1998), the infant is the recipient of the mother's penetration and becomes a penetrator by identification with the mother. To penetrate and to be penetrated form a core of sexual excitement as psychic and physical boundaries are crossed. Otto Kernberg and David Rosenfeld (1991) reiterate that these polymorphous perverse features are a crucial aspect of normal sexuality. Males have an early bodily experience, a receptive excitement and enlivened sense of interiority, which then closes down and leads to a masculine focus on externality.

Other theorists such as Bowlby (1960) postulate that the hatred of women results from the boy's grieving the maternal loss and the loss of a part of himself as a man. The male must then identify with the powerful phallic father on whom is projected the mother's original omnipotence. Maternal sexual activity is appropriated to the masculine and infantile passivity is attributed to the mother, the feminine sexual object. Bowlby noted that the denigration of women confirms male power over women and masks any dependency, need, and vulnerability.

Benjamin Schmidt (2015) underscores that narcissism is centrally involved in fostering the son's identification with a powerful father, who has a significant stake in his son's identification with him. The penis then becomes imbued with magical qualities, power, and phallo-centrism. Operating as a combined defense against maternal omnipotence and male fears regarding the inner body and castration, the penis is frequently used as a manic defense against mourning the intolerable loss of the mother. In the face of fear and loss, the denigration of women wins out.

If this is indeed a war, women have only just begun to fight. At present, the sense of outrage seems relatively mild and scattered. There is not an organized mobilization in which most women can engage. Nobel Peace Prize recipient Leymah Gbowee of Liberia spoke recently at a meeting and asked, "Where are the angry American women?" (*The New York Times*, April 3, 2012).

Women who are beginning to answer the call have come forward, run for office, and been elected. Congresswomen are increasingly willing to pounce on misogyny or anything resembling it (Chozick, 2015). In November 2014, many independent and conservative women voted for Democrats. During that election, Emily's List supported and endorsed a record number of female candidates, 11 for the US Senate and 27 for the House. Emily's List doubled its membership in 2014 and raised more money for more candidates than at any other time in its 27-year history. At this writing we have a viable woman candidate for president for the first time in United States history.

The rising numbers of women in the workplace will inevitably chip away at the disadvantages that women face. And if women really do mobilize *en masse* and bring their unique characteristics to bear, it could transform the way that Wall Street does business.

If we are to be a democracy, the march toward true equality must continue down the halls of governments, corporations, academia, hospitals, law firms, nonprofits, research labs, and in every organization, large and small. We owe it to the generations that came before and those that come after to keep fighting. To create a better, more equal world, women can lead more in the workplace and men can contribute more in the home. When half our institutions are run by women and half our homes are run by men, all will benefit from the strength and diversity both genders contribute.

References

ACLU. (n.d.). War on Women. https://action.aclu.org/blog/tag/war-women

Bowlby, John. (1960). Separation Anxiety. *International Journal of Psychoanalysis*, XLI, 89–113.

Caprino, Kathy. (2013, February 12). The Top 6 Reasons Women Are Not Leading in Corporate America as We Need Them To. *Forbes Leadership*, retrieved from http://www.forbes.com/sites/kathycaprino/2013/02/12/the-top-6-reasons-women-are-not-leading-in-corporate-america-as-we-need-them-to/

Carter, Ash. (2015, December 3). All Combat Roles Now Open to Women. *The New York Times*.

Chozick, Amy. (2015, March 4). Leader of Emily's List, a Pac Built to Elect Women, Faces her Biggest Testing in 2016. *New York Times*, retrieved from http://www.nytimes.com/2015/03/04/us/politics/-2016-election-emilys-list-hillary-clinton.html

Elise, Dianne. (1998). *Gender Repertoire: Body, Mind, and Bisexuality*. New York, NY: The Analytic Press.

Erikson, Erik. (1959). *Identity and Life Cycle*. New York, NY: International Universities Press.

Guttmacher Institute Media Center, News in Context, January 5, 2012.

Hiltzik, Michael. (2015, February 2). The Cost of Defunding Planned Parenthood: Less Healthcare for 650,000 Women. *Los Angeles Times*, retrieved from http://www.latimes.com/business/hiltzik/la-fi-mh-cost-of-defunding-planned-parenthood-20150922-column.html

Hoffmann, Diane E., & Tarzian, Anita, J. (1995). *The Girl Who Cried Pain: A Bias Against Women in the Treatment of Pain.* Amsterdam: John Benjamins Publishing Company.

Kernberg, Otto., & Rosenfeld, David. (1991). *The Psychotic: Aspects of the Personality.* London: Karnac Books.

Moore, Gwen. (2012, March 28). In Her Words. *The Daily Beast.*

National Women's Law Center. "How the Wage Gap Hurts Women and Families." Calculations from U.S. Census Bureau, Current Population Survey, 2014 Annual Social and Economic Supplement Table PINC-05: Work Experience in 2013. Retrieved from http://nwlc.org/resources/how-wage-gap-hurts-women-and-families

Omi, Michael., & Winant, Howard. (2015). *Racial Formation in the United States.* 3rd ed. New York, NY: Routledge.

Rolfe, Tiffany. (2011, June 14). What We Can Do About the Dearth of Female Creatives? *Advertising Age.*

Sachs, MaryLee. (2014, June 30). Recasting Marketing to Women. *Forbes.*

Schiebinger, Londa, & Gilmartin, Shannon K. (2010). Housework is an Academic Issue. How to Keep Talented Women Scientists in the Lab Where They Belong. American Association of University Professors. Retrieved from http://www.aaup.org/article/housework-academic-issue#.Via7EsvD85s

Schmidt, Benjamin. (2015, February 6). Is the Professor Bossy or Brilliant? Much Depends on Gender. *New York Times.*

Tahmincioglu, Eve. (2010, March 21). More Women Holding Down Multiple Jobs. NBC News. Retrieved from http://www.nbcnews.com/id/35912763/ns/business-careers/t/more-women-holding-down-multiple-jobs/#.VnwJwvkrJMw

The New York Times. (2012, April 3). US Culture War with Women at Its Center.

Uniform Crime Reports, Federal Bureau of Investigation. 1991.

Valenti, Jessica. (2010). For Women in America, Equality is Still an Illusion. *Washington Post,* retrieved from http://www.washingtonpost.com/wp-?

Women and Violence. (1990). Hearings before the U.S. Senate Judiciary Committee, August 29 and December 11, 1990, Senate Hearing 101–939 (pt. 1, p. 12).

SECTION II
Women and sexual trauma

COMMENTARY ON SECTION II

Women and sexual trauma

Kristin Davisson

Women's bodies and selfhoods are inexorably tangled in a cultural and relational matrix that degrades our autonomy as well as our safety. Our bodies are vessels to be penetrated, objectified, or possessed. Our minds and choices are infiltrated by those persons and systems that hold over us the power to subjugate our existence. Sexual trauma, both implicit and explicit, is all too common a plight for the female gender. Like many women, my personal feelings about this reality contain deeply held anger, fear, disillusionment, and often shock at the lack of progress we have made. These feelings are held in sharp contrast to my everyday selfhood as a woman, often perceiving to be in possession of her safety and enjoying the trust and company of others. How can both realities exist? This identity of "double consciousness" is often the result of "looking at oneself through the eyes of others," unable to reconcile the repeated oppressions occurring on a psychosocial level (Du Bois, 1903). Whether we are direct victims of violence, harassment, lower pay, reproductive control, or we live in constant awareness of these limitations on our gender, our lives as women are shaped by the irrevocable risks and inequities we face. It also bears mentioning that for women of color, this reality is a "double bind," increasing the insidiousness of the acts perpetrated against them and reducing the resources for healing and justice.

The authors in this section focus on the specific experience of sexual trauma; the violation of the female body and psyche; as well as the systems, institutions, and cycles of interaction that maintain and condone such abuses. Susan Kavaler-Adler emphasizes the complex interplay of intrapsychic factors that increase a woman's susceptibility to (male) object choices that further victimize, oppress, or subjugate her. In a poignant case, she provides an example of a woman trapped by introjects that disallow her a true object choice. This dialogue addresses the multifaceted interplay between societal, interpersonal, and intrapsychic factors leading women to accept deferential status to a malignant partner. This method of understanding provides a bridge between interpretation and victim-blaming, offering an avenue for self-empowerment, insight, and autonomy, ultimately providing an escape from the oppressive internal and external forces that constrain our choices as women.

The second chapter takes on the answer to the question: What of women who aren't direct victims of sexual violence? How are they impacted by the exposure, knowledge, and narratives of the suffering around them? The preliminary research I summarized in this chapter suggests that secondary exposure to trauma results in conflicts in self, identity, and object-relatedness for women "witnessing" sexual violence. The qualitative interviews give specific voice to the conflicts and emotional challenges women face as they support a close friend after her assault. The emotional words of these women linger with me as they suggest a lasting impact on our existential selfhood and sense of safety in an often harsh and threatening world.

Lastly, Katie Gentile considers the direct and repeated sexual assault of young women on college campuses and the systemic failure to institute restorative justice and measures of protection. She examines the process by which institutions separate themselves from the "perpetrator," and thus the violation itself, removing any accountability for repair, protection, or change. She illuminates the concept of community and bystander interventions, creating accountability and preventive efforts for the system as a whole. As a former counselor in numerous college counseling settings, this chapter resonated with me as it highlighted the tragic oversights as well as the opportunities for change reflective in most institutions of higher learning.

All three authors use psychoanalytic theory to make sense of a patriarchal society whose structures and institutions create and reinforce gender inequities, serve as obstacles to justice, and communicate to women their subservient status. Further, psychoanalytic understanding is used to gain perspective on a gendered experience that at its core must accept, or at the very least acknowledge, the daily threat to the body and autonomous self.

With roots in Freud, the relationship between psychoanalytic understanding and sexual trauma has been a tumultuous one. With the abandonment of seduction theory for his theory of infantile sexuality, Freud changed the direction of analytic inquiry away from listening to the abhorrent wrongs perpetrated against women and towards pathologizing their unconscious motivations. Of note, Freud himself appeared conflicted about this and continued to battle with the significance of sexual trauma for the remainder of his career (Freud, 1905/1953, 1915/1963). Psychoanalytic feminist voices such as Nancy Chodorow and Juliet Mitchell have set the tone for utilizing such ideas to examine the construction of gender roles and critique patriarchy itself (Chodorow, 1978; Mitchell, 1974). In their wisdom, they suggest keeping the integrity of psychoanalytic ideas while considering the context in which they were shaped as well as the intended or even misunderstood impact of their time. Authors in this section follow in their footsteps by considering psychoanalytic theory as a way to conceptualize not just the problem but also the resolutions to the overwhelming and sinister nature of sexual trauma As these injurious circumstances occur with excessive frequency in the lives of women, we can come together as survivors, witnesses, clinicians, scholars, volunteers, first responders, friends, allies, and partners to strengthen the fabric of our communities and change the dialogue around this issue.

References

Chodorow, N. (1978). *The reproduction of mothering.* Los Angeles, CA: University of California Press.

Du Bois, W.E.B. (1903). *The souls of black folk.* New York, NY: Dover.

Freud, S. (1953). Three essays on sexuality. In J. Strachey (Ed. & Trans.), *The standard edition of the complete psychological works of Sigmund Freud* (Vol. 7, pp. 135–222). London: Hogarth. (Original work published 1905)

Freud, S. (1963). *Introductory lectures on psychoanalysis.* In J. Strachey (Ed. & Trans.), *The standard edition of the complete psychological works of Sigmund Freud* (Vol. 15). London: Hogarth. (Original work published 1915)

Mitchell, J. (1974). *Psychoanalysis and feminism: A radical reassessment of Freudian psychoanalysis.* New York, NY: Basic Books.

4

DATE RAPE AND THE DEMON-LOVER COMPLEX

The divine, the deviant, and the diabolical in male/female politics

Susan Kavaler-Adler

In the four decades of psychoanalytic practice, I have frequently worked with women who are trapped by an internal world situation in which they are defined and controlled by a primal father inside of them, interacting with the dynamics of an inadequate, relatively absent, or abandoning mother figure. This situation always influences the way these women interact with, submit to, or fight with men in their current adult lives. In this chapter, we will look into the case of Sherry, a woman who suffered the ultimate seduction and control of a malignant man, a seductive male stranger, who defined her as part of his own psychic ritual in the prologue to raping her. The woman's susceptibility will be discussed in terms of early life trauma, as well as the character disorder pathology of both her parents. It should be kept in mind that her susceptibility is also symptomatic of a wider cultural dynamic of men defining women as a means to controlling them, which has mushroomed into the political polarization and polemics of the "pro-choice" female reproductive freedom issue. This chapter engages not only the issues of male dominance, but it will offer the psychoanalytic perspective on what allows a woman to develop a psychological capacity for choice. In discussing psychological development, we will zero in onto psychological reparation of "developmental arrest" trauma, as only this reparation could allow a woman to choose. Only when a woman is psychologically evolved as a separated and individuated autonomous person, can she fully embrace the "pro-choice" stance and be responsible for her body and for her own reproductive rights.

The demon-lover complex

When we look at how women may become aroused by and attached to malignant men, the interplay between the pre-oedipal and oedipal becomes profoundly important. The contributions of Melanie Klein and Ronald Fairbairn to the psychoanalytic literature illustrate how a powerful attachment to a bad object can take place. Melanie Klein's theory helps us to understand the woman's fantasy of the man as an idealized figure, which can flip to the side of the man as a demon, a "bad object" figure. This view is presented by Melanie Klein in her writings on the "paranoid-schizoid position," as opposed to the integrated view of the man that would be possible in the "depressive position" (Klein, 1935). In the meantime, Ronald Fairbairn spoke of the attachment to the "bad object" (Fairbairn, 1952) as related to a primal attachment to an inadequate and/or abusive mother. In Fairbairn's theory the internal "bad object" is not just a fantasy that is only partially related to the actual parent, but is based on an internalization of an actual bad mother parent; or one perceived in a distorted way due to the limitations of infant and childhood perception, but still related to the actual parent. Both the bad mother as an internal fantasy object and as a real internalized part object, can become compounded by the internalization of a bad father parent object. Such internalization of a father can be merged with the internal mother or it can be differentiated from the internal mother to varying degrees. Building on Klein's and Fairbairn's ideas, I speak of my theory of the "demon-lover" attachment, within one's internal psychic world, and of its manifestation in the external world as a "demon-lover complex" (see Kavaler-Adler, 1993a, 1996, 1998, 2003a, 2003b, 2005b, 2013a, 2013b, 2014, and others).

This theory of the demon-lover complex is particularly pertinent to a woman like Sherry, the heroine of this chapter. Sherry was unconsciously drawn to narcissistic and psychopathic men like her father, after just having repaired a fragile self-structure from her primal inadequate mothering. In the case to be discussed, we will see how the choice of a man, in the real-life drama to be described, is compelled by unconscious demon-lover attachment, even though the woman's behavior could look, to the world at large, as a free choice, or even as a consensual sexual act. After all, Sherry becomes the victim of rape, after consenting to go to a man's apartment!

We must also note that the Jungians speak of a demon-lover archetype that addresses the development of a demon-lover complex, from the view of a component in the "collective unconscious" (Jung, 1981), as opposed to seeing the overt contribution of the actual mother, father, siblings as the primal components of the internal eroticized bad object, which is the object relations point of view. But, the psychic magnet of Jungian demon-lover archetype is quite consonant with my object relations approach. An addiction to an internalized bad object, at a primal level, in the actual parental and family set up, can certainly interact in the unconscious psyche with a demon-lover archetype, which may or may not originate in a separate unconscious area of the collective unconscious. My first book on women writers, *The Compulsion to Create: A Psychoanalytic Study of Women Artists* (Kavaler-Adler, 1993a), explicitly relates the object relations components of the "demon-lover complex" to the Jungian theory of the demon-lover archetype form of complex.

Sigmund Freud, the father of psychoanalysis, was the first who acknowledged the role of the mother–infant dyad in pre-oedipal development. Some of his significant American and British followers in infant and child research are Beatrice

Beebe and Frank Lachmann; Margaret Mahler, Fred Pine, and Anni Bergmann; Donald Stern and Donald Winnicott. Freud (1931/1961) first expressed his aware- ness about the crucial role of pre-oedipal development in his paper on "Female Sexuality." Despite his other failings in attempting to understand women (as he had admitted in his famous quote: "The great question that has never been answered, and which I have not yet been able to answer, despite my thirty years of research into the feminine soul, is 'What does a woman want?'"), Freud unearthed the Rosetta stone of pre-oedipal derivations of the oedipal dynamics in women. In this paper, Freud had suggested that mother-deprivation (as well as the insatiable primal desire for suckling at the breast, and the primal hunger for maternal nurturance in general) affects the core psychodynamics related to women's desires for the father, as well as for father figures. Freud further indicated that severe problems at the early oral mothering stage could result in an overly adhesive tie to the father, which would be consistent with vulnerability to indiscriminate attachment to father fig- ures. By extension then, a sadistic father could be a source of a woman's intense erotic desires for sadistic men, especially when seduction arouses both oedipal and pre-oedipal cravings.

Such thinking is in line with my writings on the demon-lover complex, and with its clinical manifestation, as will be seen in the case of Sherry that follows. In an object relations view of the demon-lover complex, men who stir up oedipal lust in women for a powerful, aggrandized, and seductive father figure are also magnets for a re-enactment of the tragic lack of both maternal attunement and paternal pro- tection, both of which condition a life from its infancy. The demon-lover complex always involves a woman's destruction by a malignant man, where the woman is unable to assert her power with a man due to early pre-oedipal failings in mother- ing. When the demon-lover complex is seen in the context of well-known women artists and writers, who express the complex in their work, there is always a woman yearning to merge with an idealized male figure, who takes on the grandiose aspect of their own split-off power, and who is seen as an omnipotent god-like figure (Kavaler-Adler, 1993a, 1996).

Not only is the power of the woman split-off, but the sexual and aggressive impulses that the woman has trouble containing can also be split-off and projected onto the man, lending to the woman an exaggerated form of innocence. Some Vic- torian literature that talks about this is referenced in Auerbach's (1982) treatise on *Woman and the Demon: The Life of a Victorian Myth*. In this literature, the repression of female sexuality lends to the woman a contrived aspect of being a "lady," which drives her to seek an overly aggressive male, demonic figure, to usher instinctual life into the woman's own repressed and neutered being. In the twentieth century, this mythic "lady" can be seen in the theme of the Stepford wife.

In the demon-lover complex, the lady's yearning to merge with the male figure has various levels of psychological motivation. Since the lady yearns for a maternal nurturance from a male figure, this kind of female yearning is more oral than genital, although they are often acted out genitally. These female object needs are more like hungry craving than heartfelt yearning. They are constituted by insatiable oral hunger merged with a diffuse and eroticized oedipal instinctual lust. In addition to her cravings for a mother, the woman with the demon-lover complex also craves the erotic thrills of oedipal-level lust arousal, and its adolescent and adult instinct evolutions.

In this state of combined oral craving and oedipal yearning, the woman projects all her power onto the man. However, since she psychologically merges with the man (as opposed to marrying a whole object-differentiated man), she tries to own the idealized man's power, while she also projects the power of her own into her idealized male image, which then must inevitably turn demonic, as the projected and introjected power begins to possess her undeveloped infant feminine self. Then the lady wants the man as an aggrandized sexual object. She also wants him to offer her the compassion and maternal empathy of a highly attuned lover. Yet tragically, the early trauma of her pre-oedipal maternal failings inevitably re-occurs with the man to whom she has chosen to surrender. Surrender becomes submission as she endows the man with a hyper-masculinized (and even god-like) power. She projects her instincts (erotic and aggressive) that become combined with her idealized images, onto the man to whom she addictively attaches. In the woman's mind, the man then becomes a reflection of her own psychic fantasies.

When in addition to early pre-oedipal maternal deprivation, the woman's father has also been traumatizing, the demonic aspect of the chosen male is often significantly compounded. In the female version of the demon-lover complex, the god-father male forces submission, and he averts or precludes surrender by the woman. He attacks the woman with a manic erotic intensity and sadism that may or may not be explicitly sexual. And, when he has forcibly conquered the woman who craves merger with his power, he both imprisons his female victim under his omnipotent control, and then—emotionally or literally—abandons her. Often the demon-lover sadistically attacks his female prey with a sexualized lust, which can result in rape, beating, torture, or sometimes even murder.

In the literary examples of the demon-lover complex that women like Emily Brontë, Emily Dickinson, Anne Sexton, Sylvia Plath, Diane Arbus, Edith Sitwell, Katherine Mansfield, Virginia Woolf, and others have written about, death is the inevitable fate of the woman who is attracted to her demon-lover. This is true whether this death is achieved through murder by the male's manic erotic intensity and sadism—as in Heathcliff in Emily Brontë's *Wuthering Heights*—or by the woman's overt suicidal act—as in Anne Sexton, Sylvia Plath, Diane Arbus, and Virginia Woolf (see Kavaler-Adler 1993a, 1996, 2013b). Suicide often comes at the point when the lady has given herself to the demon-lover, both sexually and psychically, and then feels murderously betrayed.

In the case of Sherry, as we will discover here, the murder is not literal, but psychological, as it occurs through rape. Yet Sherry becomes obsessed with the writings of Marquis de Sade after her date rape by the hyper-masculinized, manic-erotic, narcissistic man. She reads about how Marquis de Sade raped, tortured, and abused his female victims to the point of death. And she becomes fascinated!

Nevertheless, due to the therapeutic process in which the early pre-oedipal mother has been dealt with through a critical "developmental mourning process"

(Kavaler-Adler, 1992, 1993a, 1993b, 1995, 1996, 2000, 2003a, 2003b, 2005a, 2005b, 2006a, 2006b, 2006c, 2006d, 2007, 2013a, 2013b, 2014), the young lady suffering date rape will be seen to survive psychologically. She will take her psychological power back from the man. A therapeutic writing group milieu becomes part of Sherry's healing process, as will be seen in her case. We will witness here that during this healing process, Sherry projects her male demon-lover rapist onto Harry, a man in one of my therapeutic writing groups, when Harry makes some comments that re-trigger Sherry's horrifying rape trauma. (This re-traumatization is frequent with PTSD, but it cannot always be talked about, as it could be in this therapeutic atmosphere.)

The abortion of surrender in a woman, and the vicious coopting of her soul: The demon-lover male defines the woman as a means to criminal date rape

Sherry comments after a date rape:

> "He didn't have to force me. I was like a budding flower, on the verge, just ready to open. His deep sensuous eroticism, his exotic culture, it all was melting me. I never before had felt anyone to be so sensual—that night in the barely lighted club, dancing, the music, his smell, his compliments—it was all working on me. . . . When I went to his apartment with him it was because I wanted to. I wanted to yield to him, to shed all my walls, and resistances. I wanted to surrender, but he forced me. He raped me. . . . "

Sherry dares to desire. She dares for the first time in her life to desire sexual surrender to a man. Her desire is, in part, for an emotional connection. She wants to be ravished by a penetrating male for the first time in her life. He rapes her instead. However, it all starts with him, the erotic stranger, defining her. The Arab male gave Sherry a Muslim female costume to wear, as he wants to define her as a part of his culture before he forcibly entered her, refusing to merge, holding on to an omnipotent dominating control. He tells her: "Now you look as you should, like a young Arab girl." He then penetrates her in an act of criminal intrusion. This is how Sherry describes it:

> "At first he spoke kindly to me, asking me to undress in the bathroom, and to put on the costume of his native country. I complied, willingly, wishing to please this man who seemed to exude an ever so powerful male presence. I did not mind being his mistress or concubine. I wished only for his approval, and for the lingering attention he was bestowing upon me—an attention I certainly never received from my father. When I emerged from the bathroom in the costume he instructed me to wear, I was expecting a kind of reverence and respect that I have never known from a man. 'Now you look as you should,' he pronounced. 'You look like a young Arab girl.'

The kindness in his tone was fleeting. When he reached out to me, his desire showed roughness, a brutal compulsion that did not modify passion with tenderness, and I intuited in a flash the forthcoming mutilation. He barely stroked or caressed me, but abruptly disrobed me, plunging his already erect penis into me, despite my protests that I was not ready! It hurt! It burned! I began to fight him, to try and force him off. My pride and heart sank into shocked despair. All my hope and faith in romance was being murdered. All sensation numbed out as my body froze, but still it hurt more intensely as he resisted backing off, and proceeded to pound himself inside of me. There was no soft liquid evidencing my free desire and modulating his entrance. There was no soothing of his painful intrusion. All I felt was my dryness, and the agony of my wounded vagina, as the blood of a harshly torn hymen flowed down my legs, and onto the sheets that my rapist had strategically and artfully laid out on a living room couch.

"As I cried out, the man pursued a faster pace. For several minutes I thought I had passed out and fainted. When I opened my eyes to consciousness, I felt bleak, dry, and empty. I felt cold, chilled, and trembling. I was abortively alone; he had stopped and withdrawn from me after a hasty ejaculation. I was in shock really—sitting half up, wanting to escape, but immobilized. Then before I knew what was happening, he grabbed me again and turned me over upon the couch. I could barely breathe and actively feared suffocation as he jammed me down on my face and stomach, entering me once more, extremely roughly, from the rear. I did not know till then that I could ever have endured such pain. The sharp edge of a knife seemed to pierce through my rectum and split my body apart on the inside. I was being violated again, he laughed as he culminated his climax. Then he pulled sharply away. This time I was left alone for good."

"Now I felt so heavy, like weights were binding me down on the couch as blood and semen streamed out from my rectal orifice. I didn't think I could ever move again, let alone get up. But he commanded me, 'Go clean up!' He arrogantly proclaimed that it was getting late. He said that I needed to leave before his girlfriend came home. It was in this travesty of a moment that I learned of his girlfriend for the first time. On top of feeling broken, undone, bruised, and seared with a phallus turned into a brutal knife, I now felt a shame and humiliation envelop me. I became all the more paralyzed. I had been totally duped. I was nothing to him. He would never want to see me again. He had a girlfriend, a woman his own age from his own country, whom he lived with."

"He barks at me, and prods me to get up. I did not think my feet would hold me as I rose from the makeshift bed, but somehow I made it to the bathroom, where it was dark, but I did not dare turn on the light. I did not want to see myself. Feeling orphaned and bereft, I stumbled around trying to find my own clothes. As I dressed, I tried to swallow my pain and felt that I might explode. I could not hold it all in. Wracking sobs escaped me, but I stopped them because I did not want him to hear my cry. I wanted to die, but I knew I had to leave the apartment. With my back toward him, I grabbed my coat from a chair and went to the door, only to be sty-mied by the resistant lock. After an eternity of terror, he came to unbolt it, laughing derisively: 'You will never forget me,' he said. 'I'm the first, the one who owns you, since I own your lost virginity. You will never forget me. I will be implanted within your brain, but I can, oh so easily, forget you!' Still not looking at him, I fled out into the night."

The crime of the man defining her

It is not just the act of date rape we need to attend to. The male rapist defines his female victim before he rapes her. She would have surrendered willingly, but then she would have been the "other," not defined by him. Sherry has to be the Galatea to his Pygmalion before he entered her through persecutory assault. Sherry had to lose her own identity, in his eyes, before he would take her over physically. The man has to possess her mind and image before he possessed (rather than encountered) her body. After the act, tossing her away as a piece of garbage, he defines her further: "You won't forget me! . . I'm your first. But it will be so easy for me to forget you!" Of course he can forget her, because she didn't exist as a "you." He dresses her and defines her to make her a reflection of his narcissistic image of an Arab sex slave. Contriving her image is an intimate part of his impulse and act of rape.

How does this kind of male "take over" relate to the female reproductive free-dom? The man not only legislates to control the female's jurisdiction over her own body, but he must define her as well. The malignancy begins with the male defini-tion of the female body. She is treated as Adam's rib, not as an autonomous female "other," as this is predominantly threatening to many men.

After the rape: He defines her again

Again Sherry's rapist defines her, when after the rape he encounters Sherry at the same nightclub where they had originally met. He speaks loudly to his friends of his possession of her. She is to listen, as he raises his volume. He defines her in his malicious gossip—right in front of her—as "easy." He spells out the tale of his "easy" virginal lay, exclaiming loudly so she can be sure to hear it: "That one's easy! You should take her home. She'll go with anyone!" Even as he speaks, his con-temptuous voice is cold and rapacious, just as his phallus was brutal and cold. Both are trenchantly destructive (and "envious") of Sherry's sense of her own being. He creates a negative mirror, to reflect back at her, derisively defining her. After the vicious act, which culminates in forced anal intercourse, Sherry is forced to take off his contrived Arab girl outfit and to leave his apartment, shunned and humiliated. The man again defines her before she leaves. He defines her as the excluded and foreign "other," in contrasting her to his girlfriend who is about to come home. This is a girlfriend from his own culture, who has also been defined by him. Sherry has no right to her own space in his space, his apartment, his mind. By contrast, the girlfriend is said to have a right there. For her this alien place is called home, even though she has just been betrayed there, and defined by her exclusion too. The girlfriend, who wears the Arab clothing full time, defined by all the men of his culture, can occupy a space in his space, in his apartment. Sherry must shed her contrived garb, which the man invited her into during the rape. Sherry is the "whore," the "easy" lay, not the girlfriend. The rapist continues to define Sherry as he speaks to his male friends in the nightclub, weeks after the rape. He speaks in his own contrived "image self" outfit. He speaks in a male tone of manic grandiosity and triumph. All the men then gather to define the women. The woman's greatest downfall is to be cast into the non-personhood role of a victim. This definition of her as the "other" and "victim" is then communally sanctioned by the male peer group.

Sherry continues to pursue her goal of becoming a writer, which to Sherry is the avenue to defining herself for herself, by giving vivid emotive voice to her experience in symbolic words. But even when words are supposedly the message, as in the writing group, other things can be going on in the tone and nuance, attitude, and arrogance of interpreting the other, when a group member or an analyst is intending to analyze and relate. The gross physical rape becomes a subtle verbal rape. The verbal behavior impacts through symbolic words, and the voice and the body are behind the words.

Then Sherry begins to read the pornographic ravings of the Marquis de Sade. She tells the writing group that she is fascinated by de Sade's intense pleasure in slowly torturing the female, sometimes until she succumbs to death. De Sade, the ultimate demon-lover, possesses through omnipotent control. A woman who tries to talk him out of his sadistic and murderous intention and who maintains her spirit half-way through the torture ultimately must give up all self-agency. De Sade is merely aroused to heights of perverse pleasure by the fighting spirit in this woman, and in the end, it is the woman's pain that most arouses him; and his arousal culminates in his own ability to totally crush the woman. Sherry reads and speaks to the group of how de Sade crushes the liveliest of female opponents, and the most psychologically minded.

What makes the woman vulnerable to the man's definition and rape? How does the woman become developmentally capable of her choice?

Now we fight for reproductive freedom for women as pro-"choice" advocates. However, as psychoanalysts we need to ask what makes women capable of having choice about the kind of men that they get attached to, as well as about whether they choose to follow a pregnancy through to delivery. The question of the kind of men they get attached to brings up the question of whether the men they choose are really their choices or men they are attracted to due to transference projections. If they are attracted due to transference, and if there has been failed mothering, compounded by the internalization of malignant father figures, women will lack the self-agency for choice, and they will be vulnerable to being defined and raped.

At the very least, they will be attracted to men who will not support them in their wishes to make their own independent and autonomous choices. Let's look at the developmental predispositions that interfered with Sherry being a woman of "choice" at the time she trusted a man to be a lover, who turned into being a rapist.

Sherry's father defined her mother; and her mother could never totally leave, despite hatred, lack of love, cruel physical and emotional beatings, and continuous betrayals. Sherry, on the other hand, would never have consciously complied with a domineering man. Yet, inadvertently she ends up in a rape scene, in the same position as her demeaned, used and exploited, and humiliated mother. She is attracted to the same psychopathic form of narcissistic man as her mother had been. For these women, the unconscious childhood trauma promotes vulnerability to the kind of male who uses all kinds of physical and mental weaponry to define the woman's choice out of existence.

As we see, Sherry manifests the demon-lover complex, a form of developmental arrest, which represents a pre-oedipal separation-individuation-stage trauma (called the "transitional phase" by D.W. Winnicott, 1971), compounded by the unavailability and/or malignancy of the oedipal-stage father figure. For Sherry, the problems of pre-oedipal failures in mothering emerged in the psychoanalytic transference, and they were largely repaired. However, Sherry remained vulnerable to the impact of the father's absence as a father, while he maintained his malignant presence as an abusive and abandoning husband to Sherry's mother. This vulnerability has manifested in Sherry's tantalization and seduction by the sadistic male rapist. Just like the rapist, Sherry's father had repeatedly betrayed the woman he was in a committed relationship with. He, like Sherry's rapist, had masqueraded as an attractive man in his womanizing with young women, using erotic seduction to mask his malignant character.

Men legislating rules for women, and this instructive date rape case

While looking at Sherry's story, we are looking at the possibilities of healing the self and revising the internalized trauma imprinted so graphically in the internal world of a woman. We are looking at the extreme effects of men defining women, as the psychological possession of the woman by men through their language can lead to profound regression into enacted sadistic behavior. This enactment can also take place through male-dominated legislation in our Congress, Senate, and the Supreme Court. Often male legislators define women as a group, seeking to reverse our pro-choice legislation in relation to reproductive rights. This case of date rape is instructive in revealing the dangers inherent in language being used by men to impose primitive and sadistic control of women; control which operates consciously or unconsciously in the minds of men. This case of Sherry also illustrates the failures in parenting that contribute to the individual woman's susceptibility to being seduced (and thus controlled), which in turn interfere with the woman having a "choice." The case also indicates the road to self-integration through reparation of the damaged relationship with the internal mother and internal father. Reparation through mourning the loss of primal and later trauma can allow for separation-individuation in women. Then these women can make true choices.

As I continue to speak about Sherry, I will illustrate how the mourning of pre-oedipal maternal failings allows for reparation with the external mother. This affects the internal world relations with the mother and begins to allow a psychological readiness for the oedipal-level heterosexual desires, and for heterosexual surrender. However, when the father has been as inadequate as the mother, and when the father's sadism (and seductiveness) has been internalized as a "demon-lover" figure, heterosexual readiness for erotic relations can result in exploitation by a malignant male character that echoes the internalized father. This kind of vulnerability can lead to the extreme dangers of masochistic submission overcoming healthy het-erosexual surrender, and overt trauma can reach the extreme of submission to a criminal rape. But this rape can be psychological as well. Hypothetically, women who collude with men controlling legislation on female reproductive rights might be seen to reflect a kind of female idealization and female romanticizing of men, which can result in a form of submission to legislative rape of the female (see Reich, 1940). This can in turn obviate the woman's rights over her own body. How does a woman "wake up" from such a state of collusion or submission? Let's learn about this through the psychological work with Sherry.

Sherry's journey to freedom and choice: Repairing the mother connection and turning female submission around

Through object relations psychoanalytic psychotherapy, Sherry re-finds her mother after a lifetime of feeling shut out, misunderstood, and emotionally abandoned. When Sherry surrenders to a critical regression in her treatment, a powerful moment of connection with her mother becomes possible.

The psychic turning point comes in a late evening session several years into Sherry's once-a-week therapy. The session begins like many others. Sherry seems tortured in the silence, unable to speak, unable to begin. Something is building up inside of her, and her facial expression shows her unspoken rage at me for not res-cuing her from what is within her.

Her body shows tremors of tension that cry out to me, reminding us both of the traumatized child within her that threatens to break into consciousness. The tremor speaks to us of the internal child, a child crying for attention in an emo-tional vacuum, with her mother withdrawn from her. Yet none of this is in Sherry's conscious awareness at the time. The child-self dissociated in her body has been trapped by a mind that is forced to carry the critical memories but cannot speak. I am only consciously aware of the tension in the room with Sherry. I am waiting, wondering if Sherry will find her way to words. I am wondering if she will find her way to feelings, wondering if it would be helpful for me to speak.

Suddenly Sherry darts out into the hall. I find myself leaving my office and going after her. I have developed an inner bond with her that compels me, urges me, to do it. I stand by the banister while Sherry stands agonized and torn apart on the top of the stairs, leaning on the wall. I watch while Sherry fights with herself, frantic with the pain and tension of indecision. She seems to be seeking release, but is also terrified of losing control. Turning a lifetime of rage inwards, against herself, Sherry begins to bang against the unyielding cement wall, as all her life she has banged her fists against the emotional wall put up by an unyielding mother. As Sherry seems about to bang her head against the wall as well, the head full of mental instruments of torture, derived from her unprocessed memories, she suddenly turns swiftly away instead. In a second, she pivots away from self-attack and enters into self-surrender. She bends over like a swan, yielding to her pain, and surrenders to the child within her who has needed to cry for decades.

When the parent is incapable of tolerating regret, and therefore of communicating a validation of early traumatic events in the family, the analyst naturally becomes primary source for the patient's validation. The analyst must also help the patient salvage her sense of reality in the face of the parent's denial of the traumatic events that have so impacted on the child's psyche and view of the world. The analyst needs to help the patient see the parent's incapacity to offer validation by helping her understand the psychic capacities needed to face the regret. This can help the patient to differentiate and separate from the parent, rather than to remain stuck in endless rage and retaliation, or in unavailing efforts to extract the yearned-for validation—like Sisyphus endlessly pushing his boulder up the hill, only to have it fall again.

Sherry's surrender is complete for the first time. On the edge of the stairs, about to run away, she stops abruptly, looks at me, and begins to vent a tidal wave of grief and yearning. She lets go and begins to sob and sob. I watch her body convulse in cathartic release. I gently suggest that she come back into my office. Having *chosen* to let go of her opposition, Sherry follows me. She also wails out loud, in a testimony to her need to purge herself.

Eventually I say the words that match her feeling, as I experience it through our emotional connection: "Mommy, hold me. Please hold me, mommy." I speak for the child within Sherry. There is no effort. I know she is inwardly responding. She does not have to speak to me. She continues to sob out her inner oceans of tears from deep down, filled with sadness and longing, so different from earlier tears. I bring her the tissues box, and hand her some tissues. We are deeply in communion, and I am struck by how effortless it all is now. The aggression that has been causing so much resistance has temporarily left us.

Sherry's transforming moment allows her to reach forward into the core of the mother whom she had to confront in the present. She and her mother are to come face to face with love for each other, a love that they had perhaps not felt since Sherry's early infancy—prior to all the conflicts and traumas of the separation-individuation stages. It is through this encounter that Sherry's mother's capacity for regret is momentarily realized. That most tender of encounters takes place when Sherry's mother comes from her Eastern European home to visit her and her siblings in New York. This is about a year after Sherry had surrendered to her inner anguish in her psychotherapy. Having opened up with me to her yearnings for a mothering response she had never had, Sherry played a major role in planning and preparing for her mother's visit with the family. She had no idea how her mother would respond.

Sherry has frequently felt abandoned by her mother, not only in childhood, but throughout her adulthood. Her mother never called her. Sherry always had to call her mother. She would call, always seeking something she could never find. On the phone, she inevitably felt the icy chill of her mother's emotional detachment, and of her mother's inability to listen. In therapy sessions—now no longer alone with her rage—she cries out her intense disappointment, rather than freezing her feelings and withdrawing, as she had done throughout her childhood and young adulthood. Sherry repeatedly relates the internal devastation that followed her attempts to reach her mother through phone calls. In Sherry's transferential reactions to me, she demonstrates her extreme sensitivity to feeling like she is not being listened to. She demands intent attention at all times, no matter how silent she would be.

As Sherry begins to internalize me as someone who could respond to her and understand her, over the years, and as I offer her psychic holding at times of her emotional surrender, she also becomes more capable of reaching out to her mother with empathy. And although her mother begins to have some capacity to listen and talk, she remains an extremely depressed woman, emotionally withdrawn and conveying an emotional emptiness to her daughter. So the transformational event I am going to describe seems almost like a small miracle when it comes about.

Sherry reports to me all of her experiences with her mother during the mother's visit in New York. Maybe being with her children, in the absence of her abusive husband, erodes Sherry's mother's resistances. Maybe the thought of going back to her emotionally starved home is beginning to threaten Sherry's mother. It appears that the combustion of both factors heats up the mother's emotional terrain until she finally experiences and expresses true grief. Just as she is approaching the pinnacle of that emotional precipice, she hesitates—intense conflict, tears behind the eyes, tears not yet cried. Sherry recognizes her own face in her mother's look, the one she had revealed during the session in which she surrendered to my emotional holding, and to her own need for relief, a year before.

Seeing her mother's entire body tense up, held back from release by a humiliating internal censor, Sherry whispers: "It's OK, Mom. It's OK to cry!" And in an instant her mother yields. She lets go of her censorship, and abandons herself to her tears of grief and yearning. Filled with the emotions she has resisted for a lifetime, Sherry's mother speaks from the depths of a new psychic stage, one born in the moment of intense anguish and its consummate release: "I hope your life is better than mine." That declaration speaks volumes about the grief of this mother's life, and about the buried love that has been blocked by intolerable regret. Only in this moment does this intolerable regret transform into tolerable regret, and only because Sherry is there to receive her mother's pain and longing, just as I had been there to receive hers.

Sherry has surrendered to her abandoned 2-year-old self. This has allowed her an internal reconnection with a surviving holding mother within her, through the mediation of a transitional object relationship with me, her analyst. Consequently, having received this (from the transitional object), Sherry now can offer the same kind of desperately needed emotional holding to her mother. In the moment—when she and her mother come together—this re-creates a mother–daughter bond that had been broken repeatedly. This makes communication possible on a verbal level and on a level of mutual empathy. It would not prevent repeated episodes of maternal emotional withdrawal and unavailability in the future, but it would stay with Sherry internally, paving the way for her to sustain a more loving and solid self in relation to others, and, in particular, in relation to men.

The internal strength Sherry derives from her mourning process in treatment begins to repair her bond with her symbolic mother inside of her. This allows Sherry some reparation with her actual (external) mother in her adulthood, which carries her through psychological analysis of her relations with men. Ultimately, Sherry comes to understand her compulsion to engage with abusive men. This allows her to have choice, to choose emotional risks with more emotionally available men.

The moment of verbal communication

Soon after Sherry's mother returns to Europe, the mother and daughter experience a moment of mutual caring. This happens over the telephone, and now some 4 years into Sherry's therapy. Her mother is warm and receptive to Sherry's call for the first time—still under influence of their New York connection. This allows for a conversation in which they both begin to appreciate and understand each other's separate identities and differences. Sherry's mother speaks of attending church daily as a refuge within her cold and emotionally isolating existence. Sherry says, "I guess going to church is for you something like my going to therapy."

Sherry's mother has never been able to understand what going to psychotherapy means. Yet for this one brief moment, Sherry and her mother do not judge one another. In fact, as Sherry and her mother come to appreciate each other's separate identities and differences, Sherry's mother accepts that Sherry has something in her life analogous to her seeking peace of mind through her visits and prayers in the Catholic Church. Likewise, Sherry relinquishes, at least temporarily, her defensive contempt, as well as her hostile views of her mother's inadequacy as a woman. She actually opens up to her mother's words, and also to the vision of her mother entering church, kneeling in prayer, and finding solace.

Sherry's father

After Sherry and her mother touch each other in New York, Sherry tries to soften the situation between her mother and father: "Mom, if dad wants to kick up his heels once in a while, let him. It's OK. We all need to have fun." Her mother does not respond, but she does not shut out Sherry's words, voice, or presence, as she has in the past. When Sherry as a child had cried out in pain and needed her mommy, the emotionally absent mother tried to placate her daughter with detached words, instead of comforting her with either the physical or emotional holding Sherry always longed for. "Go to bed," her mother would say, adding, "It will be better in the morning." It was never better in the morning, not for her, and not for her mother! However, following her mother's emotional surrender to her internal self in New York, Sherry finds her mother to be listening over the phone, actually listening to her, for the first time. To get there, Sherry had switched roles with her mother, comforting the mother who had not been able to comfort her.

After Sherry's mother returns home, her father continues to disappear for days at a time from the household, pursuing an affair with a 20-year-old, and then he returns unannounced to the family house to demand a cup of tea. All that Sherry's mother has to hold over him is her deed to their home. She has re-entered a world dominated by a demonic husband who abandoned and abused her, so Sherry's attempt to normalize her father's behavior as merely "kicking up his heels" is bound to fail. Her mother is again swallowed up by her husband's hostility and her own rage, which turn her cold when she defends against them. With the impact of this, Sherry's mother once again fails to be present when Sherry calls her from New York. Eventually Sherry feels like giving up. She has tried. She has opened her heart to her mother, and has had her moment of communion. Hopefully, this moment in New York remains with her. . .

As she opens up the affective avenues to sustained connection by opening her pain, grief, and rage in therapy, Sherry begins to see that she and her sister are always repeating the sadomasochism of their parents' marriage. In fact, when they try to live together, Sherry's sister drags Sherry across the floor and tries to beat her up, mimicking the behavior of her father towards her mother. Seeing this in her sister allows Sherry to observe her own aggression during the course of her fifth year of once-a-week psychoanalytic psychotherapy. She is able to re-own the part of herself she has always tended to project onto men. Owning her own aggression, Sherry is able to confront her sister and to love her again, when they return to separate apartments. Apparently, Sherry now carries a good-enough feeling of love from her brief period of communion with her mother, and from her connection with me, to repair her relationship with her sister. She is now developmentally ready to move more seriously towards men.

Sherry has to face the demonic visage of her father in the men she has felt seduced by, but in order to do so, she needs to rediscover some favorable views of him. Facing his dark side, as well as her own, helps Sherry gather and preserve some precious positive father images as if they are rare flowers she needs to dry, press, and preserve in a scrapbook. Before all this psychotherapeutic work, Sherry's experience of date rape with a foreign man came as an inevitable drama from the split-off dark side of her father that she carried within. She is hypnotically drawn forward in the path of the great seducer. This is not a fun seduction! This is serious! No wonder that it leads Sherry to read and speak of the writings of Marquis de Sade in my therapeutic writing group. In fact, Sherry becomes an extremely articulate female voice on the demonic lover (and on the demon-lover complex) as she does this. One man in the group then becomes the "demon" onto whom she projects her inner male demon, as she tells her whole story to the group, date rape and all.

Re-enactment in the writing group

The group members are awed by Sherry's description of her date rape, and even more awed by her detailed descriptions of Marquis de Sade and his cleverest female victim, who de Sade murdered. When Harry, the man in the writing group, returns to Sherry's own demon-lover, speaking of her male assailant as a guy who "fucked you and left you," Sherry freezes. It is not until her next individual therapy session that I learn how devastated Sherry has been by the male writing group member's words. Sherry tells me that she has not been able to stop those words from pulsating repeatedly in her mind—"fucked me and left me," she says. Sherry feels so vulnerable, exposed, and humiliated by her own shame when she heard these words, especially hearing them from a man! In fact, her subjective emotional experience is of feeling raped all over again. I encourage Sherry to share her reaction in the group, and to speak directly to Harry, whose words have provoked her into feeling so abused and assaulted.

Sherry struggles very hard before she responds to me. Her shame makes her want to hide away again. I urge her not to. I say that shame grows when the incident that ignites it is kept secret, kept hidden in the darkness. She is reminded of the dark bathroom where she had stumbled, broken-hearted and lost—to find her clothing after the rape she had endured. She knows she has to come out of the darkness into the light to cure herself. She knows she has to reveal her secret in order to find her voice. Consequently, she reluctantly agrees to confront Harry with her reaction to his words. She reluctantly agrees to share her re-provoked trauma with the group members, and to tell them what she had told me, that she was raped by a man's words as she had been raped by a man's body.

At the next writing group session, everyone is there. Everyone listens intently when Sherry speaks of Harry's words. She is able to look right at Harry when she reminds him "You said, 'He fucked you and left you,'" and goes on: "I can't stop hearing those words biting into me, over and over, searing pain and haunting obsession into my mind." Harry is surprised, but not shocked. He is quite willing to apologize for his insensitivity to Sherry's feelings, and adds that it was careless and thoughtless of him to speak so casually of something Sherry is still in the middle of feeling and suffering from. The group is relieved by Harry's response and by their collective capacity to tolerate and contain a trauma that had taken place in their midst. I know, however, that Sherry was not just reacting to Harry's words. I know she is projecting onto Harry the relationship with a male demon-lover figure that she still carries within her.

Sherry learned a great deal by becoming conscious of her susceptibility to seduction, and to seduction by such a demon-lover man. The demon-lover male was able to take mental control over her by directing and defining her, and then violating her in rape. She mourns her loss in her writing and in her therapy. She has much better relationships with men after that. She definitely believes she has a new sense of choice. She decides to leave a relationship with a man who seems to truly love her, and who wants to marry her, because this man is in a country where she could never live, although she enjoys the adventure of being there. He is in a medical residency in his country, and cannot come and live with her in New York. She makes a clear choice to leave him, despite that he is a man capable of loving her, and one who has been emotionally available in a way her former boyfriends have not been. Sherry is able to end this relationship directly, without feeling like a victim or a victimizer, even though the man feels hurt. Later she finds a man who she feels comfortable living with in New York, while she continues to find her voice as a writer. She says that she thought of being a therapist earlier because she felt psychotherapy had saved her life, as well as having been a powerful experience. However, she realizes that just because she benefitted from therapy doesn't mean she really wants to be a therapist. In wanting to define herself, and in wanting never to be the victim of a man's definition of her again, Sherry finds that she can discover her own voice in writing. Subsequently, she begins to pursue a degree in creative writing in college studies. She also begins to write for a literary magazine.

Conclusion of case vignette example of Sherry

The combination in Sherry of an inadequate mother, forced to submit to the abuse of her narcissistic husband and his sadism, and a rapacious father, who beats his wife and is indifferent to all her emotional needs (particularly her need to be loved), sets Sherry up for attraction to a malignant abuser. The early pre-oedipal internalization of the father's sadism and the mother's masochism (in relation to the father) can be seen as a malignant form of Melanie Klein's combined mother-father object that dominates the psyche of those arrested in the paranoid-schizoid position. As such a woman, Sherry is attracted to an external man who resonates with her magnetic, hyper-masculinized internal demon fantasy object (see Reich, 1940). She projects this tantalizing figure outward onto a malicious man, and thus finds him both char-ismatic and erotically arousing. She also projects onto him the power of her own sexual and aggressive instincts. Inflamed by the lust of oedipal desire, plus the ado-lescent and adult sexual desires that were naturally triggered in a sexually explicit heterosexual situation.

It would be "blaming the victim" to assume that the female who is raped is guilty of choosing her rapist, just because she has been sexually attracted and aroused by him. She does not consciously choose a man who might rape her, even if there is a demon-lover figure within her internal psyche that makes a certain man, with such tendencies, appealing to her. In fact, Sherry's arousal was unconsciously directed by her frustrated childhood yearnings and by the demonic and inadequate parental objects attached to those yearnings. Thus, we see how psychic fantasy plays a vital role in the pre-oedipally arrested person's attraction to an object of lust.

Sherry is a victim. She expects to be seduced into surrender by an erotically arousing sensual male, which is a common oedipal fantasy for women of all ages. Unfortunately, she is unconsciously compelled by her internal parents (as they existed in her psyche as dynamic visceral objects or as symbolic representations), with unconscious psychic fantasy elaborations, to choose a man who would viciously and violently deny her right to surrender. Oedipal-stage yearnings for surrender, which take place when the ego self has achieved subjectivity, self-observation, self-agency, self-reflection, and interiority, cannot not be sustained in the face of an unconsciously chosen demon-lover rapist.

In Melanie Klein's (1940) terms, psychic motivations to surrender regress downward on a developmental continuum to pathological pre-oedipal modes of sadomasochism, so that submission is compelled rather than surrender being chosen. Also, in keeping with Ronald Fairbairn's (1943, 1952) description of "bad" (demonic) objects, Sherry's internalization of her parents' sadomasochistic enactments set her up for an erotically arousing attraction to the seductive man, who then morphed into her rapist.

Sherry's attraction to this man repeats Sherry's attraction to a sadistic father. Due to her yet not mourned pathological father as an internal object, Sherry has been vulnerable to a woman's cravings and yearnings for the demon-lover male father figure. This is the demon-lover complex that compelled Sherry to direct the displacement of an oedipal dynamic toward a malicious man. Sherry's oedipal longings have not been played out with her father in childhood, due to her father's unavailability. Therefore, Sherry serves as a case in point in studying the nature of the demon-lover complex. She acts out her complex with an alluring and exotic foreign man who appears to have momentarily served the psychic function of a father or father-mother displacement.

The shocking trauma of date rape illustrates the seductive and malignant nature of the father, who was compulsively internalized by the rape victim in her childhood. The malignant father internalization had been superimposed on an internalization of an inadequate (borderline) mother. This is also the father with whom Sherry yearns to sexually connect, when she establishes a fairly solid connection with her female analyst as a transference mother. This study describes the reparation with the female analyst that also allows for some reparation with the actual mother and then, in turn, allows the rape victim to mourn the absence of sufficiently good mother and father objects in her childhood. Sherry is able to heal her trauma, and to resolve her psychic identification with a borderline masochistic mother, through developmentally progressive mourning process, which includes creative work in a psychotherapeutic writing group.

In the process of mourning her grief, the patient develops a fascination with the writings of Marquis de Sade. This fascination allows her to re-own the aggression that she has unconsciously invested in her internal sadistic father object of her childhood (not just a symbolic introject), which she has also acted out temporarily in a sadomasochistic relationship with her sister. Consequently, the patient's aggression can mature in a neutralized conscious fashion into a stronger and more separated and individuated self, a self that could express her voice in the world, as a writer, and as a human being in interpersonal relationships.

Conclusion

The case of Sherry is a dramatic example of the dangers of a woman suffering the seduction and control of men, and of men who wish to dominate women through defining who they are. Sherry's voice lives on in this chapter. She is a most vivid spokeswoman for the female demon-lover theme, and its pathological form of addiction to the demon-lover complex. She is also a willing spokeswoman for a woman possessed by the internal and external demon-lover, and who needs a route out of her psychic imprisonment. This route of facing one's internal demons through grieving one's losses, disappointments, traumas, and narcissistic injuries, is available through what I call "developmental mourning" process. My theory of developmental mourning has its roots in Melanie Klein's (1940) paper, "Mourning and its relation to manic depressive states." Also involved in the developmental mourning process is the self-reflective analysis of one's unconscious motives, and one's viscerally powerful compulsions, enacted through the traumatically dissociated areas of the psyche.

Utilizing this chapter and its case vignette, analogies are drawn between the defining of a single woman by a man and the defining of women as a group by male legislators. The issue of male dominance is engaged, but it is also looked at from the psychoanalytic position, related to that which allows a woman to develop a psychological capacity for choice, so that she can benefit from Federal and State legislation that upholds pro-choice. The extreme case of date rape, in this case of Sherry, is offered to vividly and visually comment on this interplay between male/female politics and psychological development. In speaking of psychological development, we need to remember about achieving psychological reparation of so-called developmental arrest trauma, to allow a woman to choose. Only when women are psychologically evolved to be able to "choose" as separated and individuated autonomous women, can they fully embrace responsibilities for their bodies and for their own reproductive rights. Then any interference with the female "right to choose" can be articulated and tested by the women themselves.

References

Auerbach, N. (1982). *Woman and the demon: The life of a Victorian myth.* Cambridge, MA: Harvard University Press.

Fairbairn, R. (1943). The repression and the return of bad objects (with special reference to the "war neuroses"). In *Psychoanalytic studies of the personality* (pp. 29–59), 1952. London: Routledge and Kegan Paul.

Fairbairn, R. (1952). *Psychoanalytic studies of the personality.* London: Routledge and Kegan Paul.

Freud, S. (1961). Female sexuality. In J. Strachey (Ed. & Trans.), *The standard edition of the complete psychological works of Sigmund Freud* (Vol. 21, pp. 223–246). London: Hogarth. (Original work published 1931)

Jung, C.G. (1981). *The archetypes and the collective unconscious: Collected works 1934–1954* (2nd ed.). Princeton, NJ: Bollingen.

Kavaler-Adler, S. (1992). Mourning and erotic transference. *International Journal of Psycho-Analysis, 73,* 527–539.

Kavaler-Adler, S. (1993a). *The compulsion to create: A psychoanalytic study of women artists.* London, UK: Routledge. (Republished in 2000 by the Other Press, NY; and in 2013 by the ORI Academic Press, NY as *The compulsion to create: Women writers and their demon lovers*)

Kavaler-Adler, S. (1993b). Object relations issues in the treatment of the preoedipal character. *American Journal of Psychoanalysis, 55,* 145–168.

Kavaler-Adler, S. (1995). Opening up blocked mourning in the preoedipal character. *American Journal of Psychoanalysis, 55,* 145–168.

Kavaler-Adler, S. (1996). *The creative mystique: From red shoes frenzy to love and creativity.* New York, NY: Routledge. (Republished in 2014 by ORI Academic Press in New York)

Kavaler-Adler, S. (1998). Vaginal core or vampire mouth. The visceral level of envy in women: The protosymbolic politics of object relations. In N. Burke (Ed.), *Gender and envy* (p. 221–238). London: Routledge.

Kavaler-Adler, S. (2000). The divine, the deviant, and the diabolical: a journey through an artist's paintings during her participation in a creative process group: An evolution of "developmental mourning." *International Forum of Psychoanalysis, 9,* 97–111.

Kavaler-Adler, S. (2003a). *Mourning, spirituality, and psychic change: A new object relations view of Psychoanalysis.* London: Routledge.

Kavaler-Adler, S. (2003b). Lesbian homoerotic transference in dialectic with developmental mourning: On the way to symbolism from the protosymbolic. *Psychoanalytic Psychology, 20,* 131–152.

Kavaler-Adler, S. (2005a). The case of David: Nine years on the couch for sixty minutes, once a week. *American Journal of Psychoanalysis, 65,* 103–134.

Kavaler-Adler, S. (2005b). From benign mirror to the demon lover: An object relations view of compulsion versus desire. *American Journal of Psychoanalysis, 65,* 31–92.

Kavaler-Adler, S. (2006a). My graduation is my mother's funeral: Transformation from the paranoid-schizoid to the depressive position in fear of success, and the role of the internal saboteur. *International Forum of Psychoanalysis, 15,* 117–130.

Kavaler-Adler, S. (2006b). From neurotic guilt to existential guilt as grief: The road to interiority, agency, and compassion through mourning. Part I. *American Journal of Psychoanalysis, 66,* 239–259.

Kavaler-Adler, S. (2006c). From neurotic guilt to existential guilt as grief: The road to interiority, agency, and compassion through mourning. Part II. *American Journal of Psychoanalysis, 66,* 333–350.

Kavaler-Adler, S. (2006d). Mourning and erotic transference. In J. Schaverien (Ed.), *Gender, countertransference, and erotic transference* (pp. 221–238). London: Routledge.

Kavaler-Adler, S. (2007). Pivotal moments of surrender to mourning the parental internal objects. *Psychoanalytic Review, 94,* 763–789.

Kavaler-Adler, S. (2013a). Dialectics of mortality and immortality: time as an internal and transitional object experience: and time as a persecutory versus a holding object. *Issues in Psychoanalytic Psychology, 35,* 47–61.

Kavaler-Adler, S. (2013b). *Anatomy of regret: From death instinct to reparation and symbolization through vivid clinical cases.* London: Karnac.

Kavaler-Adler, S. (2014). *Klein–Winnicott dialectic: Transformative new metapsychology and interactive clinical theory.* London: Karnac.

Klein, M. (1935). A contribution to the psychogenesis of manic-depressive states. *International Journal of Psycho-Analysis, 16,* 145–174.

Klein, M. (1940). Mourning and its relation to manic depressive states. In *Love, guilt, and reparation and other works: 1921–1945* (pp. 219–232), 1975. New York, NY: The Free Press.

Reich, A. (1940). A contribution to the psychoanalysis of extreme submissiveness in women. In A. Reich (Ed.), *Psychoanalytic contributions*, 1973. Madison, CT: International Universities Press.

Winnicott, D.W. (1971). *Playing and reality*. London: Tavistock Publications.

5

SECONDARY SEXUAL TRAUMA OF WOMEN

Female witnesses

Kristin Davisson

In 2010, I completed my doctoral clinical research project/dissertation on the concept of secondary sexual trauma of women. This project spanned 3 years and, like many thesis subjects, was one close to my heart and lived experience. As a granddaughter, daughter, and friend to women who have suffered the staggering consequences of sexual violence, I was interested in exploring the impact of being so *close* to another woman's experience of sexual trauma. Considering the prevalence of assault against women worldwide, vast numbers of female "witnesses" may be suffering from symptoms of secondary trauma. Given this risk, what are the implications for the mental health of these female "witnesses" locally, nationally, and internationally? This was the question I sought out to address, and the answers—and personal stories—I came across in my work were significant.

Secondary/vicarious trauma

The concept of secondary trauma accounts for the negative effects of secondary trauma exposure among those in contact with primary victims and is increasingly documented in the psychological literature[1] (Figley, 1995; Herman, 1992; McCann & Pearlman, 1990; Pearlman & Saakvitne, 1995; Stamm, 1999). In response to the emphasis of secondary traumatic states in the mental health field, Kadambi and Ennis (2004) identified a central error in the assumption that secondary trauma is an experience that has been so "warmly embraced by the mental health community that the publication of remediation and self-care strategies has preceded the performance of empirical research investigating the occurrence and etiology of the phenomenon" (p. 7). In this way, although considerable research has expanded the concept of secondary trauma to include indirect exposure to events of global terror including war, political torture, environmental disasters, and the events of 9/11, the emphasis on mental health and health care workers has excluded investigation of secondary trauma in the general population.

Female risk for secondary trauma

As my research focused on investigation of this phenomenon with respect to women in the general population who encountered secondary exposure to sexual violence, literature regarding the increased risk of women to develop secondary traumatic states is relevant.

Several empirical studies have demonstrated that female caregivers experience increased risk for developing secondary trauma symptoms when working with victims of sexual assault (Pearlman & MacIan, 1995; Schauben & Fraizer, 1995; Wasco & Campbell, 2002). In their study assessing the effect on female counselors working with sexual violence survivors, Schauben and Fraizer (1995) found that working with victims of sexual violence was associated with disrupted beliefs, symptoms of posttraumatic stress, and an increase in self-reported vicarious trauma. Moreover, these results were not associated with a female counselor's own history of victimization, suggesting that a past experience of victimization is not required for development of secondary trauma.

Research suggests that women display empathy at a higher rate than men, increasing the likelihood of exposure to trauma via empathic attunement. Empathy is described by Gold and Rogers (1995) as "accurately perceiving the internal frame of reference of another," requiring primary consideration of another's thoughts and feelings rather than preoccupation with the self (p. 75). Further, Pearlman and Saakvitne (1995) specify that long-term empathic attunement increases risk of secondary trauma, as empathy increases openness to feel what another is feeling. Gender socialization and cultural stereotypes support the notion that women are more empathic than men (Klein & Hodges, 2001; Surrey, 1991). An empirical study by Toussiant and Webb (2005) supported the commonly held belief that women behave and view themselves as more empathic than men do. In addition, Shihui, Yan and Lihua (2008) investigated gender differences in the electrophysiological brain effects of empathy in response to painful experiences of others. They found that women showed greater long-term responses than did men, comprised of subjective experiences of others' pain and changes in view of self. Empathy being the central component in relational experiences, self-in-relation theories of feminism emphasize the importance of relatedness as a crucial piece of female identity (Surrey, 1991).

Sexual violence against women

Given women's increased risk for development of secondary trauma, consideration of the prevalence of sexual violence becomes significant in understanding the extent of this exposure. The World Health Organization (2005) found that next to telling no one, friends and neighbors are the most common confidants following an incident of sexual violence.

Sexual violence against women remains a critical social issue as the frequency of sexual coercion, intimate violence, sexual assault, and rape impacts vast numbers of women each year. Of equal concern are the mental health correlates that accompany the direct and indirect effects of such widespread gender violence. With examples resonating throughout history, gender inequality has perpetuated sexual violence against women for centuries. As a widespread global concern, definitions of the acts of sexual violence differ. The National Institute of Justice (2007) defines sexual violence as "as constellation of crimes including variations of sexual harassment, sexual assault and rape." Characterization of sexual violence by the World Health Organization (2005) includes positive indication of any of the following three criteria: physical force to have sexual intercourse against a person's will, sexual intercourse due to fear of harm, or the force of sexual acts that are experienced as humiliating and/or degrading. Crimes of sexual assault encompass actual or threatened physical force, genital mutilation, and the use of weapons, intimidation, or coercion that may or may not result in rape (National Institute of Justice, 2007). Legal definitions of rape within the United States differ by state, generally referencing nonconsensual oral, anal, or vaginal penetration by body parts or objects and including rape by coercion, intimidation, threats of violence, and sexual intercourse with individuals unable to consent (National Institute of Justice, 2007).

As statistics indicate, the likelihood of female contact with a victim of sexual violence is extensive. As confidants bear witness to the direct suffering of the primary victim, they observe firsthand the direct effects of sexual violence including but not limited to experiences of depression, anxiety, posttraumatic states, dissociation, suicidality, somatization, sexual difficulties, personality disorders, lower overall health, increased risk of substance abuse, sleep disorders, nightmares, and symptoms of posttraumatic stress (Briere & Jordon, 2004; Herman, 1992; Pico-Alfonso et al., 2006; Krakow et al., 2002). Looked at together, the overwhelming statistics suggest that vast numbers of women worldwide know another woman who has suffered the direct consequences of sexual victimization. Given the empirical support for the impact of secondary exposure to trauma in addition to the research detailing women's empathic attunement to one another, one could reasonably presume that women "witnessing" the sexual victimization of others with whom they are close (and thus empathically attuned) would be at increased risk for development of secondary traumatic states.

Research study

My research consisted of a mixed-method qualitative and quantitative study described here in brief. Thirteen women were included in the study who met the following inclusion criteria: (a) over the age of 18; (b) known the victim for a minimum of 6 months with incident of sexual violence occurring between

1 month and 5 years earlier; and (c) known the victim during the period in which the violence occurred. In addition, there was a 1-month waiting period between the primary incident and data collection. Efforts were made to focus on non-mental health care providers to expand the literature on persons experiencing secondary traumatic stress and participants were chosen who did not report a primary history of sexual violence. In addition to assessment instruments given, participants responded to a qualitative semi-structured interview in which they were asked to describe their experiences in their own words, focusing on their subjective emotional responses to their relationship, the sexual violence in question, and overall feelings of personal safety, danger, and/or distress.[2] Quantitative findings revealed that this sample of women displayed markers of secondary trauma consistent with disturbances in relatedness, affect, and identity at significantly higher rates than they displayed behavioral symptoms associated with PTSD.[3]

In this chapter, I will be focusing on the *qualitative* findings from participant interviews and the meaning derived from analysis of women's personal narratives. The reason I chose to focus on this aspect of my research is that in the time since completing it, the qualitative interviews have remained in my consciousness, containing rich emotional and clinical relevancy. The narratives of these women have created a foundation from which we can start to explore the conscious and unconscious impact of vicarious exposure to sexual violence.

Participants

Thirteen women were included in the sample ranging in age from 19 to 55 with a mean of 28. Ten (77 percent) identified their race as White/European American, one woman identified as Biracial, one as African American, and one as Asian American. Religious affiliation of the sample was diverse with five women identifying as Protestant, one as Catholic, and one as Catholic/Buddhist. Two women identified as atheist, three as agnostic, and one as a humanist. Nine indicated they were single and four reported they were married. Seventy-seven percent of the women sampled identified as heterosexual/straight, one as bisexual, and two as unlabeled.

All women sampled had exposure to education at the college level: two completed some college coursework, six were students at the time (five graduate students and one undergraduate), four women were working with a 4-year degree, and one was working with a master's degree. [4, 5]

Nature of traumatic stimulus: Sexual violence

All women sampled met criteria for friendship with a female victim of sexual violence; the violence in question occurred between 1 month and 5 years earlier, and all women were in contact with their friend when the violence occurred. Across individual accounts, the nature of sexual violence varied. Table 5.1 includes frequency of exposure to various types of sexual violence reported by women sampled.

TABLE 5.1 Frequency of various types of sexual violence (experienced by friends)

Type of sexual violence	n	%
Gang rape	2	15.0
Rape motivated by discrimination	1	8.0
Rape inside a relationship	3	23.0
Suspected use of "date rape" drugs	3	23.0
Sexual coercion/threats	1	8.0
Raped/assaulted by friend/acquaintance	7	54.0
Raped/assaulted by stranger	3	23.0
Other sexual contact	1	8.0

Note: Incidents may be included in more than one category.

Themes and sub-themes

In this segment, themes and sub-themes are introduced, derived from the "coding" process.[6] The following themes and sub-themes of interest will be explored:

  I The stories
 II Emotional responses

    i   Anger and guilt
   ii   Feelings of responsibility and helplessness

III Strength of the victim

    i   Is strength overtaken by assault?
   ii   Admiration and idealization

IV Identification

    i   A sense of sameness
   ii   Identification or empathy?

  V Personal feelings of safety and danger

      i   Hypervigilance and decreased sense of trust
     ii   Inhibition of behavior and/or compensatory actions
    iii   Recalling safety pre-exposure: a sheltered life
    iv   Myths maintained: blaming the victim and feelings of safety

VI Shifts in worldview

    i   Increase in social awareness
   ii   Hopelessness/disillusionment

VII Factors of influence

      i   Multiple relationships with victims
     ii   Distance in time from the traumatic stimulus and phase of life
    iii   Closeness
    iv   Revisiting personal trauma

The stories

To open the qualitative interview, women were asked to recall how they became aware of their friend's experiences of sexual violence, followed by an inquiry of their feelings/reactions to this disclosure.[7] This allowed participants to "retell" the story of sexual violence as they first experienced it. It was not uncommon for participants to experience strong emotions as they recounted the details of the trauma stories themselves. One woman tearfully shared:

> It's very sad . . . He told her he had a gun . . . turns out he didn't, but she didn't know that. He tells her to take him to her car or he'll shoot. She said she tried to decide if she should scream but she didn't, which she ended up regretting, although who's to say he wouldn't have hurt her. So, he takes her to her car. There is no one around. He forces her into the backseat and rapes her. (crying) She said she was actually relieved that he raped her and left. He didn't drive her anywhere; he didn't kill her . . . And she said she didn't really fight; she felt resigned to her fate. She said he wasn't too rough with her physically, but that he kept calling her dirty names and asking her did she like it. She said she cried the whole time and begged him not to hurt her.

In describing her own emotional reaction to this, she stated:

> Well I felt completely helpless. So sad for her, for the fate she endured on behalf of all women I guess. And angry. Damn angry . . . I thought about it constantly. I dreamt about it the week after. Even talking about it now, again I feel paralyzed.

Another woman recalled a "hysterical" phone call from her friend in which she disclosed the ongoing physical, emotional, and sexual violence occurring in her relationship:

> She told me that he choked her until she blacked out; that she had marks all over her neck; that he was screaming at her and threw her into the wall; that he would call her really horrible sexually-based names; and that if she didn't want to have sex with him, he would make her feel bad about it and coerce her into doing it. Really bad stuff . . . the first time she called me, it was this huge pouring out of everything that had been going on for quite some time . . . I felt very powerless in that situation and scared for her.

In all but a few cases, participants recounted similar details of the traumatic encounter, giving me a sense of just how close they were to the incident of sexual violence. Distance in time from the event (ranging from 1 month to 5 years) did not appear to be a factor in the few cases wherein participants did not relate such details; rather there was an apparent correlation to closeness with the victim.

Emotional responses

Women reported a range of emotional responses when asked to recall their initial reaction to their friend's disclosure of sexual assault. Every woman interviewed (100 percent) reported initial reactions of shock, often (though not exclusively) tied to feelings of helplessness, anger, fear, or guilt. One participant reported physical symptoms of nausea, vomiting, and lack of appetite, lasting for several days. For many women, emotions tended to be clustered together, leading to feelings of confusion or conflict. One woman shared, "I was shocked. Pissed at him but also at her. Angry that she hadn't told me, angry that she let him to do that to her. Then I went from feeling angry to feeling guilty." Like this participant, most women interviewed described experiencing a *sequence* of emotions. By far, the most common sequence was shock→anger→guilt, with approximately 60 percent of women reporting this succession of emotion. Most women reported that strong initial reactions subsided after several weeks, or sometimes months. A small number of women indicated that strong reactions of shock, anger, fear, and/or helplessness remained present in their lives for years following the incident. The impact of these feelings was most strongly related to shifts in worldview, which will be discussed in a subsequent subsection.

Anger and guilt

Of the ten women who reported feeling anger, 40 percent endorsed anger toward both the victim and the perpetrator. Most of the women in this category directed their most intense anger towards the perpetrator and described anger or frustration towards the victim for reasons of not sharing their assault sooner, not reporting the incident to law enforcement, or for "not fighting back." Generally, anger in response to "not fighting back" or "staying in the situation" existed in the context of a victim–perpetrator long-term relationship. Reacting to this, one participant shared:

> She always had healthy relationships in the past, so I just didn't see it happening and then I just couldn't understand, like, "Why do you think this is acceptable? Are you in the twilight zone?" You know, it was like a feeling of helplessness, frustration, anger . . . and then you feel guilty because you're mad at them. Then you tell yourself, "come-on, don't punish the victim."

Like this participant, most women who expressed anger towards the victim reported subsequent experiences of guilt. For many women, harboring anger towards the victim created cognitive dissonance and feelings of conflict or confusion. Some women noted their awareness of the frequency of sexual violence; two participants referenced the idea that there exist "myths" around rape. Correspondingly, their feelings of anger toward the victim appeared to feel "off limits" to them. In their case, guilt may be a result of "turning anger against the self," a mechanism of defense whereby feelings of aggression are redirected towards oneself due to some aspect of unacceptability (White & Gilliland, 1975).

Of the remaining six participants who endorsed feelings of anger, half reported anger directed exclusively toward the perpetrator, and half spoke of anger directed toward the victim. Generally, anger towards the perpetrator also included some reference to "anger at the world" or "anger on behalf of all women." Unlike anger towards the perpetrator himself (all perpetrators were reported to be men in this study), anger directed towards "the world" seemed not to be transient and was clearly connected to conscious feelings of helplessness, often leaving a lasting impact on women's lives. Perhaps the most direct example of this (and most extreme) is evident in the following participant's remark.

> Three women got raped by where I live, from September to March, in the same block. And I think about that all the time. Like when I think of incidents like that, or if I'm walking home alone at night, I just feel really angry that I would have to . . . that patriarchy has placed a curfew on me for being a woman, and if I break that curfew, I suffer consequences of rape. And how I want to kill people. I want to kill a man. I get so angry, that I could kill a man if he approached me. Like instead of feeling afraid, I just feel angry.

I asked this woman if she had ever acted on these feelings, or felt close to acting on them. She responded, "No, I think in those situations, I feel completely help-less. Like I don't have the strength to stand, let alone. . . . " Notably, her friend's experience of sexual violence occurred 4 years prior to the interview, ruling out initial shock as cause for her intensity. What appeared to be furious anger, rage even, was transformed (or gave way) to profound helplessness for this participant and was associated with multiple elevations on the Inventory of Altered Self-Capacities (IASC). Similarly, other women reported heightened awareness of sexual violence and described changes in their feelings of personal safety and/or worldview.

Interestingly, anger alone (when not tied to helplessness) seemed to act as a protective factor in the conscious distress of the interviewee. That is, by her report, if a woman felt anger that separated her from the victim (i.e., "it's her fault for putting herself in that position; how could she do that?") she was more likely to report less conscious distress. (Notably, this did not always coincide with symptoms as measured by the IASC and TSI.) Reactions characterizing "blaming the victim" are addressed in more detail in a subsequent section.

Feelings of responsibility and helplessness

Feelings of helplessness were referenced almost universally in the sample. Helpless-ness is noted in the literature as a central facet of trauma, relating to a felt loss of control, powerlessness, fear of annihilation or surrender (as cited in Herman, 1992). For women who did not respond to their helplessness with feelings of anger, it was common for them to reference personal feelings of responsibility for their friend's assault. Approximately 50 percent of the sample noted some variation of feeling accountable for their friend's assault. These women were less likely to reference conscious experiences of anger, and seemed to place blame on themselves. Three women reflected on this below:

> I remember feeling like I could have done something, that I could have prevented it, that I should have known.

> I wasn't there. So I felt guilt for . . . I always feel like I'm always sort of a protector of people, so that fact that I didn't go that night . . . there are thoughts of, "oh, If I'd have gone, I usually don't drink, I could have kept my eye on her." But I realize that's a false sense of control really.

> I felt like I should have been there for her—or doing something, but the whole time, I had no idea it was happening. I should have known. I feel like it was my fault.

Though only one woman connected her feelings of personal responsibility to a "false sense of control," one wonders if feeling a sense of personal accountability might be a defense against intolerable experiences of helplessness. Not uncommonly, women described "keeping an eye on" the primary victims following the assault or increasing care-taking behaviors toward other women in their life. To this effect, one participant in her 40s remarked:

> I felt almost as if I was her mother and wasn't there to help her. I have always been there for her. . . . I have a ten-year-old little cousin who is developing now. And the thought of her—I tell her every day, "Don't let nobody look at you. If you feel, you know, the way somebody's looking at you and you don't feel comfortable, scream, holler, fight." I check on her all the time. Every day.

In her case, a conviction to help another young woman avoid or protect herself from sexual violence consciously follows feeling in some way "not there" for the primary victim. This may suggest that increased hypervigilance and care-taking, while adaptive responses to feelings of helplessness brought on by the traumatic incident, are indicative of a "false" sense of control.

Strength of the victim

Among the thirteen women sampled, eight (61 percent) talked about the strength of the female victim. Most commonly, this was voiced in conjunction with feelings of shock, surprise, or personal vulnerability. Often, participants remarked they "never expected" this could happen to a woman like their friend. Several participants reflected on this below:

> She was always such a very goal-directed, strong, smart person—very athletic, always had lots of friends. I guess people always say this with violence, but I just didn't see it happening to her. You know, she wasn't the vulnerable type.

> She is one of the strongest women I've ever met. Just hearing that could happen to her—a strong independent woman . . . was so impactful.

> She is so strong on her own; I was left feeling more despair about it.

These responses reflect an interesting idea: the concept that personal strength, drive, or autonomy may serve as a protective quality for women (or enhance a self or other perception of safety) and that, when it comes to sexual assault, there is a specific reaction to this "quality" of a woman being overtaken. This begs the question: Did participants feel the "strength" of their female friends was lost or "stolen" by virtue of their victimization?

Is strength overtaken by assault?

In response to this very issue, two participants offered contrasting remarks. One woman, when discussing her friend's rape inside a relationship, commented, "She is still that strong girl . . . maybe wounded but strong." Another participant said of her close friend who survived a gang rape, "She's a very strong person and she projects herself very well and it made me very angry that someone would take that away from her." The first participant notes the presence of her friend's co-occurring strength and vulnerability; here we see the idea that a woman can be wounded and strong simultaneously. In the second participant's remark, we see the discernment of loss, the idea that a woman's strength can be "taken" from her. This loss of "strength" may occur *literally* through the act of sexual assault and/or *symbolically* through its scope and impact.

Another participant stated:

> She's a very strong person. She's strong-spoken and demands respect . . . it's really troubling to me because I look up to her and how much she can demand respect and take control of a situation. And I feel like I can be that way too, but she is so much more so—like that's something that defined her. That was her identity.

Once more, the implication of loss is embedded in this person's comment with specific reference to the last phrase, "that *was* her identity." This same participant spoke of witnessing her friend struggle for several years following the assault, striving to "let go of" the incident and eventually turning to substances to cope. Several women echoed similar experiences, emphasizing difficulty in "watching" their friends' psychological turmoil following the assault(s). Perhaps the perception of strength and resolve of the primary victim is impacted by their contextual *resiliency*, and, as we understand psychological trauma, their access to resources (both external and internal) to cope with their situation (Pearlman & Saakvitne, 1995).

Admiration and idealization

An additional point of interest from the last quote is the introduction of *admiration* (referenced in the phrase, "I look up to her and how much she can demand respect"). Similarly, another participant stated, "She is that girl who wears the pants, takes control. She is not passive at all the way I can be. She is adventurous and bold, and really when we were close, I wanted to *be* her."

Wanting to *be* someone may be analogous to the concept of idealization, derived from self-psychology. Through idealization, one is able to nourish the self by merging (in fantasy) with an object of strength, power, omnipotence, and wisdom (Kohut, 1977). In this way, idealization becomes a vehicle for self-worth—we "want to be" like those we respect. Both participants quoted above acknowledge the quality they respect in their friend(s) to be their ability to "wear the pants," "demand respect," or "take control" of a situation. In this way, "strength" (for lack of a better term) seems to be a characteristic widely admired among women sampled. This alone may suggest that women tend to covet strength as a protective factor against violence.

This brings up a question of relevance; that is, what is the impact of an "idealized other" being victimized, and further, if women "idealize" the primary victim, are they more likely to experience secondary trauma? Twenty-three percent of women sampled obtained clinical elevations on the IASC scale of "Idealization–Disillusionment." This result, in conjunction with conscious impact reported by women sampled, seems to suggest that idealization of the victim can be an important factor in development of vicarious trauma. Over half the sample had a specific reaction to reconciling the "strength" and "victimhood" of an admired friend. To this effect, one participant stated:

> She is such a strong woman though . . . which is funny that is something that even stands out to me, like as if someone weak is the only person this would affect. But there is something so sad about seeing her strength overcome by pain. By pain that someone took advantage of her—of her ability to say yes. Now she will be haunted by it . . . so will I, I suppose.

If we were to describe this in a masculine context, we might use the term "emasculate" to speak to the quality of strength or control being stricken away. Webster's Dictionary defines "emasculate" as "to deprive of strength, vigor or spirit" or "to deprive of virility or procreative power" (*Merriam-Webster Online Dictionary*, 2010). Certainly, this definition seems to fit with women's depictions of their reactions to "strength" of other women being overcome by sexual assault. Unfortunately, there is a not a term denoted to the female corollary of this experience.

Identification

A sense of sameness

Of women sampled, many indicated feelings of closeness to the female victim, informing a felt sense of "sameness" between them. As the literature reviewing empathy in women suggests, this kind of "identification" in close female relationships is common (Surrey, 1991). Interestingly, approximately 50 percent of participants seemed to link (in discussion) their feelings of "sameness" to a personal fear or vulnerability following their friend's assault. This might suggest that identification with a female victim can extend to identification with her traumatic event. Two women make this connection below:

> It just makes you feel really vulnerable. If this can happen to her, it can happen to anyone . . . and I see so much of myself in her. I'm afraid I could be in a situation like that. This is so close to home. It's very troubling.

> Realizing this could happen to her—a girl from a small town—you know, a girl who's pretty much just like me. That really scared me.

For the two women above, the realization of "sameness" ("I see myself in her") is intimately linked with recognition of risk to the self. In psychoanalytic theory, secondary identification is defined as "an automatic, unconscious, mental process whereby an individual becomes like another person in one or several aspects. It is a natural accompaniment of maturation and mental development and aids in the learning process as well as in the acquisition of interests, ideals, mannerisms, etc." (Moore & Fine, 1968, as cited in Basch, 1983, p. 104). As one might expect, the closer the woman interviewed was to the victim, the more likely she was to speak of this felt sense of sameness. Identification is also considered to be a mechanism in providing satisfaction to the self via adoption of aspects of a loved person, ultimately making separation or loss more tolerable (Basch, 1983; Freud, 1917/1957). The frequency with which these feelings were reported may suggest that identification with the traumatic event may serve to maintain a "needed" connection between two women (victim and "witness").

Identification or empathy?

In reacting to her friend's violent sexual assault, one woman commented, "If it could happen to her, then who among us are safe?" She goes on to say, "I felt sad, like a part of it happened to me." Certainly, feeling the pain of another can be likened to the experience of empathy, an important and desired quality in a close relationship. For these women, this proposes the inquiry: Where is the line between *empathizing* with the victims and *identifying* with them? Which of these experiences makes it more likely that they will exhibit symptoms of secondary trauma? In differentiating between these two (often similar) states, Basch (1983) makes reference to the temporary nature of empathy, sometimes called "trial identification" (Reich, 1960) versus the more enduring transformation of identification. Presumably then, empathy by itself does not imply adoption of the victim's traumatic feelings.

Correspondingly, one participant shared, "It was very sad for me to think that she experienced that intrusion, and she kept it inside. And then sad like a part of it happened to me . . . the second I knew she had been hurt like that, I felt hurt." Another remarked, "I certainly hurt for her (begins to cry) and I hurt for myself and other women."

Perhaps a function of identification, the two women above obtained the most profound elevations on the IASC, suggesting significant dysregulation of affect, relatedness, and identity in their lives in the six months preceding their interviews.

Feelings of personal safety and danger

Nine of thirteen participants (69 percent) identified a noticeable decrease in their personal sense of safety following their exposure to the traumatic stimulus. In all nine cases, women reported current impact in their lives. For these women, time from the event ranged from 6 months to 5 years and did not appear be a factor of significant influence in their reaction (that is, women who were closer in time to the traumatic event did not generally report heightened concerns of safety in comparison to other women). Though many women endorsed alterations in their perceptions of safety, the depiction of their experiences varied, as did their responses.

Hypervigilance and decreased sense of trust

Five women (38 percent) identified enhanced awareness of their surroundings, often manifesting as hypervigilance and collectively relating to feelings of discomfort. This was occasionally spoken to in conjunction with a hesitance to trust men. To this, one woman remarked, "I wish I could get to that place where I have a 'healthy' sense of awareness. Instead, I freak out. I look at every man who walks by. Is he a rapist? Is he capable of this? My nervousness has skyrocketed." Like this participant, several women spoke of increased vigilance and distrust towards men. One factor of influence here appeared to be the relationship status of the participant. Generally, single women appeared more likely to struggle with diminished trust towards men, and women in established relationships were less likely to endorse this specific concern.

One 31-year-old single women with an MBA shared:

> I am a single woman. And it's hard enough to meet a man when you are a successful woman in your early thirties. Who's to say I can ever meet a man and feel safe, trusting, or protected? It's like I have to sum up all my courage just to think about it. Not a great feeling. So I think what has replaced hope about my relationship future is sadness and fear. Maybe women can't have it all . . . maybe I was foolish to think I could.

In this woman's response, we can discern a sort of resignation and hopelessness alongside her questions about safety, trust, and protection. It seems she is referencing the difficulty successful, educated women can encounter in the heterosexual dating world, joined with (or complicated by) her newfound feelings of distrust related to her friend's assault (occurring six months prior to the interview).

There also appeared to be subtle differences relating to trust in relation to victims that were brutally assaulted within a "trusting" relationship. A 29-year-old, unlabeled female reported that her friend was assaulted in a dating relationship. The participant recalled her friend confiding in her that she was tied up and anally raped by her boyfriend at the time. In regards to her personal safety, the participant shared:

> I definitely feel less safe. I feel like my eyes are open to it now. It's really sad. And what am I going to do about it? Live my life in fear? Or have fun and hope that I don't get raped? I guess I don't have the answer. I try to ignore all my fears and feelings of distrust, but inside, I'm terrified.

This brings up a dilemma that several women alluded to: the idea that following their exposure to the traumatic event, they seem, at times, unsure of how to live their lives. When asked how this dilemma made her feel, this participant responded, "It makes me uncomfortable. Really uncomfortable."

A 29-year-old woman whose friend experienced physical and sexual violence inside a committed relationship shared:

> I think it makes you understand that sexual assault is not the serial rapist, or the person in the shadows; it's the person you know. And it reminds you that you can never be safe. You can't trust anyone completely. People who do those things and act in those ways are very good actors.

Inhibition of behavior and/or compensatory actions

Several women talked about how they are less likely to walk alone after dark, have curtailed their social activities (particularly in reference to alcohol, as was true in several cases where the victim was believed to be drugged), or have added caution-ary behaviors to their routines. Two referenced making sure they traveled in groups and called friends to inform them of their whereabouts. Notably, participants who reported compensatory behaviors like those above obtained relatively lower scores on the TSI and/or IASC. One women with no clinical elevations on either scale remarked:

> Well I definitely think about my safety more. I feel less safe than before. I do. But, I try to think about it a lot, and I take more preliminary steps to protect myself than before. I may recommend to friends, if they're going on dates, to be prepared and be safe—and talk to them about that. And for me too, when I was dating after I heard about this, I was more cautious. I'd make phone calls to people so they would know where I was and walking late at night. Just general safety as a female.

Most women who addressed behavior changes shared statements similar to those above and echoed feelings of uncertainty and caution. As a whole, women seemed to express doubt that anything they could do would actually "ensure" their safety.

To this, one woman (who disclosed a personal history of sexual assault 7 years prior to her friend's incident) remarked:

> To a certain degree, I think there are definitely certain things you can do—like how safe are you? What area are you in? Who are you with? But it is so highly situational though because you could be at home in bed and it could be your father; it could be your boyfriend, your uncle—so it's highly unfortunate. I think that we're probably not as safe as we would like to think we are. That illusion of safety can keep you from totally breaking down, but when I think about it seriously, I think there is only so much you can do.

This participant discussed in detail the way she believed her own history of trauma impacted her reaction to her friend's assault. Though her words here may certainly allude to her own history, they also capture a shared fear among the sample, the concern that women can never be "completely" safe. Taken together, this information may suggest that women with a prior history of trauma are less likely to enact compensatory behaviors, seeming to diminish feelings of helplessness and enhance a personal sense of agency.

Recalling safety pre-exposure: A sheltered life

Five women (38 percent) identified a "sheltered" sense of safety prior to coming into contact with the traumatic event. Perhaps surprisingly, these women were not insulated from other types of trauma in their lives, with four of the five identifying some type of personal trauma in their life history. With regard to sexual assault, however, these women noted they had some sort of "naïveté" before encountering their friend's experience of sexual violence. Several shared their feelings about this below:

> I think my general feelings of safety as a woman were higher before. I think maybe part of that is the youth idea of "nothing's gonna happen to me; I'm invincible," but the more I heard stories like this and the more I've been educated, the more I feel hesitant and think about my safety. When this happened to XXX, it only made that feeling bigger.

> I guess I always had the attitude that, "I'm not going to worry about things." My family was always cautious and strict. I didn't really hear about this stuff. In that way, my worldview is more realistic than it was before.

> I guess I felt sheltered. Most of the things I learned about sex, I learned from her [friend who was assaulted], or another friend I had. I didn't realize this was so common. It totally changed my point of view.

The three women above experienced a shift in their outlook and sense of personal safety through exposure to their friend's experience of victimization (also likely influenced by educational experiences). This inundation of harsh reality upon a naïve (and safe) sense of oneself may represent an important aspect of vicarious trauma for these participants.

Myths maintained: Blaming the victim and feelings of safety

Of the thirteen women sampled, two reacted unlike the rest of the sample in a few key ways. They did not reference feelings of helplessness and directed anger (almost) exclusively toward the victim. As outliers, their responses are included for relevance and for the significant questions they suggest. Both women endorsed numerous experiences of personal trauma in their backgrounds and are aged in their twenties. In various respects, both women appeared to harbor current myths about sexual assault and blame the victim for her assault.

Both women shared their reactions to their friend's assaults below:

> She puts herself in a lot of risky situations, and she's a very flirtatious individual. And when she described the story, it's not that I didn't believe her, but she puts herself in these situations. I've known her to. I felt bad for her; I wanted to be there for her, but then there was this voice in the back of my head saying, "this girl . . . she puts herself in these situations that I don't and my friends don't, so she is different in that sense." So I didn't. I felt for her and I believed her, but I think there were things she did. How long did she flirt with the guy before she said no? I mean she still said stop, but she has to take accountability.

> I just can't believe she would let that happen and not say anything. I guess I don't think she's that strong of a person. She kinda comes off as brash and argumentative and she dyes her hair black. I think she hides her emotions a lot. I mean, how could she let this happen? Especially if she's that kind of a person. Wouldn't you push him off—be loud? I would. Why wouldn't she want to do that? Does she like that? (Interviewer: "What's it like for you to wonder that?") I don't know. It's weird. I feel guilty, but I don't at the same time. I think she should stand up for herself and be less passive. That's how I feel.

Sex-role stereotyping as described by Burt (1980) appears in the excerpts above. When asked about feelings of safety, both women denied current or previous concern and/or fluctuation in their feelings of personal safety. In response to this, one female remarked:

> I would say I felt safe before. I still feel safe because I'm not the kind of person that would let someone do that. I'll kick his ass. I mean, yeah, it can happen, but I know myself; I would take care of it. I'm not gonna let someone

do that to me. (Interviewer: "What do you mean by 'take care of it?'") Like get him off me. Fight. Hit him and get away and report him of course. Call the police.

This participant expressed intense frustration and anger towards her friend for not actively defending herself. In fact, she believed her friend to have "lied there" while the rape occurred. One wonders if her attributions about the incident are adaptive or protective for her in some way. This participant reported three previous traumatic experiences and it seems reasonable to assume that "fighting back" and/or identifying with a personal feeling of strength was an important resource for her in overcoming her past. Interestingly, she attained fewer elevations on the IASC and TSI than most women sampled. Consistent with her self-report, she did not appear to experience conscious distress and/or symptoms associated with primary or vicarious trauma. Her self-concept did not include feelings of fear and/or danger, seeming to provide her with a sense of control.

Though these two women differ in their responses, and present with varied personal histories, their stories suggest that holding the victim accountable for her assault may foster a sense of personal safety, offering insulation from feelings of helplessness and maintaining a sense of control.

Shifts in worldview

As alluded to in previous discussion, approximately half of the sample spoke to modifications in their worldview. According to McCann and Pearlman (1990), vicarious trauma can alter one's view and sense of oneself in the world. Participant statements corresponding to worldview generally reflected two themes: an increase in social awareness and/or a perception of hopelessness/disillusionment towards the world. Conscious shifts in worldview were consistently associated with multiple elevations on the IASC in all but one case.

Increase in social awareness

Four (31 percent) women spoke about a shift in their social awareness following their friend's assault, such that they better understood and were cognizant of power dynamics, the likelihood of sexual assault for women, and/or sociopolitical factors influencing gender violence. One woman sought a volunteer position at a domestic violence shelter a year following her friend's assault. She shared the following related to her experience:

That experience (volunteering) made me capable of examining the relationship and what had been going on with her. Like the power cycle of it all. I became very aware and educated about how common this is. It didn't make the pain go away, but it helped to understand.

Of her academic work in liberal arts, another woman remarked:

> It made real some of the things that I read. The statistics, the cycles of violence. It reminded me it is so easy to get taken advantage of and so easy to get frustrated with the victim. And that these cycles are so real. So powerful.

Other participants referenced gains in their understanding of power and gender dynamics in an overarching way. Two women reflected on this below:

> There are so many subtle ways that women are overpowered and taken advantage of. Like little ways like women who just want to please their boyfriends and they don't even realize there is a power differential and that they're playing to it. It makes me angry a lot.

> It makes it real, that you hear on the radio that one in so many women get raped, or so many are hurt by violence. You know as a woman, that's you . . . that's us. Like, my heart goes out to them and me, and I really know how common it is now. The gender dynamics of it all, the power of it. It's really sad. I look at every relationship differently now.

Both women above were between the ages of 25 and 32, identified previous "sheltered" lifestyles, and reported decreases in their perception of personal safety. Their responses suggest that in addition to feeling less safe, some women may undergo drastic changes in their view of gender interactions. Women were not directly questioned about the influence of this change on their personal relationships or sense of themselves, which opens up questions about the continued impact on their lives.

Hopelessness/Disillusionment

Five women (38 percent) identified a shift in worldview that corresponded to feelings of hopelessness, disillusionment, or disappointment. Time span from the event ranged from 2 to 5 years for the women in this category, speaking to continued impact of the traumatic event. Two women speak to their changed worldview:

> It reminded me of what people are willing to do to other people without regard of how it will affect them. I think I am more aware of that now. How people can hurt other people. And they're going to do it no matter what—I mean, there's nothing I can do about that; I just have to watch out for me. . . . So in that way, I think my worldview more realistic than before.

> It just feels so hopeless now. I mean in the age of match.com and speed dating . . . you can't know you are protected from this. It is everywhere. I don't know how to deal with that. . . . Just an overall sense of sadness I think. I feel like maybe I have been down since and can't shake it. It's disappointing, and I don't think it will ever change.

In these reaction statements, we can discern a kind of resignation in the face of a perceived "harsh" reality. In describing the impact of rape, Herman (1992) writes, "Thus women discover an appalling disjunction between their actual experience and the social construction of reality" (p. 67). It seems possible that in addition to holding true for primary victims of sexual assault, this experience of dissonance can be true for her close friends as well. The five women who identified these sorts of worldview changes seemed to view social realities quite differently following their exposure to the traumatic stimulus. Correspondingly, a 55-year-old woman spoke of her experience:

> It's more of a resigned sadness. Disappointment with the world. I want things to change, but I don't think they will in my life. I hope they will in my daughter's life. I hope she will see difference . . . I mean, the sadness with the world . . . maybe that's part of a realism? Maybe when I was younger, I would try to see the world through rose-colored glasses. This event definitely reminded me that is not the truth.

This woman was the only participant to endorse changes in worldview in the absence of clinical elevations on the IASC and/or TSI. She seemed to differ from other participants in both her phase of life and her hope for her daughter's generation. She appeared less despondent than she was realistic and hopeful. This may be a tentative suggestion that experiences of hope are important adaptive responses to trauma exposure.

Experiences of disillusionment and hopelessness echoed in participant statements (implicit and explicit) seem linked to the subjective perception that things may never improve and that the world is a sad, dark place. Disillusionment and hopelessness are experiences linked to suffering and trauma in the work of Viktor Frankl. Frankl (1959) underscored the importance of what he termed "tragic optimism," the capacity to retain the meaning of life despite its "tragic aspects" (p. 137). The participant quoted above seems to speak from this vantage point. Frankl's idea that absence of "tragic optimism" intensifies or maintains suffering seems consistent with IASC results strongly associating (conscious) statements of worldview shifts with multiple clinical elevations. Of the clinical scales on the IASC, Idealization-Disillusionment was elevated in 3 out of the 5 women who denoted hopelessness in worldview. These results suggest that a percentage of secondary victims experience worldview modifications and that such dramatic frame of reference shifts are not limited to primary victims of sexual assault.

Factors of influence

In examining reaction interview transcripts and coding the data, it became clear that several factors appeared to influence the data. That is, at least in some cases, certain variables seemed to significantly impact participant reaction. Some of these variables were pre-identified as potential "predictors" in the research questions (closeness of relationship, previous trauma), whereas others were not considered in this way. This section will explore the qualitative association of such variables as they were discussed or revealed in reaction interviews.

Multiple relationships with victims

Though the study focused on one "close" relationship, it became clear during reaction interviews that a number of participants had exposure to multiple female victims of sexual assault. (Five of thirteen women indicated they had previous exposure to victims of sexual assault, though these data were volunteered, not asked.) Although not a focus of the interviews, participants often volunteered reflections of their reactions to multiple exposures.

A 55-year-old participant remarked of her experience, "I knew more women in college, but I haven't known of any for about 20 years, so I guess it was a shock to my system in some ways."

Other women referenced closeness to the victim as an important indicator in their reactions. A 24-year-old woman reflected on her contact with two friends who were assaulted:

> The other friend, I felt more protective of her and defensive for her. I worried about her more. This friend, my closest friend, I feel like she was so strong on her own that I was left feeling more despair about it.

In this case, closeness and "strength" of the victim appeared to be relevant in distinguishing this participant's reactions between multiple exposures.

Several women who reported feeling responsible for their friend's assault noted they were (physically) with the victim prior to her being attacked. In this way, they experienced a "proximity" to the traumatic event, which by their report, they had not experienced before.

Though there were no consistent patterns, all women who indicated multiple exposures noted the relationship in question as the "closest" of their friendships to female victims of sexual assault.

Distance in time from the traumatic stimulus and phase of life

Distance in time from the traumatic event did not appear to drastically shape reactions overall. As noted in the previous discussion, most participants reported a decrease in the acuity of their initial emotional responses after several months. Distance in time from the event did not appear relevant for participants who reported continuation of intense emotional experiences.

Phase of life (with reference to age and/or developmental life stage) seemed at times to overlap with distance in time from the event, additively influencing participant reaction. The youngest participant, a 19-year-old freshman in college, encountered the traumatic event 5 years earlier. The participant remarked, "I don't feel really impacted now because it was so long ago. I would probably be more likely to notice if something like that happened to me, but I was so young." It seems reasonable to assume that distance in time from the event, coupled with the partici pant's age and the reported nature of the assault, shaped her subjective perception that she was not significantly impacted.

In other ways, phase of life seemed an important factor in the life experience of the participant. Participants aged 25 and older were more likely to report multiple exposures to sexual assault. They were also more likely to be engaged in advanced education or established careers. As noted elsewhere in discussion, single women were more likely to report distrust of men than were women who identified as partnered or married.

Closeness to victim

As noted in the preceding discussion, participants indicating closeness to the pri mary victim were more likely to recount details of the traumatic story during the interview. They were more likely to admire/idealize the victim, reporting concord ant feelings of helplessness and despair. Closeness with the primary victim was likewise qualitatively associated with feelings of sameness/identification. Corre spondingly, of the two women who obtained the lowest closeness coefficients, one engaged in victim blaming, and the other reported her feelings of closeness to the primary victim decreased on account of the victim's psychological struggle follow ing the incident.

Revisiting personal trauma

Ninety-two percent of participants endorsed prior trauma exposure and one par ticipant indicated a personal history of sexual assault. She acknowledged her previ ous traumatic experience as "triggered" by her friend's victimization. In describing her reaction to the vicarious incident occurring 2 years prior, she stated:

> After my friend's incident, things became triggered in me as well. I became hypervigilant as well. So in addition to trying to be there for her, I was strug gling with some of the same reactions like walking down the street and being very hypervigilant and things like that. That has lessened much since then.

Her candid report of conscious impact strongly suggests the re-surfacing of her former traumatic experience, though with less reported intensity than when she was in a primary victim role. For this participant, her previous experience of sexual victimization cannot be separated from her reaction in the present.

Concluding thoughts and suggestions for exploration

The participants in this study described their experiences serving as "witnesses" to their friends' experiences of sexual violence. They frequently began their narratives by recounting the traumatic event, giving voice to the primary traumatic stimulus. Their descriptions incorporated dynamic and often complex emotional responses including various manifestations of anger and guilt directed towards themselves, the perpetrator, and/or the victim. Their stories spoke to the changes that occurred over time in their emotional responses, perceptions of themselves, and view of the world around them.

Within these descriptions, the theme of helplessness emerged alongside a longing for control/protection. The strength and/or admired qualities in the victim served as a source of struggle for the group overall as they wrestled to reconcile their illusions of safety with their feelings of sameness and/or idealization towards the victim. The group made connections to their personal feelings of safety and danger as women, the majority identifying decreases in their feelings of safety following the traumatic event. While the group varied in their responses to perceived reductions in safety, they tended to struggle with the idea that "nothing they could do" could keep them completely protected. A small number of women appeared to deal with this ambiguity by aligning themselves with rape myths and blaming the victim. Shifts in worldview were associated with long-term changes for some women in the sample including increases in social consciousness and/or feelings of hopelessness/disillusionment. Finally, factors of influence (multiple relationships with victims, participant phase of life, closeness to the victim, and personal history of trauma) were spoken to as they seemed to emerge in participant descriptions.

An important theme that was explored in the present qualitative analysis was worldview. Results indicated that this theme emerged as an important aspect of women's conscious reaction to the traumatic incident. In a study by Banyard and colleagues (2010), female friends were described as experiencing "anger at society" in response to the sexual assault of a friend. This can be discussed in light of worldview shifts in the current study. Shifts in worldview were often associated with the adoption of a "realistic" stance and loss of naïveté, including increased social awareness of gender violence or dynamics of power. It was not uncommon for women in the sample to report feelings of anger in accordance with this "newfound" knowledge. Worldview shifts of participants were likewise observed to include hopelessness, disillusionment, and/or disappointment. These experiences alluded to a kind of resignation and despondence towards the world, accentuating a cognitive and emotional dissonance that, for some women, negated experiences of hope and optimism.

Constructivist Self-in-Development theory views frame of reference (worldview) as a necessary structural force through which one organizes and understands one's experience in the world (McCann & Pearlman, 1990). Disruption of this central psychological force is one manifestation of trauma to the self, resulting in confusion, fragmentation, and disruption in the perception of a secure reality (Kohut, 1977; Herman, 1992; Pearlman, 1998). Women in the study demonstrated interruption of cohesion (by virtue of self-report and the Inventory of Altered Self-Capacities), further suggesting that dialogue is warranted to fully understand the implications of this life change.

Many participants in this study recounted with strong emotions the traumatic details of their friends' assaults, linking themselves emotionally to the pain and suffering of the victim. Identification and empathy emerged as processes by which women seemed to *feel* the anguish of their friends. Given their various shifts in worldview and strong emotional ties to the victim, participants struggled to organize and make meaning of witnessing such violence and destruction first-hand.

In *Civilization and its Discontents*, Freud (1930/1961) commented on human destruction as follows: "The fateful question for the human race seems to be whether, and to what extent, the development of its civilization will manage to overcome the disturbance of communal life caused by the human drive for aggression and self-destruction" (p. 81).

As a group, participants struggled to resolve this reality; they fought to regain composure and confidence in the world around them. Amidst reactions of helplessness, they longed for control and protection, citing particular hardship with the perception that "nothing could keep them safe" as women. The strength and admired qualities in the victim served as a source of struggle for the group overall as they attempted to reconcile their illusions of safety with their feelings of sameness or idealization towards the victim.

As with any qualitative study, potential investigator bias is a limitation of research design (Kazdin, 2003). I aimed to eliminate biases and personal prejudices with potential to sway research findings. Nonetheless, as Kazdin pointed out, this is a reality that cannot be completely overcome. As related to this limitation, the mixed-method design of this study provides a "check and balance" to qualitative analysis (Creswell, 2003) and objectively confirms the presence of symptoms (by self-report) separate from results viewed through the lens of the investigator.

Clinically and diagnostically, findings of this study raise implications for treatment and conceptualization of women's issues. Mental health practitioners need to be cognizant of the potential likelihood for secondary trauma in the lives of women. In consideration of the community impact of this exposure, it can be assumed that communities of women are dealing with the phenomenon of secondary trauma. The extent of their suffering may be in connection to the unique context surrounding sexual violence in differing cultures and communities. Further studies in the domain of community trauma and gender violence may be interested in the extent to which global communities of women respond uniquely to this exposure as well as identifying and clarifying resiliency and protective factors.

Notes

1 Material in this chapter is cited from Davisson (2010). For the purpose of this chapter, *secondary trauma* will be used as an all-encompassing term, referring to reactions experienced via secondary exposure to a traumatic event; the focus will be women who bear witness to the sexual victimization of their close friends. It is noted that the terms *traumatic countertransference, burn out and compassion fatigue*, and *vicarious traumatization* have been used to describe this experience in different and overlapping ways.

2 Participants were given two assessment instruments to assess symptoms of secondary trauma, The Trauma Symptom Inventory (TSI; Briere, 1995), and the Inventory of

Altered Self-Capacities (IASC; Briere, 2000). Participants were also given a demographic questionnaire, the Stressful Life Events Screening Questionnaire–Revised (Goodman *et al.*, 1998) to assess lifetime exposure to traumatic events, and the Norbeck Social Support Questionnaire (Norbeck *et al.*, 1981) to assess closeness to the victim.
3 Quantitative findings are summarized as follows: TSI scale means were not clinically significant, with 5.92 percent exceeding the clinical cut-off ($T = 65$) on each scale and a mean number of elevations for each participant of 0.77. Six participants (46 percent) exceeded the clinical cut-off on one or more TSI scale. IASC scale means were clinically significant, with 28.92 percent exceeding the clinical cut-off ($T = 70$) on each scale. Ten participants (77 percent) exceeded the clinical cut-off on one or more IASC scale. With 62 percent of the sample exceeding the clinical cut-off, Instability was the most frequent clinical elevation followed by Affect Dysregulation and Skill Deficits at 46 percent.
4 It is noted that women sampled were mostly (though not exclusively) located in proximity to an educational institution (either by student or alumni status) and their academic knowledge likely impacted their feelings about issues addressed in the current study. Moreover, women in these academic fields may be more responsive to the subject of study than the general public.
5 All but one participant (92 percent) indicated a significant history of trauma during oral administration of the SLESQ. One participant disclosed a personal history of sexual assault that was not reported in the screening process and her data was included in the sample for relevance.
6 Analysis of qualitative data was based upon the blending of phenomenological and ethnographic research frameworks, integrated into a general coding process detailed by Creswell (2003).
7 All research participants consented to their unidentified data being used for publication and further analysis. Raw data were destroyed after 1 year and participants underwent a debriefing after the interview wherein resources for psychological services were made available.

References

Banyard, V., Moynihan, M., Walsh, W., Cohn, E., & Ward, S. (2010). Friends of survivors: The community impact of unwanted sexual experiences. *Journal of Interpersonal Violence, 25*(2), 242–256.
Basch, M.F. (1983). Empathic understanding: A review of the concept and some theoretical considerations. *Journal of the American Psychoanalytic Association, 31*, 101–126.
Briere, J. (1995). *Trauma Symptom Inventory professional manual.* Odessa, FL: Psychological Assessment Resources.
Briere, J. (2000). *Inventory of Altered Self-Capacities professional manual.* Odessa, FL: Psychological Assessment Resources.
Briere, J., & Jordon, C.E. (2004). Violence against women: Outcome complexity and implications for assessment and treatment. *Journal of Interpersonal Violence, 19*(11), 1252–1276.
Burt, M. (1980). Cultural myths and support for rape. *Journal of Personality and Social Psychology, 38*(2), 217–230.
Creswell, J.W. (2003). *Research design: Qualitative, quantitative and mixed methods approaches.* (2nd ed.). Thousand Oaks, CA: Sage.
Davisson, K. (2010). *Secondary sexual trauma of women: Closeness with sexually victimized women as a risk factor.* Unpublished doctoral dissertation, Argosy University, Chicago, IL.
Figley, C.R. (1995). Compassion fatigue as secondary traumatic stress disorder: An overview. In C.R. Figley (Ed.), *Compassion fatigue: Coping with secondary traumatic stress disorder in those who treat the traumatized* (pp. 1–21). New York, NY: Brunner/Mazel.
Frankl, V.E. (1959). *Man's search for meaning.* Boston, MA: Beacon Press.

Freud, S. (1917/1957). Mourning and melancholia. In J. Strachey (Ed.), *The standard edition of the complete psychological works of Sigmund Freud* (Vol. 14; pp. 237–258). London: Hogarth.

Freud, S. (1930/1961). Civilization and its discontents. In J. Strachey (Ed. & Trans.), *The standard edition of the complete psychological works of Sigmund Freud* (Vol. 21, pp. 64–146). London: Hogarth. (Original work published 1930)

Gold, J.M., & Rogers, J.D. (1995). Intimacy and isolation: A validation study of Erikson's theory. *Journal of Humanistic Psychology, 35*, 78–86.

Goodman, L.A., Corcoran, C., Turner, K., Yuan, N., & Green, B.L. (1998). Assessing traumatic event exposure: General issues and preliminary findings for the Stressful Life Events Screening Questionnaire. *Journal of Traumatic Stress, 11*(3), 521–542.

Herman, J. (1992). *Trauma and recovery.* New York, NY: Basic Books.

Kazdin, A.E. (2003). *Research design in clinical psychology* (4th ed.). Boston, MA: Allyn & Bacon.

Kadambi, M.A., & Ennis, L. (2004). Reconsidering vicarious trauma: A review of the literature and its limitations. *Journal of Trauma Practice, 3*(2), 1–21 [electronic version].

Klein, K.J.K., & Hodges, S.D. (2001). Gender differences, motivation, and empathic accuracy: When it pays to understand. *Personality and Social Psychology Bulletin, 27*, 720–730.

Kohut, H. (1977). *The restoration of the self.* New York, NY: International Universities.

Krakow, B., Germain, A., Warner, T.D., Schrader, R., Koss, M., Hollifield, M., . . . Herlitz, A. (2002). Sex differences in face recognition: Women's faces make the difference. *Brain and Cognition, 50*(1), 121–128.

McCann, L., & Pearlman, L.A. (1990). *Psychological trauma and the adult survivor.* New York, NY: Brunner/Mazel.

National Institute of Justice. (2007). Violence & victimization research division's compendium of research on violence against women: 1993–2007. Retrieved from http://www.ojp.usdoj.gov/nij/vawprog/vaw_portfolio.pdf. For an extended report to 2015 see https://www.ncjrs.gov/pdffiles1/nij/223572/223572.pdf

Norbeck, J.S., Lindsey, A.M., & Carrieri, V.L. (1981). The development of an instrument to measure social support. *Nursing Research, 30*, 264–269.

Pearlman, L.A. (1998). Trauma and the self: A theoretical and clinical perspective. *Journal of Emotional Abuse, 1*(1), 7–25.

Pearlman, L.A., & MacIan, P.S. (1995). Vicarious traumatization: An empirical study of the effects of trauma work on trauma therapists. *Professional Psychology Research and Practice, 26*(6), 558–565.

Pearlman, L.A., & Saakvitne, K.W. (1995). *Trauma and the therapist.* New York, NY: Norton.

Pico-Alfonso, M.A., Garcia-Inares, I., Celda-Nivarro, N., Blasco-Ros, C., Echeburua, E., & Martinez, M. (2006). The impact of physical, psychological and sexual intimate male partner violence on women's mental health: Depressive symptoms, posttraumatic stress disorder, state anxiety and suicide. *Journal of Women's Health, 15*(5), 599–611.

Reich, A. (1960). Further remarks on counter-transference. *International Journal of Psychoanalysis, 41*, 389–395.

Schauben, L.J., & Frazier, P. (1995). Vicarious trauma: The effects on female counselors of working with sexual violence survivors. *Psychology of Women Quarterly, 19*, 49–64.

Shihui, H., Yan, F., & Lihua, M. (2008). Gender difference in empathy for pain: An electrophysiological investigation. *Brain Research, 1196*, 85–93.

Stamm, B.H. (Ed.). (1999). *Secondary traumatic stress: Self-care issues for clinicians, researchers, and educators* (2nd ed.). Lutherville, MD: Sidran Press.

Surrey, J.L. (1991). The self-in-relation: A theory of women's development. In J.V. Jordan, A.G. Kaplan, J.B. Miller, & J.L. Surrey (Eds.), *Women's growth in connection: Writings from the Stone Center* (pp. 51–66). New York, NY: Guilford.

Toussiant, L., & Webb, J.R. (2005). Gender differences in the relationship between empathy and forgiveness. *Journal of Social Psychology, 145*(6), 673–685.

Wasco, S., & Campbell, R. (2002). Emotional reactions of rape victim advocates: A multiple case study of anger and fear. *Psychology of Women Quarterly, 26,* 120–130.

White, R.B., & Gilliland, R.M. (1975). *Elements of psychopathology: The mechanisms of defense.* New York, NY: Grune & Stratton.

World Health Organization. (2005). WHO study on women's health and violence against women: Initial results on prevalence, health outcomes and women's responses. Geneva, Switzerland: Author.

6

CHASING JUSTICE

Bystander intervention and restorative justice in the contexts of college campuses and psychoanalytic institutes

Katie Gentile

In 2011, after a great deal of agitation on the part of female students and risk to themselves, the United States Department of Education filed charges against Yale University for its failure to provide women students with equal access to education. The suit was the culmination of years of complaints from women students. These students endured an educational culture shaped by verbal and physical violence against them. Instead of continuing, and failing, to gain justice through the common route of the criminal justice system—reporting incidents and trusting the university would investigate sexual misconduct[1] as it would any other crime—the students instead leveraged Title IX. Title IX, passed in 1972, addresses access to education in general, although it is most famously known for its applications to college-based athletics. Using Title IX in this context put the university on notice in a new way. Federal funding is linked to Title IX. If a college/university is shown not to support Title IX, federal funding is in jeopardy. Calling upon Title IX shifted the focus from the sexual misconduct itself; instead it was on the process of investigation by the campus. The school, not individual students, became identified as culpable and an offending party. Instead of having to prove an incident did or did not occur, under Title IX, the students had to show the campus failed to investigate reports of sexual misconduct. The students claimed the university's refusal to address or investigate reports of sexual harassment, stalking, rape, and attempted rape on campus was not merely the toleration of, but the creation and sustaining of a hostile environment for female students, limiting their access to education.

This same year the US Department of Education's Office for Civil Rights issued a "Dear Colleague Letter," outlining specific guidelines for colleges to apply to incidents of sexual misconduct. It described "42 different forms of sexual violence and misconduct—mainly though, legal terminology of physical sex acts perpetrated against a person's will or where a person is incapable of giving consent" (Ali, 2011, cited in Koss *et al.*, 2014, p. 243). As such, the Dear Colleague Letter mandates a "quasi-criminal justice" (Koss *et al.*, 2014, p. 242) approach to managing misconduct. Actions emanate from individual, usually masculine identified bodies. Options may vary but the problem is contained within an individual who is identified as the one who has transgressed. As such, a campus is able to split off the offence into the perpetrator (or the victim) and, through a system of justice, purge the community body of the danger.

In this chapter I am attempting two things: to use psychoanalytic theory to better understand the potential roles of bystander intervention and restorative justice for campus sexual misconduct and to turn this around to use these approaches as an external example to better identify and understand similar issues in the psychoanalytic space. I am interested in the potential these campus-based interventions hold for breaking the vicious cycle that perpetuates the victim–perpetrator dynamic that is rampant not just on campuses and in criminal justice literature, but within psychoanalysis itself. Even though most psychoanalysts know such limiting dyadic projections merely silence and paralyze the potential response of communities to address problems in their midst, such paranoid/schizoid (Klein, 1958; Ogden, 1994) "all or nothing" splitting is a common response of psychoanalytic training institutes. I am not claiming a direct comparison between sexual boundary violations in the psychoanalytic setting with the various kinds of sexual misconduct that occur on college campuses. However, I am using the wide variety of campus responses to imagine and create space within psychoanalysis, and in turn, using psychoanalytic theory to potentially deepen our understanding of community-based campus response. Both are social bodies and both are struggling to address sexual misconduct.

When an analytic couple is stuck in a clinical impasse, the emergence of a "third" position can create the space necessary for reflection and meaning making (Benjamin, 2004), enabling the dyad to come to a new way of being. This triangular positioning creates a space for reflection, pulling the dyad out of a rigid dynamic. Temporally linear repetition is shifted by this opening of the space. In this chapter, I use a similar temporal/spatial approach to describe what could seem as a "sudden" explosion of cases of sexual assault on college campuses. Of course an increase in media coverage is not an increase in incidents. They have always been too frequent. Like any stuck dyad, or shamed family, college campuses have, for the most part, chosen repetition and the practice of relying on their own disciplinary boards to "police" their own, keeping the family secret. This chapter is one attempt at creating an outside position from which we might be able to compare, contrast, and look inside psychoanalytic and campus responses.

Framing psychoanalytic sexual misconduct

First, as written elsewhere, there are vast differences between a college community and the psychoanalytic setting (Gentile, in press). Psychoanalysis depends upon privacy and confidentiality. According to Baranger and Baranger (2008) the contract of therapy is that the therapist will provide "help in resolving conflicts through interpretations and promises confidentiality and abstention from any intervention in the other's 'real' life" (p. 796). This promise determines behavior so that analytic interactions maintain an "as if" quality, which they compare to seeing a play. As they note, an analyst should be able to differentiate the actor playing Hamlet from Hamlet, or, as I have written, the analyst should be able to differentiate the patient playing a seducer from a seducer. The analytic situation, then, is akin to a dream to be held and examined but not to be acted out.

Within psychoanalysis, the erotic is one space that is often conceptualized as being out of our control. Certainly this is a common trope in the cultural narrative where erotic attraction has been captured in song, poems, dance, and visual art as being an external force driving our most spontaneous and, perhaps enlivening, interactions. Diane Elise has described erotic transference to be akin to a riptide (Elise, personal communication). This analogy differs with that of the slippery slope (Gabbard, 2001) also common in psychoanalysis. On a slope there is a point of no return, a point where one forever loses one's footing and cannot help but slide to the sexual conclusion. As Elise observes, the slippery slope also conjures a clear visual gradation. The implication being that with "careful footing, where one does not stray" from the clear non-slope path, one can safely avoid slipping. Of course, as she observes, there is no clear path to avoid the slope altogether.

As I have described elsewhere (Gentile, in press), the riptide is a much more apt description. Anyone who has had the pleasure of swimming in an ocean knows the danger of rip tides and the ways they are often invisible to the untrained eye. Pleasure and danger, life and death blend in a tide that only becomes apparent once you are caught in it, being pushed and pulled out to sea. It is a visceral panic felt as the body is pushed, pulled, stretched away from comfort. Strong swimmers are no match for a riptide. Most beaches now feature instructions of exactly how to swim out of a riptide. One must swim in the riptide, not against it, to make one's way free. This can feel counterintuitive. The idea is to respect the force of erotic transference, reminding oneself of the conditions: it is transference. Swimming in the sea while keeping a firm eye on the shore embodies the "as if" quality of the analytic space. One may be able to predict the conditions for a rip tide, but not the exact location and force of one, how it will tug at the body and destabilize. One can imagine in advance what to do, train oneself to swim out of it, use knowledge and theory as a "life-jacket" to stay afloat (Elise, personal communication), but doing so in the moment is a scary challenge. We can learn theories about erotic transference and read papers from clinicians who have a facility for working with it, but each tide will present unique and frightening challenges. Furthermore, it is just these theories and the frame, Elise's "life-jackets," that are often disavowed, thrown out, or manipulated to justify boundary violations. These acts reinforce what Honig and Barron (2013), Foehl (2005), and Levine (2010) have observed that analytic boundary violations damage the psychoanalytic community and profession at large, and are aggressive acts against the profession. As such, they need to be conceptualized and understood to be community-based transgressions demanding a community-based response.

Colleges do not have the same responsibility for holding a relational process, and they do not usually understand the multiplicities of self-experiences and conscious and unconscious motivations and intentionalities (Bromberg, 1998; Mitchell, 2000). Indeed, having sat on a cross-college multidisciplinary behavioral intervention team[2] for years, I can safely say most college investigations proceed with a "doer–done to" mentality. Psychoanalysts, on the other hand, are supposed to understand multiplicities as well as the concept of mutuality (see Aron, 1996) and how these demonstrate that we never really know how our colleagues interact with patients. We really do not know what happens behind any closed door. Yet these generative theories of multiplicities seem to leave us when we are asked to comprehend transgression. We find ourselves caught like the neighbor of a perpetrator who can only repeat "but s/he was such a nice person, prolific writer, wonderful mentor, fantastic supervisor ..." or, more terrifyingly, "how could this happen to me?" (Foehl, 2005).

Despite these procedural and structural differences, just taken as cultural bodies, psychoanalysis and colleges have both chosen similar tactics to deal with violations, either disavowing and victim-blaming, or policing, investigating, and disciplining one's own behind closed doors. In most cases the danger is contained to either the victim or the offender and whoever gets this projection is safely split off from or silenced within the particular social body. Even though both psychoanalysts and academics critiqued this tactic when taken by the Catholic Church and the US military, (one of the lead military prosecutors was recently arrested for sexual assault himself), and many US police departments—boundary violations within psychoanalysis have been dealt with (if they were dealt with) by peers and/or internal institutional and professional ethics committees. Perhaps a state ethics board is notified—*perhaps*. But the protection of the institute's reputation and the identity of the accused take precedence. Similarly, the reputation of the college campus is protected. Parents calling the college president with fears for their child's safety is a powerful and potentially costly event. In both settings the traditional form of victim-blaming in cases of sexual violence is institutionalized, as the main protections often go to the accused. The accuser, by mentioning the accusation, can be sued for defamation and treated by both institutions as crazy, trouble-making or just hysterical.[3] Despite these informal protections for the accused, both universities and analytic communities have recently been exposed to high-profile lawsuits.

Discussion of sexual boundary violations cannot help but be shaped and limited by the familiar doer–done to, Judeo-Christian-based, judicial structure (Butler, 1997; Benjamin, 2004; Cornell, 1995, 2010) for participants. There is limited capacity to imagine one side without the other. Psychoanalytic notions of enactment and trauma have helped us better understand how these positions may shift and how the abuser can become the abused and vice versa (Davies & Frawley, 1992). But in these theories the binary oppositions remain firm even as participants themselves change roles. Using examples from these two settings, I hope to create some space outside this judicial binary, where accountability and shame can be held, fostered and reflected upon.

Sexual violence and misconduct in the college context

Research indicates that dating and sexual violence is common among college students, with prevalence rates from 14 percent (DeKeseredy & Kelly, 1993) to about 40 percent (White & Koss, 1991). A mixed method study of dating violence, sexual assault and stalking indicated that local commuter students at an urban campus had violence rates of 40–50 percent (Gentile *et al.*, 2007). Until recently most colleges considered such violence a problem best addressed by women's centers and similar underfunded and understaffed student services. But, as mentioned earlier, when the university/college's response to sexual violence is approached as a Title IX issue, there is suddenly a financial need to develop an institutionalized systematic response.

I was the director of a college women's center for over 10 years. The position was part clinical, part programming for students and the community, and part faculty—research and teaching. Like most college women's centers, I dealt with countless cases of intimate partner violence, rape, and sexual assault. The women's center, like many such centers within college campuses, gradually became responsible for the development and implementation of violence-prevention programs around issues of sexual and intimate partner violence and harassment. Now under the Dear Colleague Letter, most campuses have hired a Title IX prevention specialist, who may or may not be housed within a women's center. It is important to understand the ramifications of locating prevention within women's centers or within a prevention specialist. Most women's centers are significantly underfunded, most receiving no operational funds from colleges. Most women's centers have limited staff and space to undertake a school-wide prevention effort. Similarly, although many now hire a Title IX coordinator, funding for prevention and intervention may be limited. Lastly, many women's centers are not highly respected on campus either because of their identified mission (i.e. women's empowerment, activism, and feminism) or/and because of the traditional Cartesian split between body and mind: Student activities are considered the touchy feely body, split off as separate, unrelated to the intellectual academic mission of the college. Thus, situating prevention within women's centers or with a single person can send a message to the campus that this effort is not considered important.

Ideally, under Title IX, schools have a great deal of responsibility to act in the face of accusations, not just proven incidents, of rape, sexual assault or harassment, and intimate partner violence. Colleges are supposed to follow the "knew or should have known" standard of intervention. This makes colleges responsible for violence based on the atmosphere and conditions of the campus. Given the usually private nature of rape, sexual assault and harassment, and intimate partner violence, this means schools have a responsibility to act, to do something, even if there is not clear evidence to prosecute. Obviously, this does not mean all schools respond. Consider the Columbia University student who carried a mattress to her classes to publicly remind the campus that the University had not investigated properly her allegations of rape. This woman claimed the school's refusal to investigate or/

and discipline perpetrators not only reinforced violent behaviors but constituted discrimination that hindered the woman student's participation in her education. Using Title IX in this way also shifted the discourse of college prevention work, focusing on the realities that the atmosphere of a campus can limit women students' access to opportunities. This gender-based violence approach for Title IX is also now being used by LBGTQ students to attempt to address homophobic violence on campuses. Again, ideally the college/university has a responsibility to create an *atmosphere* wherein violence is unacceptable, but this requires a clear definition of what constitutes violence and threat—tricky tasks within a patriarchal culture. Each campus has to develop adequate support and advocacy for victims, accountability for students and the college at large, and the development and implementation of prevention-based curriculum for all incoming students.

Ideally this approach creates an epistemological shift as sexual and intimate partner violence should be recast not as private issues between students, but as significant problems that the university/college have a legal (and ethical) responsibility not only to address, but to prevent. This approach is challenging not least because it disrupts Western culture's comfortable split between public and private spaces. Here colleges would have to find ways to influence the private spaces of interpersonal interactions and actively prevent certain behaviors occurring in those spaces.

This tide of prevention and intervention was only heightened by the media attention on Yale University, which at the time was facing huge fines based on Title IX. This attention resulted in the now public list of colleges and universities that are being investigated by the Department of Education.

The policy I was involved in creating defined and identified sexual violence, campus points of entry for students, how cases would be investigated, and disciplinary steps that could be taken. This might seem cut and dried, but consider the seemingly simple part of identifying entry points. We knew from experience that students sought out the assistance of professors, counselors, coaches, mentors in student activities, women's centers, security personnel, and their student peers. This meant that all these constituents needed to be trained on how to identify cases of sexual violence and to intervene at their respective levels of responsibility (i.e. a counselor would intervene differently from a security officer). Additionally, training curriculum needed to address potential biases about different forms of sexual violence (including trainee's potential tendencies toward victim-blaming, downplaying certain forms of violence, and ignoring harassment, including homophobic and misogynous hate speech), while communicating an established protocol for reporting sexual violence. In practice, this gets very complicated; for instance, when cases began in the Counseling Center, confidentiality trumped any reporting protocol. Identifying campus Title IX or prevention experts to develop and implement prevention and training curriculum is one thing but making such trainings a campus-wide priority is another. There needs to be top-down support so other obligations do not trump trainings.

Title IX and the Clery Act make it clear that campus police cannot be the only investigators for crimes and victims must be urged to contact local police on their own. Nationally, many universities and colleges had pressured students not to call local police, hiding the crime. They kept investigations internal, allowing them to pad statistics and create a fantasy of a safer campus. Universities and colleges sometimes took months to investigate accusations, leaving the accuser in a potentially dangerous physical and psychological limbo. For instance, does a student continue to go to a class with an offender or choose to drop the course, losing money and credits? What about the student who fears returning to campus and seeing her perpetrator? Investigations must occur in a "timely manner" but what does this mean? What about students whose campus jobs are at risk if they have to avoid specific areas in order to comply with restraining orders or to avoid running into an offender? What are the rights of an offender to educational access? Can they be denied access to the campus or to their classes or extracurricular activities during the investigation? Indeed, like the analyst, students too can sue for discrimination when accused. These are real-life examples that only hint at the complications involved in seemingly simple steps.

As I write this chapter, the policy on which I worked, in effect until around 2014, has been a bit gutted in favor of a stricter, more criminal justice-focused policy that follows the dictates of the Dear Colleague Letter. In this new policy, victims no longer get an advocate. A pathology model prevails in which victims are urged to seek mental health counseling instead. Campuses must have a Title IX Officer (the campus legal counsel) and a prevention expert; however, the prevention expert is not a single job, but encompasses additional responsibilities for someone who is probably already overtaxed. There is no mention of campus-based services or programs like Women's or Gender Centers as potential sites for prevention or advocacy. The new policy, like the Dear Colleague Letter, contains the problem of sexual violence on campus and its corresponding solution, within individual, discrete bodies. While the campus atmosphere is addressed, it is one lone person, the Title IX advocate, who is responsible for change

Disrupting binary dynamics of victim–perpetrator

Although the new policy and the Dear Colleague Letter focus on individuals, they do also mention the importance of bystander intervention. This addition of a campus-based intervention to a policy so focused on individuals is interesting. Bystander intervention is based on the idea that people act depending on the behaviors of those around them. It is founded on the assumption that most people are not violent, yet stay silent when faced with violence because they lack the confidence or knowledge to intervene. Bystander intervention is based on the ontological assumption that people want to intervene and would if they understood how to do so.

As social psychologists know, the more witnesses there are, the less likely it is that individuals will respond. Bystander intervention examines and addresses some of the reasons people choose not to respond in certain situations. The approach disrupts socially reinforced habits of victim-blaming, thereby helping to shift social norms. Ideally, it also spreads responsibility to both men and women, but does so with an understanding of differential positions of cultural power. Women may have a specific and substantial role, but it is understood that within a patriarchal system, most men are more influenced and moved to action by the opinions and behaviors of other men. Thus male bystanders become particularly important in prevention work.

By focusing on the bystander, the third party, this form of intervention can deconstruct the gendered binary of doer–done to, victim–perpetrator. The oppositional victim and perpetrator positions fade to the background and the bystander is elevated and made the agent of change and action. Students are not identified as potential victims or perpetrators but instead identify as a bystander. Students may be asked to recall situations where they saw violence occurring and are asked to identify the violence. They are then asked to describe how they felt as witnesses to the violence. Most recall intense and shameful feelings of vulnerability, helplessness, and powerlessness and they are able to identify and describe these most often because they were not the direct victim or perpetrator. Students are walked through ways they might intervene (if safe), or alert an authority; how they might talk to a friend who was assaulted or harassed; and, most importantly, how they can talk to friends who crossed the line themselves. Having organized and implemented these trainings, I have found students respond quite positively to being coached to help victims. But when I open up the idea of intervening with a perpetrator, the discussion initially falls silent. Gradually, students open up about experiences they have experienced with friends who perpetrated some physically or verbally violent act where they did not know what to do. Not surprisingly, students described wanting to disavow and avoid any future feelings of powerlessness, helplessness, and vulnerability, meaning they employed strategies that allowed them to avoid acknowledging future micro/macro aggressions and/or supported their own use of such aggression in their own interactions. Providing tools for intervening, even if the tool was just an active reflection of that powerlessness, results in a disruption of the victim–perpetrator dynamic. It can create a space for a third position that is not completely devoid of the others, but at the very least, has more space for reflection.

Again, ideally bystander intervention impacts individual student behaviors while it creates a shift in the campus culture. The bystander may be the third, the witness, but it is clear that the bystander position comes with close proximity to both the victim and perpetrator. Here the knowledge that we could all be victim or perpetrator is held and used not to fuel dissociation, but reflective and realistic action to become an agentic bystander. Accountability within this model is shared with the bystander, who has a responsibility to intervene in some way. The pressures on the victim–perpetrator dyad are diffused as the bystander, and thus, the community body, shares the shame and accountability.

Although I have used some psychoanalytic ideas to translate the functions of bystander intervention it is important to note it is not built upon the traditional notion of psychoanalytic or clinical witnessing. Certainly psychoanalytic ideas of witnessing can generate a similar third space, a "live" or "moral third" (Felman &

Laub, 1992; Benjamin, 2009; Boulanger, 2012; Gerson, 2009) and can provide a way of entering another's subjectivity (Benjamin, 2009). The bystander enters into both the victim and perpetrator's respective subjectivities, attempting to engage both if only in thought. Ullman builds on Margalit's (2002) idea of moral witnessing (as cited in Ullman, 2006), where the witness reports on and documents "a reality of human suffering inflicted by evil policies" (p. 183) could be seen as a form of bystander intervention.

Analysts writing about witnessing, however, do not always see or focus the impact of this witnessing on the cultural or community body. Again, as mentioned earlier, as long as the individual body identified as the perpetrator or boundary violator contains the badness, the underlying systemic issues fueling patriarchal violence can remain untouched. Communities do not have to change. Many theories of psychoanalytic witnessing split off the offender, the identified "evil," locating it squarely in the "other," a third party, not-me, not-you, but "them" (Poland, 2000; Grand, 2002, 2003; Boulanger, 2012). Here the third is the body of accountability but it is disembodied within the relationship. No one is truly responsible. As observed elsewhere (Gentile, 2013a), this can function to triangulate, pulling the patient close through a presumed identification of goodness and distance from perpetration. We-together are not-them, not bad. Bystander intervention demands evil and goodness be held together within the bystander. We are all offender and victim and agentic bystanders. In psychoanalytic witnessing the violence is conceptualized as having happened outside the dyad (albeit potentially being re-enacted within it). The culpability of the analyst is typically missing in most accounts (see Gentile, 2013a). For the bystander, goodness or ethical relating has to be earned through the process of intervening and actively challenging a violation or attitude. It is an obligation that opens up the potential space for others to respond (Oliver, 2001), and allows for a restoration of dignity (Ullman, 2006) to each party. This response-ability and restoration of dignity requires holding people and institutional bodies accountable for what may be shame-full actions.

Restorative justice and campus accountability

Any potential space for restorative reflection within psychoanalytic institutes, however, can be seen as a luxury in the college and university setting. Institutes, unlike colleges and universities, do not rely on federal funding, thus they are not beholden to the government in the same way. Because the Dear Colleague Letter was in large part a response to campuses not addressing sexual misconduct, it should come as no surprise that it holds to a black and white criminal justice approach to dealing with it. Although mediation is mentioned, it is not detailed.

Koss *et al.* (2014) describe a number of different forms of mediation. They observe, most mediation relies on the terminology of "disputant," which tends to indicate the main issue involved is really just that of different takes on realities, and not a violent sexual crime. Restorative justice, on the other hand, aims to hold and address the needs of the offender, the victim, and their respective communities. This form of intervention focuses on both the individual and the social. According to Koss *et al.* (2014) restorative justice involves multiple routes for reporting an incident. The identified offender is then invited to accept responsibility for some behavior. There is then an investigation. The repair stage follows where the victim receives validation and reparation for harm. Included are indirect victims who may have been impacted. The offender is engaged with counseling to help identify behaviors that may lead to violence and reoffending. This stage also focuses on identifying and shifting norms of the community. Restorative justice may also include "circles of support and accountability" (Koss *et al.*, 2014, p. 247), having a circle of peers create support for the offender while also outlining a form of sentencing. It is based upon Quaker beliefs in transformation through community-based interventions. Although accountability is also key here, the victim is not necessarily present or central. Instead the offender, his/her actions, accountability, and tracking the ongoing behavior of the offender are the focus. Koss *et al.* (2014) observe that this form of community intervention has proven effective at reducing recidivism among sex offenders.

In this model neither victim nor offender are isolated or left alone, and thus, offenders are potentially less apt to recreate the abusive dynamic. As Koss *et al.* note, it is oriented to the future and to creating a form of reconciliation.

While feminists are represented on both sides of the restorative justice debate, my take would be that restorative justice extends too much empathy to perpetrators. Daly (2002, 2006) outlines a number of key issues when it is used with youth offenders. First, as she notes, the general cultural narrative of justice is that of a courtroom. One cannot assume participants know what restorative justice looks like, how they should act during the process, or what results might be considered—including the necessity for accountability and responsibility. Daly observes that not everyone has the psychological skills or the empathetic concern for others that is assumed and required. In her analysis of restorative justice cases with youth offenders she found most young people "did not think in terms of what they might *offer victims*, but rather what they would be *made to do by others*" (emphasis in original, Daly, 2002, p. 16).

Certainly the success of any restorative justice intervention rests upon the success of perspective taking and the capacities of the offender to experience empathy and remorse. Such a shift can be effective in prevention work around bystanders but it is trickier when working with offenders and victims. Additionally, the offender has to admit the offence. This is a huge shift from either the criminal justice or mediation model where it is assumed there is a dispute about what actually occurred. That said, if the conditions are met, the conference process is potentially extraordinary. When there is compliance with the process, decisions are left with the empowered victim who witnesses remorse for the offence itself and the harm that was caused. This is something few courts provide to victims. In turn, by witnessing the harm they caused, recognizing their impact, the offender is supported to hold shame, agency, and hope for change. Because the offense is situated within a cultural context, a community that is also identified as offensive, the offender is able to share a form of rehabilitation.

Chasing justice

> An ethics of entanglement entails possibilities and obligations for reworking the material effects of the past and the future understanding there can never be complete redemption and justice is always a "justice-to-come."
>
> *(Barad, 2010, p. 266)*

Postcolonial theorists (Mohanty, 2004; Spivak, 1988), philosophers, and legal scholars (Tronto, 1994; Oliver, 2001; Cornell, 1995, 2010) describe perpetrator accountability as being central within witnessing and testimony. This accountability is integral to the creation of a third space of resolution, healing, or what psychoanalysts would also identify as moving out of enactment. Shame, here, is not to be avoided like a hot potato. Of course the act of avoidance and the shame itself can close down psychic space for reflection, but we are ruled by our own narcissism when we insist it can only do that. We grant it tremendous power. Shaming, as Mary Douglas (1966) observed years ago, is one of the most important and effective tools of social organizations. As I have written elsewhere (Gentile, in press), to avoid shame is to shield perpetrators from the effects and impact of their actions, which denies them their dignity. It denies the pain and dignity of the victims, including the pain of the community. After all, there is no space to make amends without shame. Accountability then is not just about "shaming" the perpetrator; it is a necessary component of recognition for both victims and the community as a whole. Philosopher Kelly Oliver (2001; 2004), referencing postcolonial and critical race theorists, describes how the "other" functions to hold and embody the shameful affects for the colonizers. Thus, creating the capacities to shift shame back to the transgressor who shares it with the potentially enabling community body, is key. They must be supported to hold their own shame, to examine it, to move through it.

A psychoanalytic bystander

Identifying the bystander within a campus community automatically also requires identifying the crime or potential crime that is about to be committed. After all, a bystander is a bystander to a specific form of criminal event. This location of the bystander is complicated in the psychoanalytic setting. Psychoanalysis by its very nature is confidential and takes place behind closed doors. Additionally, consent, the line articulating some forms of sexual misconduct, becomes even more powerful and confusing in the context of psychoanalysis. For all mental health workers, consent is so important we have even created an additional level for research and clinical work, called "informed" consent. Legally, consent can only operate between positions of equal cognitive capacity and implies a subject with only conscious and non-contradictory motivations and intentions. In this legal context there is no evolution of desire (Saketopoulou, 2010) or temporal multiplicity of experiencing (Gentile, 2013a, 2015). But in the psychoanalytic context where regression is taken quite seriously, patients can only exercise consent initially, when the frame of the analytic treatment is being negotiated. Once the treatment is in progress, consent to any changes in the relationship could be seen as a function of transference or/ and countertransference.[4] Blechner (2014) describes seduction as the patient's role, and the analysis of it as that of the analyst. If the analyst enacts this transference it is not the patient who has seduced the analyst but the analyst who has seduced the patient. A psychoanalytic dyad could be seen as a means to the development of the capacity for consent for the patient, but by definition, the relationship is not based on equal capacities in the moment.

Certainly withholding this capacity for consent from patients can be disempowering and patronizing. This can sting in a neoliberal world that clings to the fetish of self-regulation and unfettered individualistic agency (Layton, 2010; Gentile, 2013b). In this cultural context to question consent is to undermine coherent and legible subjectivity. But we are not individual subjects, as relational psychoanalysis in particular knows (Bromberg, 1998; Mitchell, 2000; Aron, 1996) and many other theorists also espouse (Deleuze & Guattari, 1977, 1987; Barad, 2010). Most important, the frame is based on unequal power. It is the analyst who defines the time, the fee (even when negotiated). Moreover, the psychoanalytic relationship is one formed by dynamics of power that are carefully articulated by "the frame." Even in the most relational approach, it is the analyst who ends the session after 45 min and collects the fee. In boundary-violating sexual misconduct the professional fails to uphold their end of the bargain. Consent is irrelevant.

Clearly college settings differ from psychoanalytic spaces in a number of ways, but training institutes can take note of what the academy has found helpful and most effective (understanding that efficacy in this area is complex and difficult to measure). Given the requirements of patient confidentiality, the legalities of boundary violations, and the threat to one's livelihood, bystander invention might be easier to apply than restorative justice (although I think the latter is important to conceptualize). Just imagine an institute successfully engaging a form of restorative justice to address a boundary violation. What would it look like to have an offender held within the community, not exiled as the identified cancer to the otherwise "pure" and "innocent" community? Could there be remorse, apology, and a community circle holding the offender accountable? Could the patient/supervisee/victim work with the community to create forms of apology? If offenders are held in the community, wouldn't that make it so much easier for someone on the slippery slope, someone struggling in the rip tide, to ask for help? And such an atmosphere would make the work of a bystander so much easier in terms of identifying, engaging, and addressing a potential offender.

Using what we know from psychoanalytic theory about the repetition of violence and trauma it should not come as a surprise that situating prevention and intervention within a community can be effective. After all, community based interventions hail community members through their capacities to be agentic and powerful bystanders. Additionally, such a model of organizing communicates clearly articulated procedures for reporting (including transparent ramifications and consequences of reporting), transparent protocols for intervention and accountability that is consistent and apparent to the community, including maintaining a clear channel of communication throughout the "timely" investigation. This transparency is extremely important within a cultural context of confidentiality. Modeling how confidentiality is generative (through psychoanalytic process) and when it needs to be dispensed with for the good of the community is therapeutic in and of itself. Holding secrets and/or being inconsistent collapses the bystander agency, pulling the community back into the rigid position of victim/perpetrator, and functions to create more anxiety and dissociation (Wallace, 2007). It renders the community helpless. This is extremely important since it is the body of the community that needs to be used to collectively contain and process shame, accountability, and remorse.

Community-based accountability, as described in the college setting, requires the capacity to create and sustain an atmosphere that does not tolerate abuse in any form. Maintaining this cultural atmosphere requires engaging in a continual ongoing process as groups, like individuals, will typically retreat to positions and interactions that are familiar, even when they are the positions of oppression and violence (Bion, 1961/1989). As mentioned, my college community has changed our policy to one where victims are urged to get support not from an advocate who could ease one through the process or reporting, but from a counselor who will be bound by confidentiality. Indeed, community accountability is an ongoing process that requires a great deal of vigilance.

The bullying of candidates, younger members, and those with less professional prestige (Levin, 2014), and the "cult of personality" that develops in institutes, can position certain members above the law, destroying community building and accountability. Institutes as communities can punish a less powerful victim with threats to professional growth including opportunities to teach, publish, and present, and/or to receive patient referrals. For bystander intervention to be effective, speaking up cannot come with professional or personal retribution or punishment. Thus, all members of the community not only have to be aware of the procedures of speaking up and reporting, these procedures need to be implemented by a committee of people at varying levels of professional development and prestige, including candidates. There also need to be strict, clear, adhered-to guidelines for disciplining attempts at retribution. This is extremely important. Many cases I have worked on were turned to the victim's favor when the perpetrator or community members began harassing the person who reported. Retribution is a violation that is easier to prove as there is usually evidence of contact.

A community-based response, though, also requires intervention for the perpetrator or professional at risk of violation. As mentioned previously, colleges have to have a multi-department committee that takes reports from the community, works to identify students at risk, and helps determine appropriate interventions. Institutes could have similar committee-based intervention teams. However, due to the confidential and private nature of psychoanalytic work, the most important form of intervention is interpersonal, helping members operationalize risky behaviors, identify them in themselves and others, and learn appropriate forms of intervening for the psychoanalytic setting. This needs to be done while holding the fact that psychoanalysis historically has used the confidential nature of the work as an excuse for special rules, codes of ethics, and processes of investigation and reporting. It may be a unique setting but the operations of power, privilege, and abuse are fairly universal.

Although the academic setting is different from the clinical setting some basic ideas of bystander intervention, namely the emphasis on community building, the roles of community members to act and respond and in turn create conditions for responding, can help shape institutional approaches to dealing with sexual boundary violations. In this context, ethics training would focus on creating the conditions for responding—response-ability. Violations would be seen not only as the destructive actions of an individual, but an indication of the shame-full and destructive atmosphere created and sustained by the institute and community. This would be an ethics based on integration, not dissociation and identifying the individual aggressor. It would be a model based on our theories of how groups evolve, how trauma is enacted, and how affective engagement can be best used toward transformation.

Although sexual boundary violations with psychoanalysis and sexual violence on college campuses each have some unique factors, both communities have been shaped by strong patriarchal systems that have rendered making sexual violence visible a challenge. Thus it is important for us to look at what each can bring to the other in hopes of creating transformative and preventative interventions in both settings.

Notes

1 Following Koss *et al.* (2014), I will be using the term sexual misconduct to describe incidents of sexual violence. I like the term sexual misconduct. Terms like sexual assault, abuse, harassment, and rape focus the action of the word on the victim's body and the impact of a behavior. Sexual misconduct seems to me to keep a focus on the offender, the perpetrator of the misconduct, and the offender's behavior.

2 After the Virginia Tech shooter there was a nation-wide push for the development of prevention specialist task forces on campuses. These teams are known as BIT—Behavioral Intervention Teams. The national guidelines recommend members be representatives from academic affairs, students services—including counselors and liaisons with women's centers—security personnel, and legal council. BIT teams meet regularly to discuss any students who have been identified as being disruptive or potentially at risk for failing academically. It is a prevention-based model of intervention.

3 In fact, Blechner (2014) refers to Celenza's (2007) research indicating that psychoanalysts who do sue the accusing patient receive more favorable responses from ethics boards than those who do not respond aggressively.

4 Harry Smith took the opposite stance and defended himself against accusations of sexual boundary violations with a patient by saying because the patient was a psychologist herself, she understood the power of transference and countertransference and thus, exercised consent to a sexual relationship (Herman, 2012).

References

Aron, L. (1996). *A meeting of minds: Mutuality in psychoanalysis.* Hillsdale, NJ: The Analytic Press.

Barad, K. (2010). Quantum entanglements and hauntological relations of inheritance: Dis/continuities, spacetime enfoldings, and justice-to-come. *Derrida Today, 3*(2), 240–268.

Baranger, M., & Baranger, W. (2008). The analytic situation as a dynamic field. *International Journal of Psychoanalysis, 89,* 795–826.

Benjamin, J. (2004). Beyond doer and done to: An intersubjective view of thirdness. *Psychoanalytic Quarterly, LXXIII*(1), 5–46.

Benjamin, J. (2009). A relational psychoanalysis perspective on the necessity of acknowledging failure in order to restore the facilitating and containing features of the intersubjective relationship (the shared third). *International Journal of Psychoanalysis, 90,* 441–450.

Bion, W.R. (1961/1989). *Experiences in groups and other papers.* New York, NY: Brunner-Routledge.

Blechner, M. (2014). Dissociation among psychoanalysts about sexual boundary violations. *Contemporary Psychoanalysis, 50*(1), 1–11.

Boulanger, G. (2012). Psychoanalytic witnessing: Professional obligation or moral imperative? *Psychoanalytic Psychology, 29*(3), 318–324.

Bromberg, P. (1998). *Standing in the spaces: Essays on clinical process, trauma and dissociation.* New York, NY: Routledge.

Butler, J. (1997). *The psychic life of power: Theories in subjection.* Stanford, CA: Stanford University Press.

Celenza, A. (2007). *Sexual boundary violations: Therapeutic, supervisory, and academic contexts.* Lanham, MD: Aronson.

Cornell, D. (1995). *The imaginary domain: Abortion, pornography and sexual harassment.* New York, NY: Routledge.

_____. (2010). The ethical affirmation of human rights: Gayatri Spivak's intervention. In R.C. Morris (Ed.), *Reflections on the history of an idea: Can the subaltern speak?* (pp. 100–114). New York, NY: Columbia University Press.

Daly, K. (2002). Mind the gap: Restorative justice in theory and practice. Downloaded November 3, 2014.

_____. (2006). Restorative justice and sexual assault. *British Journal of Criminology, 46,* 334–356.

Davies, J.M., & Frawley, M.G. (1992). Dissociative processes and transference countertransference paradigms in the psychoanalytically oriented treatment of adult survivors of childhood sexual abuse. *Psychoanalytic Dialogues, 2,* 5–36.

DeKeseredy, W., & Kelly, K. (1993). The incidence and prevalence of woman abuse in Canadian university and college dating relationships. *Canadian Journal of Sociology, 18,* 137–159.

Deleuze, G., & Guattari, F. (1977/2009). *Anti-Oedipus: Capitalism and schizophrenia.* New York, NY: Penguin Classics.

_____. (1987). *A thousand plateaus.* Minneapolis, MN: University of Minnesota Press.

Douglas, M. (1966). *Purity and danger.* New York, NY: Routledge.

Elise, D. (2014). Personal communication. March 1, 2014.

Felman, S., & Laub, D. (1992). *Testimony: Crises of witnessing in literature, psychoanalysis, and history.* New York, NY: Routledge.

Foehl, J.C. (2005). "How could this happen to me?": Sexual misconduct and us. *Journal of the American Psychoanalytic Association, 53*(3), 957–970.

Gabbard, G. (2001). Boundaries, culture, and psychotherapy: Commentary. *Journal of the American Academy of Psychiatry and the Law, 29*(3), 284–286.

Gentile, K. (2015). Generating subjectivity through the creation of time. *Psychoanalytic Psychology*, *33*(2), 264–283.

_____. (2013a). Bearing the cultural in order to engage in a process of witnessing. *Psychoanalytic Psychology*, *30*(3), 456–470.

_____. (2013b). Biopolitics, trauma and the public fetus: An analysis of preconception care. *Subjectivity*, *6*(2), 153–172.

_____. (in press). When the cat guards the canary—A new look at sexual boundary violations in psychoanalysis. In C. Levin (Ed.), *Boundary trouble: The ethics of psychoanalytic intimacy in relational perspective*. New York, NY: Routledge. In press.

Gentile, K., Raghavan, C., Rajah, V., & Gates, K. (2007). It doesn't happen here?: Eating disorders in an ethnically diverse sample of low-income, female and male, urban college students. *Eating Disorders: The Journal of Treatment and Prevention,. 15*(5), 405–425.

Gerson, S. (2009). When the third is dead: Memory, mourning, and witnessing in the aftermath of the Holocaust. *International Journal of Psychoanalysis*, *90*, 1341–1357.

Grand, S. (2002). Between the reader and the read: Commentary on paper by Elizabeth F. Howell. *Psychoanalytic Dialogues*, *12*(6), 959–970.

Grand, S. (2003). Unsexed and ungendered bodies: The violated self. *Studies in Gender and Sexuality*, *4*(4), 313–341.

Herman, C.M. (2012). Sex with patient caused no harm, doctor says. *CommonWealth: Politics, Ideas, & Civic Life in Massachusetts.* January 26, 2012. Downloaded September, 2013.

Honig, R.G., & Barron, J.W. (2013). Restoring institutional integrity in the wake of sexual boundary violations: A case study. *Journal of the American Psychoanalytic Association*, *61*(5), 897–924.

Klein, M. (1958). *Envy and gratitude and other works, 1946–1963*. New York, NY: Delacorte.

Koss, M.P., Wilgus, J.K., & Williamsen, K.M. (2014). Campus sexual misconduct: Restorative justice approaches to enhance compliance with Title IX guidance. *Trauma, Violence, & Abuse*, *15*(3), 242–257.

Layton, L. (2010). Irrational exuberance: Neoliberal subjectivity and the perversion of the truth. *Subjectivity*, *3*, 303–322.

Levin, C. (2014). Trauma as a way of life in a psychoanalytic institute. In R.A. Deutsch (Ed.), *Traumatic ruptures: Abandonment and betrayal in the analytic relationships* (pp. 176–196). New York, NY: Routledge.

Levine, H. (2010). The sins of the fathers: Freud, narcissistic boundary violations and their effects on the politics of psychoanalysis. *International Forum of Psychoanalysis*, *19*, 43–50.

Margalit, A. (2002). *The ethics of memory*. Cambridge, MA: Harvard University Press.

Mitchell, S.A. (2000). *Relationality: From attachment to intersubjectivity*. New York, NY: Routledge.

Mohanty, C.T. (2004). *Feminism without borders: Decolonizing theory, practicing solidarity*. Durham, NC: Duke University Press.

Ogden, T.H. (1994). The analytic third: Working with intersubjective clinical facts. *International Journal of Psycho-Analysis*, *75*, 3–19.

Oliver, K. (2001). *Witnessing: Beyond recognition*. Minneapolis, MN: University of Minnesota Press.

Oliver, K. (2004). *The colonization of psychic space: A psychoanalytic social theory of oppression*. Minneapolis, MN: University of Minnesota Press.

Poland, W.S. (2000). The analyst's witnessing and otherness. *Journal of the American Psychoanalytic Association*, *48*, 17–34.

Saketopoulou, A. (2010). Consent, sexuality, and self-repsect: Commentary on Skerrett's "Beyond consent." *Studies in Gender and Sexuality*, *12*, 245–250.

Spivak, G.C. (1988). Can the subaltern speak? In C. Nelson & L. Gorssberg (Eds.), *Marxism and the interpretation of culture* (pp. 271–313). Basingstoke, U.K: Macmillan Education.

Tronto, J.C. (1994). *Moral boundaries: A political argument for an ethic of care.* New York, NY: Routledge.

Ullman, C. (2006). Bearing witness: Across the barriers in society and in the clinic. *Psychoanalytic Dialogues, 16,* 181–198.

Wallace, E.M. (2007). Losing a training analyst for ethical violations: A candidate's perspective. *International Journal of Psychoanalysis, 88,* 1275–1288.

White, J.W., & Koss, M.P. (1991). Courtship violence: Incidence in a national sample of higher education students. *Violence and Victims, 6,* 247–256.

SECTION III
Women defining motherhood

COMMENTARY ON SECTION III

Women defining motherhood

JoAnn Ponder

The chapters in this section of the book focus on whether to become a mother, and the psychological processes of becoming one. Until the mid-twentieth century, it wasn't always easy for women to prevent pregnancy. Things changed in 1960, when the Federal (United States) Drug Administration approved the oral contraceptive that came to be known simply as "the pill." It is a highly effective form of birth control that a woman can choose to take in private, thereby giving her control over reproduction, or the freedom to engage in heterosexual intercourse without becoming pregnant. Women subsequently embraced the pill not only to aid in family planning, but also to challenge the authority of doctors, lawmakers, and men in general (May, 2010). In this sense, I believe that birth control pills heralded the second wave of feminism in the US. Whereas first-wave feminism focused on voting and property rights, the second wave emphasized a wide range of issues, such as sexuality, reproductive rights, family, workplace, and legal and de facto inequalities (Dicker, 2016, 2008).

The childfree women's movement, as described in the chapter by Adi Avivi, is associated with second-wave feminism. As the second wave brought more options in roles for women, along with improved contraception, an increasing number of women have chosen not to have children. These women typically refer to themselves as "childfree" rather than "childless" in order to denote their choice and liberation as opposed to their lack or lesser status. Nonetheless, Avivi's research and personal experience revealed that there is still a tendency in American culture to pathologize them. The prejudice may be as subtle as questioning their choice, though we seldom question a married or adult woman's choice to have a child. It is as if childbearing is the normal baseline not to be questioned or considered, even though most theorists view the desire to have children as having both biological and social antecedents (Chodorow, 1999, 1978). A contemporary and innovative intervention for childfree women is internet chat groups. Avivi found these groups to be a viable, accessible means of providing emotional support and consolidating identity.

The Birth Rights Movement, as described in Helena Vissing's chapter, also is associated with second-wave feminism. The movement challenges the authority of obstetricians and advocates for natural childbirth free of medical intervention. In prior centuries, children were valued as farm and factory laborers. According to Chodorow (1999, 1978), birth rates were high, but so were infant and maternal mortality rates. With the development of capitalism and industrialism, birth rates declined, and medical care and mortality rates improved. According to birth rights advocates, however, there are too many unnecessary medical interventions for a mother giving birth, which may dampen her joyousness in the occasion and potentially her bonding with the baby. Based on a careful reading and analysis of the literature, Vissing contends that the advocates essentially are restricting maternal choice by substituting their dogma for medical dogma. She further suggests that the birth rights rationale serves to defend against the expectant mother's underlying fears about the dangers of childbirth by idealizing the experience.

Medical advances over the past half-century include not only improved contraception, but also assisted reproduction techniques. Nevertheless, many women postponed pregnancy until it was too late. My chapter explores women's reactions to infertility and their transformation to motherhood following adoption. I interweave memoir, clinical material, and professional literature to explore how the adoptive mother's psychological journey is the same and different from that of a biological mother. Whereas most of the adoption literature focuses on adopted children, this chapter focuses on adoptive mothers. Traditionally, psychoanalytic literature emphasized mother as object, referring to her role as a self/object or someone who provides a facilitating environment for the baby to develop. It is only recently that psychoanalysis has considered maternal subjectivity, or the mother's own coming into being through relationship with the infant (Baraitser, 2008). This chapter will add to that body of psychoanalytic literature, as well as the adoption literature.

The three chapters in this section provide only a small sampling of the possible range of topics about women and their relation to mothering. Like appetizers that whet the appetite for more, each author speaks in her own voice from her unique vantage point, doing so in a culturally sensitive manner. A major criticism of second-wave feminism is that it fails to consider the voices of women of color, working-class women, and lesbians (Dicker, 2016, 2008). Unfortunately, that same criticism could be levied against this section of the book. While these women were not purposely omitted, they did not respond to the call for proposals, and several declined direct invitations to submit. Hopefully, their voices will be heard in another volume in the future. In the meantime, these chapters offer engaging ideas and satisfying food for thought.

References

Baraitser, L. (2008). *Maternal encounters: The ethics of interruption.* London: Routledge.

Chodorow, N. (1999, 1978). *The reproduction of mothering: Psychoanalysis and the sociology of gender.* Berkeley, CA: University of California Press.

Dicker, R.C. (2016, 2008). *A history of U.S. feminisms.* Berkeley, CA: Seal Press.

May, E.T. (2010). *America and the pill: A history of promise, peril, and liberation.* New York, NY: Basic Books.

7

CHILDFREE WOMEN

Surviving the pushback and forming an identity in the internet era

Adi Avivi

"But why not? You are so good with kids!" My friend's guest at a dinner party was incredulous upon learning that I did not want any children of my own. Years of being challenged about this lack of desire to bear or raise children had made me think about the "Why?" question in depth; still, I had not found a concrete answer. "I just don't. I never did. I don't have—I don't need a reason," I managed. "I just don't want kids." So there we stood, unable to communicate on the subject. The interaction seemed to cause her significant anxiety, and feeling that side of myself yet again rejected caused me anxiety as well.

Being criticized and rejected in this way was a recurring experience for me; other childfree women have similar experiences. I knew I did not want to have children from a very young age. In the childfree community, I am what would be called an "early articulator." Most childfree women go through a longer decision-making process, but I always knew. As a young person, I did not have the words "childfree" or "early articulator" at my disposal, so I would just say that I didn't want to have children if the topic arose. Naïvely, I expected it to be accepted like other things about me: I like art, I want to study psychology, I don't want to have children.

I remember vividly the first time I realized that not wanting children meant others would question my femininity and even my well-being. I stated it, in passing, to a group of my friends in my late teens. "What is wrong with you?" asked my male best friend, alarmed. "Why must you say such unfeminine things? You present yourself as completely weird and repulsive!" I was surprised. Why would anyone think me less a woman, less desirable, or less normal, simply because I don't want kids? It did not occur to me that I was expected to want kids. My internal experience was of not wanting them. I recognized I broke some social rule . . . but what rule was that?

Studying psychoanalytic and feminist theories and volunteering in a rape crisis center gave me a clue. I was threatening to others in multiple, complex ways. I was threatening patriarchy by refusing to accept my role as a female-born woman. I was threatening cultural, political, and economic dogmas: in the complex Israeli society, well-educated Ashkenazi women are the "right kind of people" to have children. I found that in the US, women are generally expected to have children as well. And I was threatening to other women, as my childfreedom implied there was a choice involved in childrearing. The paved and familiar path for womanhood was not a must. I learned that some people are uncomfortable with unusual choices. But I also learned that being outspoken moves others. Women who demand public space despite being a sore spot for the hegemony might be appreciated and even loved by some, even needed for those who are different as well but for whatever reason could not be out (yet).

I was very lucky to have tremendous support from my family and my partner. Although my childfreedom has not been necessarily celebrated, it was accepted or at least tolerated by most of my loved ones. A while ago, my mother told me that when I was a young girl, pre-teen, I stated in front of her and her friend: "I am never having kids!" The friend said, trying to comfort my mother: "Oh, she's just a little girl. She'll change her mind." My mother said: "I know my daughter. She will not change her mind. She won't have kids."

My mother has always been exceptionally accepting of my non-conformism. A combination of an easygoing nature, her own individualism, unusual for a woman born in the 50s, and her general desire for her children to "do whatever they want" gave me the freedom to disregard certain social norms without feeling rejected or punished by her. Learning that she recognized childfreedom as an integral part of me at such a young age was heartwarming. Being known by my mother was empowering. I believe that part of my naïve expectation, that others would accept me too, stemmed from her loving attitude toward me.

I am more at peace with this aspect of my identity, now that I am approaching 40 years of age, than I was before. As I get older, people are less demanding that I conform. Finding a childfree partner who shares my non-desire to parent and creating our life together on our terms has been lovely. No less important, researching and writing about childfreedom has been an affirming experience. It helped me understand myself better, and I hope these insights will be helpful to other childfree women and their allies.

Women who purposely live childfree are often invalidated by others regarding their choice not to have children. Exploring one's identity as childfree could therefore be challenging. In an internet era, childfree (CF) women who are actively reading and writing about childfreedom online might find like-minded others who would allow them to explore this topic more freely than "in real life." The need to interact with accepting others was borne out in qualitative research that I will present in this chapter, revolving around the notion of childfreedom as an identity and culture, its practitioners constituting a minority group. This chapter will present data showing that online communication can be a tool for interactive self-exploration and a safe haven in which the CF identity could develop.

Research project

Unlike many of my peers who struggled to recruit subjects for their dissertation projects, I was flooded with enthusiastic volunteers for my study of women who chose to remain childfree. They explicitly articulated their desire to contribute to CF research, to have their voices heard, and to present their positions to the professional community. Their reasons for volunteering were remarkable. For example:

S16: If clinical research were done, then people would (hopefully) have an unbiased, truthful picture of who the CF are. I hope I can help the CF and the researcher in this instance.

S4: We need to get our voice heard. It is important that people understand that there are other lifestyles out there that are just as natural as starting a family and that every lifestyle is a choice. I hope that by being part of studies that look at objective, empirical research, it will help dispel common myths that are often attached to CF women.

S22: My reason for volunteering was to broaden out the pool of respondents and to show that you can get to disgraceful middle-age being CF and have no regrets, you can still find CF love as an older CFer [childfree individual] and live life with no fear of the future.

The dedication and commitment these women showed were incredible and turned out to be directly related to the research question that this project sought to answer—"What are the functions of internet communication for CF women?"—because the answers the women provided showed how the internet addressed in different ways their deep desire to be heard by others and to listen to their CF peers.

Introduction to childfreedom

In *The Baby Matrix*, Carrol (2012) discusses how US culture supports and encourages bearing children, using the term *pronatalist* culture (i.e., supporting and encouraging having children) and the social devices it uses to promote parenthood as inevitability. In pronatalist culture, having children is not only the expected norm but considered a sign of health and happiness. Moreover, bearing and rearing children is perceived as each individual's natural destiny. Carrol reveals myriad techniques used by media, political groups, and religious institutions to promote pronatalism. In such a culture, not having children renders one "the other," leaving the diverse group of those who do not want to partake in parenting in a minority status. Both as the choice not to have children and, for some, a subculture that supports that choice, childfreedom has received growing attention in the past few years. For example, the August 12, 2013, cover of *Time* featured childfreedom. Yet, as Carrol points out, the childfree are not accepted as an integrated part of society, or as a group holding a place deemed equal to those who choose to parent.

Despite an increasing proportion of individuals and couples choosing to remain childfree, parenthood is typically considered an essential part of "creating a family" as well as a key stepping stone of maturity (Gold & Wilson, 2002; Letherby, 2002). Most women still become mothers, although the percentage of women who do not has doubled since the 1980s, with a slight decrease in that trend over the past few years (Monte & Ellis, 2012; Mcquillan *et al.*, 2012).

In a culture that considers parenting the key to happiness, adulthood, and normality, women who lead CF lives are marginalized. They have been described as sick, insensitive, uncaring, unkind, aberrant, immature, unfeminine, egotistical, cold, materialistic, peculiar, abnormal, and/or unsatisfied in marriage (Calhoun & Selby, 1980; Coffey, 2005; Giles *et al.*, 2009; La Mastro, 2001; Letherby, 2002; Mollen,

2006). The decision to remain childfree is pathologized and attributed to childhood trauma, poor parental role models, oppressive childrearing, too many siblings' child-care responsibility, and negative identification with one's own mother (Reading & Amatea, 1986, as cited in Hird & Abshoff, 2000).

In fact, being dismissed and criticized when talking about one's childfreedom is so common that it has a term in the CF community: "getting bingoed." The phrase was coined when a humoristic bingo board (West, 2006) was published online, making light of the frequency with which CF people encounter unpleasant reactions when sharing that they do not want children. Instead of numbers to be matched from randomly drawn balls, CF people could collect dismissive statements plotted on the board, such as "You will regret it," "Only selfish people don't want children," "If everyone thought like you, the human race will be extinct," "Children are the future," and "Who will take care of you when you're old?"

The academic world has taken note of the increased popularity of CF choice. A wide variety of disciplines, including sociology, gender studies, feminist theory, political science, communication, and biology, have researched aspects of this phenomenon. Existing studies have examined reasons for remaining childfree (Agrillo & Nelini, 2008; Coffey, 2005); perceptions of people who are variously childfree, childless, or parents (Hird & Abshoff, 2000; Lampman & Dowling-Guyer, 1995; Rowlands & Lee, 2006); and characteristics, gender differences, representations, myths, and realities of people leading CF lives (Boyd, 1989; Giles et al., 2009; Kenkel, 1985; Seccombe, 1991; Somers, 1993). Although some of these studies address counseling for this population (Gold & Wilson, 2002; Mollen, 2006), psychology overall has been more invested in exploring motherhood than in studying those who choose not to parent.

Making the decision

In a recent article published in Sweden, Peterson and Engwall (2013) interviewed twenty-seven women exploring their CF identity formation. Much like me in the anecdote that opens this chapter, their participants referred to their choice not to mother as "natural." The women struggled to provide a reason for their choice, even stating that this was not "a decision" but an inner knowledge they had about themselves for a long time, with one of their subjects stating, "I simply have no desire to have children" (Peterson & Engwall, 2013, pp. 380–381).

With that said, it makes sense that a culture that expects childrearing would seek to question the decision not to conform to that expectation. Studying the decision-making process, Scott (2009) identified eighteen reasons her participants chose to remain childfree. The most common reason for couples was simply that they enjoyed life and their romantic relationships as is. Additional reasons included valuing freedom and independence, not wanting the responsibility of children, having no wish to have children, lacking parental instinct, concerns about the world being overpopulated, and having goals that conflict with the project of raising children. Mollen (2006) found that CF women experienced resistance to complying with their expected gender role and gender identity; they received discouraging messages from their families through early interactions; and some experienced the responsibilities of childcare at an early age. In addition, Mollen's interviewees mentioned needs for personal freedom, fear for their body's safety, concern for their child's genetic heritage, and a view of the world as an unsafe place to raise children.

Contrary to a common misconception that CF women make this choice as a single person, Safer (1996) made her decision not to have children within the realm of a happy marriage, with a partner who would have supported her decision either way. Safer also researched the process of deciding to remain childfree. She claims that most women experience conflicted feelings and uncertainty during the decision-making process. According to her research, some find the decision painful because of conflicted feelings, while some are uncomfortable with others' expectations and demands. Although a few women decide effortlessly, Safer suggests they are in the minority. Bartlett's (1995) interviewees found it hard to identify a specific moment in time or an experience that led to the decision. Like Safer, Bartlett found that some women made the choice again and again, vacillating, reassessing their commitment to childfreedom, and sometimes having to choose it "on a daily, weekly, or yearly basis" (p. 97). These findings are somewhat different than those of Peterson and Engwall (2013). It stands to reason that there are cultural differences between European and American women in terms of making the choice not to reproduce. The time gap between the studies might also be of significance.

Ireland (1993) suggested the presence of three subgroups among women who do not have children. The first group is "Traditional." These are women who did not mother due to poor health or infertility, rather than by choice. Another group is the "Transformative," referring to those who actively chose to be childfree, and by that, transform womanhood for themselves and others. Finally, women who delay the decision until they cannot have children make up the "Transitional" group. Callan (1984) categorized CF women as "early articulators," referring to women who made a decision not to have children before marriage, or "postponers" who remain childless due to circumstance. The most distinct difference between the two groups was in their experience of discussing their decisions with relatives and friends. Early deciders were more likely to be perceived as nonconformists, confronted about their decision, and accused of selfishness, disliking children, or infertility (Callan, 1983, p. 267). Postponers were less likely to be treated in this manner: their childfreedom was perceived by others as transitory.

Expanding on Callan's categories, Scott (2009) distinguished four categories, depending on how and when a person arrived at the decision to refrain from having children: "Early Articulators," who make the decision early in life; "Postponers," who delayed having a family and remain childless for life; "Acquiescers," who make the decision because their partner wants to be childfree; and the "Undecided," for whom the choice is not yet certain (p. 16). These terms became part of the CF lingo, similar to "being bingoed," and are used to identify subgroups among the childfree.

Regardless of how or why women decide to be childfree, nearly all report that having a supportive community is a crucial aspect of their process (Bartlett, 1995; Donat, 2011; Durham, 2008; Durham & Braithwaite, 2009; Mollen, 2006; Safer, 1996). Indeed, in studies that addressed the clinical needs of participants attempting to decide whether to raise children, the researchers chose a group model for their work (Russell *et al.*, 1978; Daniluk & Herman, 1983). Pelton and Hertlein (2011) argue that CF women need to form an identity regarding this aspect of their lives within a supportive relationship—such as the therapeutic relationship. In short, CF women need to be able to talk about their choice and status. However, research has shown that they are presented with substantial obstacles to doing so.

Discussing the CF lifestyle with others

To thoughtfully make the decision whether or not to live a CF life, it is crucial that women receive the empathic support of others. However, they often find others to be unsupportive and critical. As mentioned above, childfreedom is typically stigmatized. This is especially true for women (Park, 2002). Research by Durham (2008) and Donat (2007) revealed that when others reacted negatively to the topic of childfreedom, such reactions were frequently influenced by the view that childfreedom is deviant. The childfree, by acknowledging their status, were therefore at risk of being criticized, insulted, and alienated in important relationships. Park (2002) claimed, referring to Veevers (1980), "Those who are childless by choice are stigmatized by their blemished characters, while the sterile or infertile are stigmatized by their physical abnormalities" (pp. 30–31).

Donat (2007) found that, despite some openness to challenging the pronatalist dogma in Israeli media, her subjects still found little room to publicly discuss their CF identity:

> While the subjects in this study describe their choice not to be parents, as producing a tremendous amount of freedom in their personal life—most of them report a subsequent reduction, or even a total loss of freedom in the public arena, due to the explicit and implicit restrictions of the people around them, that point them out as "out of place" anomalies.
>
> (p. 9)[1]

Donat portrayed this group experience as "living in the closet," and the discussion with others who comply with the pronatalist hegemony in Israel as a "coming out" process. Durham (2008) reported similar wording in his participants' testimonies of disclosing their choice.

Internet, identity formation, intersubjectivity, and childfreedom

> Taking responsibility for the social relations of science and technology means refusing an anti-science metaphysics, a demonology of technology, and so means embracing the skillful task of reconstructing the boundaries of daily life, in partial connection with others, in communication with all of our parts.
>
> (Haraway, 1985, p. 100)

I decided to approach my research from an intersubjective psychoanalytic view-point. The radical notion that reality is co-constructed and molded by the meeting of minds implies a call for responsibility, acknowledgment of both privileges and weaknesses, and striving to truly see others and truly let them see us. Human identity is formed in the ongoing dance between I, thou, and the third (Ogden, 1994), the mutual recognition (Benjamin, 1995; Aron, 2001) that allows the parties in interaction to fully experience themselves in connection.

This position evoked my curiosity regarding the CF experience of self and other. When a CF person has not yet fully consolidated that part of her identity, how could it be created, separated, and connected to others if that part of her is unknown or lacking language to signify itself? How could the childfree play with that aspect of her identity without sympathetic others who would reflect it as a positive possibility? The answer, I found, was *online* (Basten, 2009). While "in real-life" childfreedom remains marginal, online there are blogs, message boards, chat rooms, and informational websites dedicated to the issue, inviting visitors to discuss the topic in an environment of like-minded others. In fact, many of the women who participated in my study used the term "safe haven" when referring to their discovery of CF online forums. From a self-psychological stance, these online venues provide opportunities for mirroring and validation.

I explored CF women's experiences online and used intersubjectivity and gender identity theories to discuss my findings (Avivi, 2012). I will present the core findings of my qualitative data analysis (Auerbach & Silverstein, 2003), which generated four theoretical constructs: *The CF identity is complex and dynamic; being a CF woman influences interpersonal relationships; CF-dedicated websites are powerful tools of communication, support, information, and socialization; and for CF women, the personal is political.* Each construct will be presented with special regard to those aspects most pertaining to clinical applications, using direct quotes from my participants.

It is important to note that, despite a relatively large number of participants ($N = 29$) for a qualitative study, my sample did have some limitations. My inclusion criteria were: being a woman, identifying as childfree, using CF-dedicated websites, and being literate in English. Although I believe my sample is a good representation of the group of CF women who are active online, my criteria exposed me to a very narrow sample within the Western CF population at large since being part of a group does not necessarily mean consuming its related literature or conversing about it actively on social media sites. Possibly because of that, most of the women were self-identified as leaning toward a liberal political and social standpoint; White; had at least an undergraduate degree; and all were American, Canadian, or European. Most were also either married or cohabitating with a significant other. This does not necessarily mean that being childfree is reserved to women from within these demographic categories. It stands to reason that White, educated, and Western women might be the first wave of open "representatives" of childfreedom, so to speak, possibly much as in other movements, where those who have social privilege are often the first to be acknowledged. Demographic exploration of the CF community at large has been scarce thus far. Hopefully this will be remedied in the near future by further research, which would allow the voices of more diverse racial, ethnic, gender, and SES groups to be heard.

First construct: The CF identity is complex and dynamic

The women in my study reported on their experience meeting other CF individuals online, receiving support, information, and a safe place to discuss their thoughts and feelings regarding childfreedom. They discovered that although they were all childfree, they reached that identity through different paths. Becoming self-aware and introspective about the CF identity was a process some made quickly while others were still engaging. Some viewed childfreedom as a defining part of themselves, while others claimed it was not necessarily the most significant piece of their identity. As one of the subjects said:

> S18: I think it is important to note that you can't paint all CF women with the same brush. We have all made the same decision, but we have all had drastically different paths that led us to that decision. It's very interesting to speak with other women who have had very different life experiences than I have, but who have also decided not to bring another person into this world.

One of the aspects within this construct was the sense of confusion many of the subjects felt due to the gap between what they wanted or considered preferable— namely, not to mother children—and what they thought was possible and acceptable. Although some of the women—especially those who knew from a young age that they did not want children—responded with frustration and anger toward others who questioned and criticized them, others questioned themselves and assumed motherhood was a must.

> S20: I think that until I was about twenty-five, I absolutely dreaded the possibility of having children and felt no desire whatsoever for it, but I still assumed that it was going to happen someday, simply because there seemed no other option (certainly not in the society in which I grew up, which is totally fertility-obsessed).

The self-identified "early articulators" expressed confidence in their lack of desire to have children; however, they did not necessarily believe they would be able to follow that desire. Growing up, these individuals were aware that their choice was unfamiliar as they did not have examples of women who elected not to mother in their respective cultures. Others' reactions were often dismissive or critical, leaving the CF child or teenager without role models or mentors to guide her in discovering the CF aspect of herself.

> S21: I didn't have anyone—a mentor, teacher or family member—once tell me, "You have a choice in the matter, and whatever you choose is okay." I looked at parenthood as something that was necessary—something to dread.

The lack of familiar examples, such as famous people, pop-culture references, or texts that normalized childfreedom, could account for the above-mentioned assumption of some participants that parenting was a must. The lack of CF cultural content may also explain the experience of participants who were not sure about their childfreedom from an early age. For them, the decision was more complicated, requiring deep self-exploration before coming to terms with not having children. They sought therapy, talked to friends and family, had long discussions with their spouses, and sometimes had to cope with emotionally challenging soul-searching processes. Such an emotional process was presented in Safer's (1996) account of her decision not to have children. She described a long journey in which she and her spouse engaged in continuous conversations until they decided to remain childfree. Safer also talked about a period of mourning over the lost opportunity of mother-hood, although she was content with her choice to remain CF.

Psychoanalysis and psychology in general also provide little information for the childfree. Even in critical and feminist psychoanalytical theories, the focus on mother-hood did not change; rather, the perspective on parenting expanded, included fathers to a larger extent, and incorporated social, political, and cultural ideas that viewed motherhood in context (Chodorow, 1978; Benjamin, 1988; Fast, 1984). There are some indirect notes on the possibility that motherhood is not for all women. Ben-jamin (1988), in her criticism over psychoanalysis's association between femininity and nature, stated that some feminists' equation between womanhood, mother-hood, and nature was a problem rather than a way to empower women because, just like men, women were social and not just biological, and their intersubjectivity lay within their social interactions (p. 80). Chodorow (2003) also noted that she did not believe motherhood is a "natural destiny" (p. 1185) for all women. Furthermore, she stated that she did not believe that not-mothering is inherently pathological. This being said, she chose to explore the experiences of women who regretted choosing not to mother and analyzed the psychological dynamics that played a part in their arriving at the conclusion that they wanted children when it was too late. Chodorow can hardly be accused of seeing motherhood through a traditional and patriarchal lens (see Chodorow, 1978), and one could safely assume that she would support CF women and legitimatize their choice. Still, there appears to be a lack of space to explore the CF choice as positive and promising of happiness. As one subject in my study stated:

> S21: I think that younger women need us older gals to step up and say, "Hey, you CAN get through this stage of life. Don't let it get you down!" Hence, why I drop into CF forums.

It is also important to note that despite often being warned that they will regret their childfreedom, CF individuals do not typically experience regret, even later in life (DeLyser, 2011).

One psychoanalytic article that concentrated on women who chose not to mother is Hird's (2003) "Vacant Wombs." In this article, Hird explored the psycho-analytic approaches to reproduction and motherhood and gave a psychodynamic viewpoint to her prior work on childfreedom (Hird & Abshoff, 2000). She advocated for an inclusive approach that took into account CF women within psychoanalysis, claiming that such inclusion would enrich the field and create space for diversity. Such inclusion might allow women to reach their childfreedom with less turmoil, as some of the women in this study experienced:

> S21: Sometimes I still get that feeling that there's something "wrong" with me for not wanting to be a parent. Checking in with other CF folks makes me feel more "normal."

> S9: [Engaging in CF forums] also helped me to stop beating myself up for not being "normal." I felt less like a freak of nature.

For many of the women in my study, finding a CF community online was the first encounter with others who did not want to parent. With the discovery that others were like them, they also discovered how different they were, sometimes finding that they had nothing else in common. Much like parenting, non-parenting is a choice that evolves in a plethora of ways and is uniquely executed in each individual's life. This variety could attest to the wellbeing inherent in this choice; it is not the product of some misfortune or failure but a natural outcome for a range of life routes.

Another interesting aspect of CF identity was the approach the women took to their bodies' potential for pregnancy. As one develops her identity and finds that she does not want to have children, she is faced with some decisions regarding her body (Peterson & Engwall, 2013; Richie, 2013). The mature female body is not physically consistent with the wish not to become pregnant, if biologically healthy. Thus, for most, the CF identity requires significant prevention measures. For some of the participants, cementing their choice through sterilization became part of their journey. Richie (2013) explores personal, legal, and medical aspects of sterilization for CF women. She notes: "Barriers to the chosen method of birth control are constantly being encountered by capable women who are certain that they do not want children. This is seen in both the stories of women who seek support for finding a provider to sterilize them and in the sparse data on childfree sterilized women" (p. 42).

The topic of sterilization is fascinating when considering queer theories (Hird, 2004; Sullivan & Stryker, 2009) that offer rich discussions about changes to the human body as an act of claiming one's identity despite biology. In this sense, sterilization is a bold act of self-actualization that allows one to be who she is despite cultural and social boundaries imposed on her because she was born to a certain anatomy. In her discussion of body-transforming art, Knafo (2009) talks about the transformative and defensive qualities that could both explain a decision to defy the limitation of the body and use technology to modify it. The act of changing one's body could be the result of defending against childhood wounds, but it could also be "a postmodern brave refusal to be bound by traditional and cultural definitions of femininity, health, and beauty" (p. 156).

The participants in my study who chose sterilization expressed positive and reaffirming feelings regarding their choice. Some of them had to obtain the approval of a therapist (or a few therapists) in order to become sterilized. Their accounts are a testimony for the position of alterations of the body as part of becoming the self one wants to be:

> S27: When I was in my early to mid twenties, I always just assumed that I would eventually want kids later on when I was older. Finally at age thirty-five, I came to terms with the fact that I did not want kids at all, and I was not ever going to want them, so I made an appointment for a tubal consult and got permanently sterilized a few months later. That was three years ago, and it was one of the best decisions I have ever made in my life.

> S12: I was one of the lucky ones, apparently. I only had to go through two psychologists before being approved for the procedure. I planned ahead and started ~six months before I turned twenty-one (my state, Illinois, pays for sterilization with the healthy woman's card) and only got hassled in the form of "are you sure?" (all the way up to the operating table ...) after laying down all the reasons why I don't want offspring in the bluntest manner.

Second construct: Being a CF woman influences interpersonal relationships

> S15: My parents and in-laws are all supportive of our decision and I realize that is something to be so grateful for. I've seen a lot of discussion online from other CF individuals who are afraid to tell their parents, are constantly badgered by parents or in-laws, etc.

In his discussion of intersubjective relationships, Gerson (2004) claimed that meaning in each person is not created independently, but it is rather entangled in the inevitable interactions with others. In his discussion of different usages of the concept of "the third" or "thirdness" in psychoanalysis and specifically in intersubjective discourse, he found numerous definitions of this abstract notion variously employed by different writers. He identified three main usages of the concept: "the Developmental Third, the Cultural Third, and the Relational Third" (p. 64). When talking about the Cultural Third, he notes that this is a third entity that intrudes on the dyad and shapes its interaction. It is not a product of the meeting of two subjects but what colors that meeting. By that, the third is the creation of a connection that contains cultural forces (Benjamin, 2004).

Gerson (2004) states that the Relational Third is not a third entity, concept, language, or person interacting with the dyad, but rather a product of the dyad (p. 78). This, he claims, is the most common use of the "third" concept in intersubjective discourse. I understand the Relational Third as a process created by the ability of each subject to contain her own desire to both connect and maintain independence at the same time, as well as contain the other's desire to both come close to her and maintain distance. In that, I feel mostly influenced by Benjamin's (1988) writing about intersubjectivity as the ability to tolerate the "paradox of recognition" (p. 36); that is, the movement between the wish to control the other and the need to experience the other's humanity, independence, and freedom. It is of note that intersubjectivity in this sense is a process, a dynamic interaction—not an end result. According to Benjamin (1988, 1995, 2004), in order for an intersubjective encounter to unfold, individual similarities and differences must be tolerated.

The CF women in my study face a unique challenge in creating a Relational Third with others because the expectation and assumption that they will mother—furthermore, that they want to mother—color their meetings with other subjects. That cultural message can be a form of Cultural Third that constructs the space between them and others, making their childfreedom a stranger. In their meetings with others, there is an aspect of themselves that is at times completely outside of the realm of the dyad (or group) or is incomprehensible by the other. In more concrete terms, CF individuals who shared information about their childfreedom with others were at risk of being criticized, insulted, and alienated in important relationships. In intersubjective terms, others wanted to control the CF individual, to change who she was, and to demand that she be more similar to them. Others wanted to subjugate her so that her choice would no longer threaten them, placing her in the category of "not-me" (Sullivan, 1953, pp.162–164).

Masking the CF part of a woman's identity can be interpreted as an attempt to avoid having to acknowledge the existence of more than one possibility. The idea that someone could be happy without children can be intimidating because it suggests multiplicity. In this context, the old social order has less power to restrict; choice itself emerges as an option. For those who cannot tolerate closeness to someone radically different from them, that multiplicity can be unbearable. For them, the solution might be to cancel the validity of the CF woman's difference and label her as deviant. In that, her subjectivity is denied and she becomes an object used to restore a sense of control and safety for others. As a further result, the wealth of alternatives is decreased, and with it, for those accepting the default path, so reduced is any anxiety stemming from the need to acknowledge that one's mode of operation is not necessarily the best and only one. Reduced as well is the need to mourn the loss of the unchosen option. In other words, denying the legitimacy of childfreedom prevents the narcissistic injury from the loss of omnipotence.

Indeed, the women in this study disclosed that they had to continuously negotiate whether to mask their childfreedom or demand others acknowledge their identity. They routinely had to decide between honesty and self-censorship when talking about parenthood, feeling hesitant to be open and honest, anticipating that others would try to impose the notion that parenting was the only legitimate choice. In fact, even in a group with a majority of CF friends, participants stated that they evaded the topic if they feared the discussion would make non-CF people uncomfortable:

S2: I have other friends that are CF, but as we all usually hang out together, even [with] the over-sensitive future mom, we tend to censor ourselves.

S7: I have a few close friends who are hugely supportive, and I can be very open with them, but not with most.

S10: I also want to add that communicating online with other childfree women is important to me since I know no other childfree women offline.

S15: [My partner and I] have often felt isolated because of this and spent time with only each other. That used to bother me before finding other CF people online. Simply having that connection to other like-minded people has helped me be more comfortable [as] just the two of us.

Even when participants initially felt they could communicate their preferences, they reported that close friendships, especially with other women, changed or were even lost when those friends started having children. When people around them became parents, the CF women started feeling alienated, judged, and even pitied. Talking about childfreedom became off limits, and bonds that had previously been central to their social lives were lost. Sometimes this was due to logistical reasons, such as parents' schedules changing. Sometimes parents became so absorbed in their parental roles that they were unable to make room for non-parents in their lives. Parents no longer wanted to engage in activities they had previously enjoyed; they became offended by topics that were considered legitimate and even funny before they had children; and they began criticizing the CF woman even if they had previously been supportive of her choice. Although parents felt entitled to talk about their pregnancies and children without ever feeling that they were imposing or offensive, CF women did not enjoy the same latitude in discussing their reproductive preferences.

It appears that when some women make the choice to follow the path of motherhood, they are no longer able to contain the CF choice made by their female peers. This process is painful and leaves CF women on the outskirts of their social circles. The capacity for creating mutual space is often lost, leaving no room for the coexistence of both options. In many cases, the relationship is not just altered, becoming less comfortable or enjoyable; it might foment hostility or simply end. This could be traumatizing for the CF woman, leaving her anxious when yet another female friend becomes pregnant:

S25: The first CF forum I signed up for was a little over two years ago. Two good friends had disappeared after I mentioned to them that I was planning to get sterilized. These two had been my pillars of support through some serious family drama some years prior—and seeing them disappear because of this was unsettling, disappointing, depressing, and a whole lot of other things.

S2: People who, a few years ago, were totally supportive now seem to get offended at the drop of a hat. Now that they are having babies, they take it personally that I haven't changed my stance on the subject, even though I have expressed nothing but joy and encouragement for them.

Another type of close relationships affected by childfreedom was romantic relationships. Having a CF life partner was an important aspect of the women's lives. Sometimes one's significant other was the only other CF person with whom they had an ongoing close relationship. Some CF women realized that they could not become romantically involved with someone who wanted children. Those participants looked for a CF partner because the intention to have children was a "deal breaker":

> S1: I first found a CF online community when my (then-) husband and I were deciding whether to split up because he wanted kids. The community gave me support and helped me make the oh-so-right choice to end the marriage.

Childfreedom remained misunderstood and unfamiliar to most people these subjects met. Potential partners thought that they could change the CF women's minds or that having children from previous relationships "didn't count." Having to explain the meaning of being childfree became part of the dating experience for the participants. Additionally, just being childfree was not enough to ensure compatibility. Still, when the other person was equally adamant about wanting to remain childfree, there was a mutual starting point that gave the relationship a better chance of succeeding:

> S20: I realize that the question of having children is so critical for me, that I could never share my life with someone who doesn't feel as strongly as I do about it. My current partner and I actually bonded over the decision not to have kids. This came up in a random conversation when we first met, and this was a central reason in our decision to start dating. I recommend anyone who deals with this question to target men or women who are consciously CF—that's another advantage of online forums.

Third construct: CF-dedicated websites are powerful tools of communication, support, information, and socialization

> Thus when you congratulate yourself for having met someone who speaks the same language as you, you do not mean that you encounter each other in the discourse of everyman, but that you are united to that person by a particular way of speaking.
>
> *(Lacan, 2006/1953, p. 246, paragraph 298)*

The women in my study reported a marked difference in their experience of themselves, others, and the space between them and others once they found other CF individuals online. Aside from finding like-minded, similar others in terms of childfreedom, they also discovered others who were different from them. Each woman had the opportunity to rejoice in meeting "someone who speaks her language," as well as grapple with the realization that other CF individuals were separate from her and different—they were subjects. The powerful influence of CF-dedicated websites on these women's sense of self-actualization and sense of ownership over their choice was remarkable. In addition, the participants reported diverse patterns of online activity and involvement in different subareas of interest within the CF online world. The rich personal and communal experience online was often in direct opposition to the restricted and superficial interactions about childfreedom they had in real life.

One unique aspect of finding information online was the exposure to CF lingo. Language facilitated a sense of community and culture that they could identify with. Knowing that others referred to not parenting by using the word *free* rather than *less* was refreshing:

> S14: I only learned of the term "childfree" about five years ago by coming across a childfree website. In that respect, the very vocabulary I use with respect to my reproductive choice has changed dramatically. I love and stress the FREE in childfree, for as I have learned through online forums, we are not "less" anything in our lives.

This chapter cannot, unfortunately, accommodate a discussion of signifiers, signified, and the difference between what is psychosocial, psychological, or biological (Rapoport, 2010). However, the playfulness of trying on a new word, of claiming language in the process of demanding that one's identity would be included in the shared reality of a dyad of a group, is fascinating. The joy and self-affirmation mentioned by this participant call for an exploration of the thirst to be known and to the desire to examine what is in the words used by the CF milieu. No doubt, such an exploration will reveal that the signifier cannot truly contain that which it is signifying, as it never can, especially when attempting to signify "the other."

In intersubjective terms, the internet offered CF women a space in which they were able to explore aspects of themselves that were otherwise hidden. Even when they were open about their childfreedom outside of the internet, the participants were "the other," and their environment did not allow for variations or nuances in their identities. Finding a community in which they were the majority and their childfreedom was accepted and even assumed was empowering in and of itself. In that atmosphere the participants could examine the subtleties within their identity, measuring themselves from a position of twinship (Kohut, 1971), that is, a relationship with someone like them with whom they identified. Twinship offered a connection rooted in similarity rather than in contrast. The women were also able to be mirrored by others who accepted their qualities and choices. According to Kohut, such twinship and mirroring relationships were both needed for the development of their authentic self. Offline and in person, most others mirrored the CF women as peculiar at best. Often the mirrored reflection was a distorted picture, portraying childfreedom as abnormal, sick, and unnatural. Online, however, that aspect of themselves was not only accepted but celebrated:

> S20: The first time I joined an online childfree forum I simply felt elated. I expected a group of people feeling united by a sense of persecution and loneliness, conceiving of themselves as freaks and misfits, and I found a lively and cheerful community whose members basically conducted themselves as if they are the norm and those who wish to have children are those whose actions are unfathomable and even morally questionable. This is what I love the most about the forum in which I'm a member—the feeling of complete normality that governs it. We may be exceptional in our families and in our workplaces, but in the discussion forums our choice of a childfree life is the only one taken for granted, the only one that makes sense. It is so liberating and refreshing.

Communication with other CF individuals had positively influenced the participants' identity by elevating their self-esteem, self-understanding, and confidence. They felt that their CF identities were strengthened, instilling them with a sense of self-worth and pride. Before they found the CF websites, many of them were prone to feel shame and confusion. Conversing with like-minded people helped them feel dignified and happy in their choice:

> S17: I'm a better rounded person because of the online childfree community.

> S14: Writing about childfreedom has given me a fuller understanding of what that means and how it permeates my life.

> S26: I know myself better, my identity is stronger, and I feel confident in so many ways.

> S8: The online community has helped me SO much in accepting that I really don't want them [children], and, like others, has helped me be a little more vocal and comfortable with the decision.

Relationships with others and self-presentation in real-life communities were also influenced. The women in the study felt that writing and reading online enhanced their ability to talk about their choice, providing them with articulated arguments and organized frames of reference, whereas before they only had their inner feelings as a guide. Participants felt more courageous when it came to disclosing their CF status to non-CF individuals and a new sense of confidence when they were questioned and challenged. Having clarity regarding the meaning of childfreedom and how it manifested specifically for each of them helped them intelligibly communicate about it even with unsympathetic others:

> S17: Knowing that I'm not alone in my feelings towards not wanting children has given me the confidence to answer questions by parents. I felt a sense of

empowerment coming clean about how I have felt my whole life and that I should never feel guilty about my choice.

Humor was another aspect of communal discourse that was mentioned by women in this study. Humor is known to be a positive and powerful defense mechanism, a mature tool for coping with difficulties and conflicts (Freud, 1936/1946). The internet offered a variety of cartoons, jokes, and witty blog posts dedicated to the humorous side of being childfree, giving the participants strength or at least a different perspective when facing the difficult social reality of being childfree. It helped them maintain a positive stance and reduced their hostility towards others who criticized them, especially when the laughing matter was taboo in other settings:

> S16: I continue to get joy out of it. I love laughing with them at things that society will not allow me to otherwise laugh at.

Although the freedom to vent and laugh, often at the expense of parents or children, was appreciated by participants, many mentioned that the humor sometimes amounted to too much hostility. The forums tended to be rejecting of other CF individuals as well, for example, those with rightwing leanings or strong religious convictions. Apparently, the majority of CF individuals identified as liberal or even radical on issues outside of childfreedom. This anecdotal information is not yet supported by in-depth demographic studies about CF individuals or studies that compare CF and non-CF individuals in terms of demographics or beliefs. It would be interesting to explore these dimensions of the CF community in the future.

Aside from noting that politically conservative or religious individuals were less welcome in the forums they frequented, women in this study also noted that those who were unsure of themselves sometimes felt that there was no room for their lack of conviction:

> S4: Unfortunately, there are some online CF communities that are very hostile towards those who decide to have children. I find this discouraging, as the hostility towards my CF opinions was what brought me to CF forums and the online community in the first place.

> S20: What I would have been like as a mother, what such a life would entail, what I might be missing out on, etc.—I never felt comfortable sharing that in an online forum.

Although not all websites fit all CF individuals, special aspects of the internet were important to the participants. Anonymity, accessibility, ability to walk away from unpleasant interactions, ability to take time and word oneself carefully, using writing versus talking, and tremendous variety were all mentioned as important internet communication qualities valued by the CF women in the study.

Fourth construct: For CF women, the personal is political

The fourth and last construct presented in this discussion addresses the political aspects of childfreedom. The construct's title is drawn from the feminist mantra "the personal is political," a phrase attributed to different writers of the second feminist wave. Although its exact origin might not be clear, its meaning is important. The phrase indicates that people's personal decisions and private conduct have profound political implications. When a woman makes a decision regarding work, family, dress code, or choice of language, she is choosing to express her acceptance or rejection of social norms. This is, of course, a simplistic view as the choice to perform similar acts can have different meanings for different people. For example, choosing to get married could be a defiant act if family or society disapprove of the pairing; marriage could also be an act of submission to the most rigid and oppressive social norms.

Benjamin (1988) discusses the social and political implications of her intersubjective theory. She claims that in US society, the narcissistic fear of surrendering one's power over other humans is the source of political, social, and personal cruelty and oppression. Our society idealizes the father-image, which includes aspects of individualism, separation, and domination and devalues the mother-image of connectedness, closeness, and dependency. However, both needs exist in every human, regardless of their sex and gender. The masculine image requires men to maintain rigid separation from others, and in doing so, reject their need for connectedness and closeness. If they address these "feminine" needs, they will have to acknowledge their identification with the maternal. They, therefore, can only tolerate rigid definitions that will simplify their relationships with others. Such definitions help maintain hierarchy by engendering a sense of omnipotence among those who believe they are fitting the only permissible role in the absence of choices. Other options can be classified as deviant or in some cases rejected altogether or even declared illegal. Allowing others to be different but similar, close but separate, independent but needed is impossible when one depends on narcissism and a fantasy of omnipotence in order to maintain a coherent sense of self.

However, the other continues to exist. The participants expressed a desire to contribute to the growing knowledge about CF women, adding that they wanted their voices to be heard. They hoped to dispel misconceptions and misunderstanding, helping non-CF individuals, policymakers, religious leaders, and mental health professionals to see childfreedom for what it really is: a diverse and rich community with culture and values, made up of individuals who cannot be fully understood or explained by their childfreedom alone. They hoped that social acceptance would reduce the resentment and bitterness some CF individuals felt while inviting people who might benefit from CF life to entertain it as an option:

> S8: On a less realistic note, I'd like to think that research like this is a big step in changing the way people talk to and about the childfree and the choice

to reproduce. It would be nice if people asked "are you going to have kids?" instead of "when are you going to have kids?" and say "If you have kids" instead of "when you have kids." If the dreaded "bingo" went away tomorrow, it would make life so much easier.

S13: I'm hoping to bring attention to the cruel and dismissive remarks ("bingos" and otherwise) we childfree experience on the Web and real life, and to dispel the myths behind the most common bingos. I hope research shows that we are just as human as the next woman, that there is nothing missing or wrong with us, and that parenthood is not for everyone nor should it be.

S15: I am eager to see more exposure of the experiences of those living childfree. My hope is that as information about CF living grows, that more young people will take the time to consider the choice to have children rather than just having kids without thought. So many people are brainwashed into thinking it's a rite of passage . . .

Most participants talked about being discriminated against or misunderstood, and those who did not feel this way still mentioned incidents in which they were met with bewilderment and disbelief. All participants reported that other CF individuals they met online constantly talked about the discrimination, insults, and rejection they felt. This was especially true when the women were in their mid-20s to mid-30s, if they had recently married, or if they lived in smaller, more rural locations. Participants were called weird, psychologically impaired, and selfish. Others were told that they would regret their choice, that they would "go to hell," and that they were juvenile and sick. They often felt that they had to defend their choice and that others did not believe and even pitied them:

S22: Put it this way, I've never had a childfree person accuse me of being psychologically disturbed because I don't like and don't want kids. I've had that from a parent, though. Now tell me, how do you have a reasoned discussion with that attitude?

S22: I worked for a US company for a while and was told to not mention anything about my CF views to the higher ups as this could be "career limiting." Throw in being an atheist, then it seemed I'd be making Charles Manson look like Snow White. It's a pretty sad state of affairs that something that's unimportant to my job could have a negative impact. To me, that's blatant discrimination and bigotry.

S25: When I got into my late twenties, the pressure mounted, and when I got married, I thought I had entered an alternate universe. The preoccupation of others with my uterus and what I was to do with it and my life was unreal.

The social hardships of CF women were similar to those of other minorities. Much like other minorities, they had limited social space, they were minimized to that one aspect of themselves, were robbed of legitimacy, and were constantly challenged. Some women made the comparison between being childfree and being LGBTQ. They referred to disclosing the CF status as "coming out," mentioning the potential social and professional price to pay for being childfree:

> S26: I've often made the comparison to sexual minorities: we need peer support as well, and we need to hear that there are other people like us. This is no handicap, on the contrary. Sometimes I wonder the thoughts of those people who are childfree but never communicate through these forums or other way online, and never discuss their childfreedom. What do they think of themselves? I even think they might lack something, as they don't have the CF "culture" in which to discuss various things with others.

Allowing others to be different requires a capacity to tolerate pain because seeing other options puts a spotlight on one's limitations. This, according to Benjamin (1988), is true on the individual level, the community level, and the state and country level. Throughout history, the inability to tolerate the "other" and the need to make "me" the only option have pushed nations to wipe out other groups, to deny human rights, and to demand conformity explicitly and implicitly. Benjamin states that both patriarchal hegemony and some feminist worldviews demand that women be mothers and color the maternal role as the source of feminine power. If a woman is not a mother, the patriarchal social order is in danger. Also, the unique power of reproduction as a defining symbol of female supremacy is threatened when capable individuals live fulfilling lives without reproducing. However, the participants of this study conveyed that having childfreedom as an equal option will not ruin humanity or take away feminine power. In fact, it will allow for the definition of what is human to be expanded and offer greater choice for women.

For example, some participants expressed moral and political concerns, saying that while the pronatalist culture ostensibly focuses on children, it actually centers on the *concept of future children* rather than already living children who are in need. When thinking of the consumption of resources created by every Western child in comparison to children in Third World countries, the moral implications of pronatalism in industrial countries is disconcerting. Promoting motherhood as the preferred choice for everyone is actually a failure to recognize the needs of millions of other, less visible children in communities whose resources are often abused by Western countries.

Indeed, public and political forces are involved in reproduction. That involvement manifests in campaigns around abortion rights and access, controversy over economic entitlements, workplace policies and employment benefits, and religious freedoms. Because the CF choice is not valued or even accepted in many cases, CF women suffer discrimination both socially and legally. For example, sterilization laws in many places do not support women's desire to cement their childfreedom (Richie, 2013).

> S26: I'm even more interested in judicial issues because of the sterilization law. So, I have a really increased interest in information about anything that vaguely has something to do with childfreedom and other issues, which I feel belong to my identity and are important to me. I've joined the CF association we have in Finland, and I've had my Essure done.

Religion is another public sphere that supports reproduction in ways that might erase the legitimacy of childfreedom. Participants expressed their need to conceal their decision from religious relatives, reporting a sense of alienation from religious communities. This can explain, though not justify, the intolerance religious CF women experienced in certain online forums:

> S21: I'll never forget when the priest told me that, if I quit my job, stayed home, and had babies, things between me and my ex would be OK and he would "change" and be nice to me. I wasn't stupid enough to buy that line. Not from a man who doesn't even have sex himself!

The political and cultural implications of their private choice created a higher level of interest and awareness to other social issues among the CF women in this study. They noticed that women's rights issues were often limited to "mothers' rights," leaving younger women and CF women on the outskirts of what was considered politically relevant. They became concerned with the rights of other minorities, such as the LGBTQ community and others.

> S26: I've started to become interested in human rights in other areas as well. Free thinking, atheism, gay rights, and equality in general are important to me. It is not just that I know for sure I don't want children; it has affected a lot more.

> S29: I stayed active for a good while. The political climate helped a lot—every day, it seemed like there was something new to be outraged about.

> S22: I guess I should really be looking for a site which is more of a political platform, rather than just a support forum.

Clinical implications

My research touched on a very specific subgroup within childfreedom. The women I interviewed were all internet users and their demographic background proved to be quite homogenous. CF individuals in other communities and from different backgrounds are out there, although they did not volunteer for my research sample. Despite this limitation, the body of work presented in the chapter could be used to make some recommendations. People who express a desire not to have children often feel offended and rejected if others assume that they should actually have children. Exploring both wanting and not wanting children with impartial curiosity would allow people to make parenthood choice formed more by personal desire than social expectations. Those who do not want to have children would understand that it is a choice and would not be pushed to assume a role that could negatively impact their lives and, potentially, the lives of their future children. Moreover, those leaning toward becoming parents would also understand that they, too, are making a choice, not merely fulfilling a biological or social imperative, and in doing so may glean the validity of the alternative they are foregoing.

In addition, psychotherapists might benefit from being informed about the CF online culture and what it offers to women in particular. Any mental health provider might encounter a woman who either identifies as CF, or is currently debating whether or not to live CF, or is unaware that this option exists but would benefit from considering it. The pride, joy, and confidence that this study's participants gained from their online interactions on CF websites were remarkable. Women who feel defective or abnormal because they have been told for years that they are unfeminine, sick, wrong, or childish might find a community that will normalize their identity online, especially in conservative areas, during peak reproductive ages, or when a romantic relationship has been consolidated. Awareness of the tremendous pronatalist pressures could enrich treatment and help CF individuals feel heard.

Another clinical implication of this study is the powerful and positive effect of groups. The social group of CF peers could aid women in accepting their own CF status and becoming proud and self-aware. Therapists might consider group therapy for CF clients, many of whom may not even realize there are others who explicitly share their desire to live childfree. In areas where such a group might be hard to facilitate, the internet can provide a tool for peer support. Therapists who are adventurous enough could potentially facilitate some group discussions online and even run a group with the aid of a webcam and microphone, introducing CF individuals to each other, while letting them know that childfreedom is accepted by their mental health professionals.

Note

1 My translation from Hebrew—Avivi.

References

Agrillo, C., & Nelini, C. (2008). Childfree by choice: A review. *Journal of Cultural Geography*, *25*(3), 347–363.

Aron, L. (2001). *A meeting of minds: Mutuality in psychoanalysis*. Hillsdale, NJ: The Analytic Press.

Auerbach, C.F., & Silverstein, L.B. (2003). *Qualitative data*. New York, NY: New York University Press.

Avivi, A. (2012). *Childfree women's online discussions of the choice to not have children: A qualitative study*. Doctoral dissertation. Retrieved from https://www.academia.edu/14178557/ Childfree_Women_s_Online_Discussions_of_the_Choice_to_Not_Have_Children

Bartlett, J. (1995). *Will you be a mother? Women who choose to say no*. New York, NY: New York University Press.

Basten, S. (2009). Voluntary childlessness and being childfree. Retrieved from http://www. spi.ox.ac.uk/research/oxford-centre-for-population-research/papers-to-download.html

Benjamin, J. (1987). The decline of the Oedipus complex. In J.M. Broughton (Ed.), *Critical theories of psychological development* (pp. 211–244). New York, NY: Plenum Press.

Benjamin, J. (1988). *The bonds of love*. New York, NY: Pantheon Books.

Benjamin, J. (1995). *Like subjects, love objects*. New Haven, CT: Yale University Press.

Benjamin, J. (2004). Beyond doer and done to: An intersubjective view of thirdness. *Psychoanalytic Quarterly, 73*(1), 5–46.

Boyd, R. (1989). Minority status and childlessness. *Sociological Inquiry, 59*(3), 331–342.

Calhoun, L., & Selby, J. (1980). Voluntary childlessness, involuntary childlessness, and having children: A study of social perceptions (Book review). *Family Relations, 29*(2), 181.

Callan, V.J. (1983). Factors affecting early and late deciders of voluntary childlessness. *Journal of Social Psychology, 119*, 261–268.

Callan, V.J. (1984). Voluntary childlessness: Early articulator and postponing couples. *Journal of Biosocial Science, 16*, 501–509.

Carrol, L. (2012). *The baby matrix: Why freeing our minds from outmoded thinking about parenthood & reproduction will create a better world*. Live True Books. Retrieved from http//live truebooks.com

Chodorow, N.J. (1978). *The reproduction of mothering: Psychoanalysis and the sociology of gender*. Berkeley, CA: University of California Press.

Chodorow, N.J. (2003). "Too late": Ambivalence about motherhood, choice, and time. *Journal of the American Psychoanalytic Association, 51*(4), 1181–1198.

Coffey, K. (2005). Selected factors related to a childfree woman's decision to remain childfree and her self-identified sexual orientation. *Dissertation Abstracts International, 66*.

Daniluk, J.C., & Herman, A. (1983). Children: Yes or no, a decision-making program for women. *Personnel & Guidance Journal, 62*(4), 240–243.

DeLyser, G. (2011). At midlife, intentionally childfree women and their experiences of regret. *Clinical Social Work Journal, 40*, 66–74.

Donat, O. (2007). Split pronatalism: The choice of life without children in Israel. Master thesis, Tel Aviv University at Ramat Aviv, Israel. Personal communication.

Donat, O. (2011). *Taking a choice: Being childfree in Israel*. Tel-Aviv: Miskal—Yediot Ahronot books and Chemed books.

Durham, W. (2008). The rules-based process of revealing/concealing the family planning decisions of voluntarily child-free couples: A communication privacy management perspective. *Communication Studies, 59*(2), 132–147.

Durham, W., & Braithwaite, D. (2009). Communication privacy management within the family planning trajectories of voluntarily child-free couples. *Journal of Family Communication, 9*(1), 43–65.

Fast, I. (1984). *Gender identity: A differentiation model*. Hillsdale, NJ: The Analytic Press.

Freud, A. (1936/1946). *The ego and the mechanisms of defense*. New York, NY: International Universities Press.

Gerson, S. (2004). The relational unconscious: A core element of intersubjectivity, thirdness, and clinical process. *Psychoanalytic Quarterly, 73*(1), 63–99.

Giles, D., Shaw, R., & Morgan, W. (2009). Representations of voluntary childlessness in the UK press, 1990–2008. *Journal of Health Psychology, 14*(8), 1218–1228.

Gold, J., & Wilson, J. (2002). Legitimizing the child-free family: The role of the family counselor. *The Family Journal, 10*(1), 70–74.

Haraway, D. (1985). A manifesto for Cyborgs: Science, technology, and socialist feminism in the 1980s. *Socialist Review, 15*(2), 65–108.

Hird, M.J. (2003). Vacant wombs: Feminist challenges to psychoanalytic theories of childless women. *Feminist Review, 75*(1), 5–19.

Hird, M.J. (2004). Naturally queer. *Feminist Theory, 5*(1), 85–89.

Hird, M., & Abshoff, K. (2000). Women without children: A contradiction in terms? *Journal of Comparative Family Studies, 31*(3), 347–366.

Ireland, M.S. (1993). *Reconceiving motherhood: Separating motherhood from female identity.* New York, NY: Guilford Press.

Kenkel, W. (1985). The desire for voluntary childlessness among low-income youth. *Journal of Marriage & Family, 47*(2), 509–512.

Kohut, H. (1971). *The analysis of the self.* New York, NY: International Universities Press.

Knafo, D. (2009). Castration and Medusa: Orlan's art on the cutting edge. *Studies in Gender & Sexuality, 10*(3), 142–158.

La Mastro, V. (2001). Childless by choice? Attributions and attitudes concerning family size. *Social Behavior and Personality, 29*, 231–244.

Lacan, J. (2006/1953). The function and field of speech and language in psychoanalysis. In B. Fink (Trans & Ed.), *Ecrits: The first complete edition in English* (pp. 197–268). New York, NY: Norton.

Lampman, C., & Dowling-Guyer, S. (1995). Attitudes toward voluntary and involuntary childlessness. *Basic and Applied Social Psychology, 17*(1–2), 213–222.

Letherby, G. (2002). Childless and bereft? Stereotypes and realities in relation to "voluntary" and "involuntary" childlessness and womanhood. *Sociological Inquiry, 72*(1), 7–20.

Mcquillan, J., Greil, A., Shreffler, K., Wonch-Hill, P., Gentzler, K., & Hathcoat, J. (2012). Does the reason matter? Variation in childlessness concerns among U.S. women. *Journal of Marriage and Family, 74*(5), 1166–1181.

Mollen, D. (2006). Voluntarily childfree women: Experiences and counseling considerations. *Journal of Mental Health Counseling, 28*(3), 269–282.

Monte, L., & Ellis, R. (2012). Fertility of Women in the United States: 2012—Population Characteristics. *U.S. Department of Commerce Economics and Statistics Administration U.S. CENSUS BUREAU.* Retrieved from http://www.census.gov

Ogden, T.H. (1994). The analytical third: Working with intersubjective clinical facts. *International Journal of Psychoanalysis, 75*(1), 3–20.

Park, K. (2002). Stigma management among the voluntary childless. *Sociological Perspectives, 45*(1), 21–45.

Pelton, S.L., & Hertlein, K.M. (2011). A proposed life cycle for voluntary childfree couples. *Journal of Feminist Family Therapy: An International Forum, 23*(1), 39–53.

Peterson, H., & Engwall, K. (2013). Silent bodies: Childfree women's gendered and embodied experiences. *European Journal of Women's Studies, 20*(4), 376–389.

Rapoport, E. (2010). Bisexuality: The undead (m)other of psychoanalysis. *Psychoanalysis, Culture & Society, 15*(1), 70–83. http://dx.doi.org/10.1057/pcs.2009.31

Richie, C. (2013). Voluntary sterilization for childfree women: Understanding patient profiles, evaluating accessibility, examining legislation. *The Hastings Center Report, 43*(6), 36–44.

Rowlands, I., & Lee, C. (2006). Choosing to have children or choosing to be childfree: Australian students' attitudes towards the decisions of heterosexual and lesbian women. *Australian Psychologist, 41*(1), 55–59.

Russell, M., Hey, R.N., Thoen, G.A., & Walz, T. (1978). The choice of childlessness: A workshop model. *Family Coordinator, 27*(2), 179–183.

Safer, J. (1996). *Beyond motherhood: Choosing a life without children.* New York, NY: Pocket Books.

Scott, L. (2009). *Two is enough.* Berkeley, CA. Seal Press.

Seccombe, K. (1991). Assessing the costs and benefits of children: Gender comparisons among childfree husbands and wives. *Journal of Marriage & the Family, 53*(1), 191–202.

Somers, M. (1993). A comparison of voluntarily childfree adults and parents. *Journal of Marriage & Family, 55*(3), 643–650.

Sullivan, H.S. (1953). *Conceptions of modern psychiatry: The first William Alanson White memorial lectures.* New York, NY: Norton.

Sullivan, N., & Stryker, S. (2009). King's member, queen's body: Transsexual surgery, self-demand amputation, and the somatechnics of sovereign power. In N. Sullivan & S. Murray (Eds.), *Somatechnics: Queering the technologisation of bodies* (pp. 49–64). Farnham, UK: Ashgate Publishing.

West. K. (2006). The breeder bingo card. *The seven deadly sinners: A seven headed art beast.* Retrieved from http://7deadlysinners.typepad.com/sinners/2006/04/breeder_bingo_c.html

8

A PERFECT BIRTH

The Birth Rights Movement and the idealization of birth

Helena Vissing

I grew up in Denmark where the midwifery model is integrated into the universal health care system. I therefore never experienced the chasm between mainstream obstetrics and the natural childbirth movement that I encountered after moving to California. I was completing my doctoral studies in clinical psychology when I became pregnant with my first child. Like many women in Los Angeles, I educated myself about pregnancy and childbirth and discovered the vast field of natural childbirth. At the same time, I was specializing in psychoanalysis and motherhood psychology, and I was intrigued by the ideologies and public debates surrounding the Birth Rights Movement. I was, and am, particularly intrigued by the intensity with which expecting mothers and birth workers express their beliefs in the revolutionary potentials of birth, privately as well as in the public realm. My training in psychoanalytic theory and practice inspired me to delve into the deeper layers of natural childbirth philosophy.

The Birth Rights Movement has expanded with fierce haste over the last decades. With the popularity of parenting philosophies like Attachment Parenting and the home birth movement, birth choices and rights are ubiquitous questions for expecting parents. We are seeing an upsurge of intense advocacy for women's reproductive rights, especially on the question of birth choices. In the Birth Rights Movement, birth is seen as a decisive moment in a woman's life and is viewed as having crucial impact on the baby and the attachment process. Mainstream obstetrics and hospital birth practices are fiercely criticized and understood as oppressive, profit-oriented, and inhumane.

The Birth Rights Movement began in the 1970s in opposition to the way the obstetric system in the United States had developed in an industrialized and medicalized direction (Jones, 2012). Interestingly, this rise occurred around the same time as the shift from the biological reductionism that writers like Chodorow (1978) sparked in feminist psychoanalysis, which finally broke with Freud's one-sex theory and opened up for describing the female in relation to her own body rather than the male's (Balsam, 2012). According to Jones (2012), the critique of industrialized labor presented in the Birth Rights Movement actually emerged within second-wave feminism and inspired feminist thinkers. The new focus on topics like motherhood, reproductive rights, and sexuality that emerged with second-wave feminism entailed a critique of the industrialization of birth: the medical system was seen as patriarchal structural oppression (Gaskin, 2011).

However, the philosophy of natural childbirth had its own trajectory, and a feminist counter-critique developed, which focuses on the implications of the idealization of natural childbirth (Jones, 2012). Given that psychoanalytic theory has been slow to engage and integrate feminist thinking, it is not surprising that one finds few references to the Birth Rights Movement in the psychoanalytic literature. Nonetheless, I believe that psychoanalytic theory has insights to offer in understanding the movement. In this chapter, I will engage these strands of critique through psychoanalytic thinking. I suggest that the Birth Rights Movement idealizes birth through the use of bio-essentialism and subjective accounts of birth in a way that does not thoroughly embrace the negative intrapsychic aspects, which may reproduce a controlling ideology of female reproduction. The birth experience is prescribed the utmost importance, and all subsequent parenting is seen in light of this philosophy of birth. I will begin by presenting the Birth Rights Movement and its philosophy and then unfold my analysis and discussion through the feminist and psychoanalytic literature.

The Birth Rights Movement

Over the last 70 years, industrialized societies have seen significant improvements in childbirth safety and a marked shift to obstetric methods and philosophy (Tew, 1990). The family home was the usual place of childbirth until the start of the twentieth century, but already by the late 1960s, birth had become almost exclusively a hospital event (Chard & Richards, 1992). A shift so historically abrupt yielded critical reactions. Interestingly, the inspiration for the Birth Rights Movement originally came from the works of obstetricians Fernand Lamaze (Karmel, 1959) and Grantly Dick-Read (1933, 1942) who are considered pioneers in the field of psychoprophylactic preparation for childbirth. They introduced a new approach to childbirth preparation that included education, breathing exercises, and conditioning. Using positive suggestion, psychoprophylactic techniques were developed from hypnotism (Datta, 2001).

In the 1960s and 1970s, grassroot movements and communal living created pockets of counter-culture to the established medicalized obstetric system. A central person is Ina May Gaskin, who headed the development of an independent midwifery model in a Tennessee commune called The Farm from 1971 onwards. Her writings and advocacy have significantly influenced the Birth Rights Movement. Her first book, *Spiritual Midwifery* (Gaskin, 1975/2002), introduced a mindset toward childbirth characterized by its focus on health; prevention; minimal intervention; integration of emotional, sexual, and spiritual aspects of childbirth; and a more egalitarian relationship between patient and provider.

From the 1970s and onward, new approaches to pregnancy and childbirth like Gaskin's grew and became organized; a notable example is the Lamaze Institute (Jones, 2012). The movement has also developed into academic organizations; for example, The Association for Pre and Perinatal Psychology and Health formed in 1983, which seeks to "educate professionals and the public, worldwide, that a baby's experience of conception, pregnancy, and birth creates lifelong consequences for individuals, families, and society" (2015). These organizations have indeed succeeded in impacting childbirth practices and obstetrics. Childbirth practices have been reformed to include partner-involvement and growth in midwife-led units (Jones, 2012). Drapkin-Lyerly (2012) has pointed out how the natural childbirth philosophy has influenced childbirth practices positively in two main ways: in its promotion of birth as non-pathological, which has brought attention to the harms of routine medical interventions, and in its emphasis on birth as a social process imbued with meaning.

Today, the Birth Rights Movement is a panoply of activist groups and organizations. The debates surrounding childbirth take place in academic contexts, in practitioner/activist communities, and in the public realm, namely in online forums and on social media. From 2008 onward, several documentaries and publications have sparked an upsurge of interest in birth rights, the natural childbirth philosophy, and activism. The documentaries *The Business of Being Born* by Abby Epstein (2008) and *Orgasmic Birth: The Best-Kept Secret* by Debra Pascali-Bonaro (2008) are examples of idealizing approaches to childbirth. Birth is presented as a sensual and orgasmic event that women have been too suppressed or anxious to realize. A number of organizations have been created with focus on legislative advocacy, including Human Rights in Childbirth, which was established in 2012 with the mission to "clarify and promote the fundamental human rights of pregnant people." The motivation for this advocacy is the understanding that basic human rights, like the rights to informed consent, to refuse medical treatment, to equal treatment, to health, to privacy, and to life, are violated when a woman's agency in childbirth is not secured (Universal Rights, 2015).

Birth rights and ideology

Despite the influences of the Birth Rights Movement over the past decades, we continue to see a significant increase in the medicalization of childbirth as evidenced by increasing Caesarean section rates (Jones, 2012; Malacrida & Boulton, 2014). Activists in the Birth Rights Movement believe that the issue of human rights in birth is threatened to a degree that is ultimately destructive for humankind. In an editorial from *Midwifery Today*, founder Jan Tritten states: "As we all know, nearly all motherbaby [sic] human rights are being egregiously violated around the entire world in the pregnancy and birth process, the time miracles should be happening" (2010, p. 5).

Birth rights and the natural childbirth philosophy are one side in a belligerent ideological fight with the established obstetric system. In the backdrop of decades of oppression of women's birth choices, birth becomes a matter of victory or failure in the Birth Rights Movement. A woman's individual desires and struggles to achieve her reproductive goals become political matters. If a woman perceives her birth experience negatively because her plans and wishes for the birth were changed or hindered, she may regard it as "failed." The birth experience holds the potential for victory, both on a personal and a political level. I assert that the idealization of birth is an illusory solution to the intense boundary challenge of reproduction. On the individual level, it serves to protect against anxieties about the body. On a cultural level, this defense fuels the ideological fight. When the rightness of birth choices is debated in a heated atmosphere, it happens at the expense of maternal subjectivity and emotional integration. Mothers' subjective experiences of their reproductive rights are used as testimonies in current discourses on birth rights and thereby become underpinnings in an ideological debate (Vissing, 2014).

In the tension between the Birth Rights Movement and mainstream obstetrics, a woman's reproductive rights and choices become highly charged political issues at the expense of her personal agency, subjectivity, and autonomy. Paradoxically, the current developments of the Birth Rights Movement have reproduced a culture where women's reproductive capacities are still political and ideological issues at the expense of individual rights. In this chapter, I will examine what happens with birth rights advocacy when birth and women's reproductive capacities are idealized. Can the Birth Rights Movement advocate for women's reproductive rights without idealizing birth and throwing maternal subjectivity out with the bath water?

The idea that a completely wondrous, ecstatic, and fulfilling birth experience is not only possible, but the truer nature of the female body's capacities is the epiphanic message in Orgasmic Birth. From a psychoanalytic perspective, this libidinal focus is intriguing and calls for exploration. For instance, less ideal birth experiences are attributed to hospital obstetrics and lack of a caring and sensually attuning atmosphere for the mother. Birth in and of itself is considered orgasmic in nature, if only the true nature of birth is invited and accommodated for. Along with this idealization of birth, we see signs of splitting. Death and the destructive aspects of birth are denied through an exclusive focus on the sensual, gratifying, and fulfilling aspects of birth. Women's ambivalence and negative feelings about birth are not integrated but attributed to external influence such as obstetrics and hospital maternal health care. Insights from psychoanalysis may offer a deeper understanding of the issues at play when there is idealization and splitting in relation to childbirth. We also see developments in feminist psychoanalysis that agree with the focus on sensuality and erotic empowerment in relation to childbirth, including writings by Balsam (2012) and Holmes (2008), who emphasize the interplay between female psychological developments, the reproductive function of women, and the destructive feelings related to childbirth. Their writings are based on the assumption that the female body and female psychological development are inseparable.

The critique of idealized labor

The Birth Rights Movement grew from a critique of "industrialized labor" (Jones, 2012; Malacrida & Boulton, 2014). The counter-critique of the Birth Rights Movement that has developed centers around the idealization of birth. Jones (2012) describes the latter, the critique of "idealized labor," as being concerned with articulating anxieties about the negative impact on laboring women of the discourse and practices of idealized birth. This chapter aims to engage these two strands through a psychoanalytic lens. I wish to develop a feminist psychoanalytic appreciation of the underlying motivations and dynamics of what is at stake in childbirth. Jones (2012) encourages us to exercise caution in the critique of idealized labor because of the "tendency to reductively understand the embodied experience of labor as entirely discursively produced, a gesture that risks re-performing the dematerialization of women often effected through obstetric intervention itself" (p. 99). I am therefore walking a philosophical tightrope in my arguments on how the Birth Rights Movement may be reproducing the oppressing tendencies it sets out to fight.

The mechanisms of an ideal birth fantasy can be understood through an examination of the woman's emotional life. Several analysts have contended that pregnancy is a constructive psychic crisis because it impinges on the emotional organization of the mother's psyche, thus forcing her to find ways to cope and make her own meaning of the transition to motherhood (Bibring, 1959; Holmes, 2008; Balsam, 2012). From this understanding, childbirth is then, both in its concrete event and in what it represents, a crucial moment of climax for this crisis. There is indeed a lot at stake, internally and psychologically, and in the external biological sense of life and death.

An influential example of idealized labor is provided in Debra Pascali-Bonaro's documentary *Orgasmic Birth: The Best-Kept Secret* (2008).[1] In the book that followed the documentary, the idea of Orgasmic Birth is defined:

> Our definition is broad enough to include those who describe birth as ecstatic and specific enough to give voice to those who actually feel the contractions of orgasm and climax at the moment of delivery. Many of our interviewees spoke of astounding pressure and sensation in the vagina as birth approached, followed by a flood of release and emotion as the baby emerged. *Whenever a woman can look back on these moments with joy, when the physical and emotional aspects of birth are fully experienced as pleasurable, we call this orgasmic birth.*
> *(Davis & Pascali-Bonaro, 2010, p. xi, my italics)*

This is an idea of Orgasmic Birth as mainly or only consisting of pleasurable experiences. It is the dominant feeling of both the physical and emotional aspects of birth. The Orgasmic Birth philosophy is cultivated in home birth movements, where the childbirth is understood to carry deep personal meanings of self-realization directly linked to a woman's sexuality.

The main notion of Orgasmic Birth is that culture has veered us away from the true nature of birth through the lack of support for the physiological processes that naturally lead to ecstasy in childbirth. With reference to the now commonly known "love-hormone," the authors claim that it is the best-kept secret that childbirth is orgasmic in nature: "oxytocin is the missing link between sex and childbirth" (Davis & Pascali-Bonaro, 2010, p. xii). Through the direct connection to sexuality, childbirth becomes a liberating sexual event in its true form. However, sexuality is described with a significant spiritual quality by, for example, referring to Tantra philosophy, in which "a woman's body creates the space and opens the energy field for sexuality, thus setting the pace for intimacy" (Davis & Pascali-Bonaro, 2010, p. 114). The purpose of the orgasmic state is not only pleasure: it is through her sexuality that the birthing woman embodies the bonding and intimacy that is necessary for the baby's entrance into the world. The ideals that follow from this philosophy are that true birth is ecstatic, consciousness expanding, and liberating. Furthermore, it also creates an idealistic coupling of reproductive capacities and femininity.

Idealizing assumptions: Bio-essentialism and the use of subjective accounts

In a philosophy that claims to honor, protect, and fight for both the birthing woman and her baby, how is birth then idealized? I suggest that the idealization is fueled mainly by two elements of the Birth Rights Movement's philosophy: bio-essentialism (or reification) and the use of (maternal) subjective accounts. I believe these notions may be contributing to a reproduction of control of women's reproductive rights since they carry a moral imperative for women to fight against a perceived external and essentially political reproductive oppression through their personal birth choices. The personal thus indeed becomes political, but with a significant cost of subjectivity. In the following, I will account for the expression of these two elements and how they contribute to the idealization.

The term "natural" is widely used in the Birth Rights Movement, coined in the term "natural childbirth" by Grantly Dick-Read (1933). In the idea of "normal" or "natural" birth, the birth process is seen as an inherently natural biological, psychological, and potentially also spiritual process, that, if left undisturbed, will unfold itself (Dick-Read, 1933; Gaskin, 2002). Natural childbirth proponents have argued that the unnecessary or questionable interventions, like excessive fetal monitoring and induction that can lead to a cascade of interventions, are disturbing to the natural process of birth (Kitzinger, 1981). More radical voices of the Birth Rights Movement, who practice and advocate for unassisted childbirth (with no use of professional help), state that birth is so natural and normal that is should be protected from any kind of intervention (Haydock, 2014). Haydock, who represents this approach, states:

> My experience tells me that birth is a completely natural process which requires no intervention, no observation, and no tools. Birth happens with or without your ideas or plans . . . Birth happens, and if you let it, birth can happen in a way more beautiful and blissful than you could ever imagine.
>
> *(Haydock, 2014, p. 11)*

This statement shows how the ideology of Natural Childbirth in its more radical form ultimately sets an ideal of birth being completely untouched by cultural factors. Another widely used argument in natural childbirth philosophy is the idea of trusting birth (Davis & Pascali-Bonaro, 2010; Gaskin, 2002). The notion is that the obstetric paradigm wrongly teaches women that they neither trust their own bodies nor the process of birth.

What is understood as the "natural" and "normal" here is quite far from the realities of general childbirth practices. Using the terms "normal" and "natural" create an implicit judgment of women who need or chose to use medical technology and interventions in birth (Drapkin- Lyerly, 2012). Mothers' negotiations of their personal experiences and their wishes for and choices of birth methods are profoundly influenced by cultural ideals and expectations and, in particular, ideas about what is normal. Drapkin-Lyerly (2012) has voiced concern about this, arguing that the "normal birth becomes (in hearts and minds) the good birth, potentially leaving women who use technology to conclude that they have somehow failed or missed out during their entrée to motherhood" (p. 316). I agree with Jones's (2012) contention that the bio-essentialist view of the birthing woman is indeed what makes the Birth Rights Movement ideological when she states:

> Given that we may understand reification—or the posing of the cultural as natural—to be the hallmark of ideology, the positioning of a culturally constituted natural body as natural in a straightforward sense reveals a normative ideological operation at work in the rhetoric of "natural" childbirth.
>
> *(p. 107)*

The use of birth stories is a cornerstone of the literature of the Birth Rights Movement. First-person accounts of birth are often the main focus of literature; for example, in Gaskin's influential book on midwifery (2002), several birth stories are used to illustrate aspects of the philosophy and experience-based beliefs. Often birth stories are picked because of their particular relevance to a topic. Short introductory reflections are added, which tie the birth stories into the author's statements. In this way, the birth stories become crucial testimonials of the philosophy that Gaskin is conveying. Throughout the literature on natural childbirth, the philosophy is often presented with the authors' personal accounts of birth experiences and how these experiences inspired them (for example, Davis & Pascali-Bonaro, 2010; Haydock, 2014).

However, the use of subjective accounts is particularly problematic when the subjects in question are mothers. Maternal subjectivity has been intensively debated because of its tendency to slip away just as we think we are able to grasp the mother's perspective. The disappearance of the mother as a full subject in theoretical developments became a major topic in feminist critiques of psychoanalysis in the 1970s and 1980s (Baraitser *et al.*, 2009). The challenge of asserting maternal subjectivity becomes further problematic when there is idealization at play, as it is namely the idealization of the maternal that makes it hard to connect with the reality of the mother subject (Benjamin, 1988; Parker, 1995). I therefore find it concerning to see mothers' subjective experiences widely used in literature of an ideological nature. Mothers' subjective experiences risk getting lost in the ideological discourse because they are fitted into a specific narrative and used as underpinnings. With that we lose the voice of the individual mother's intrapsychic and complex experience.

Psychoanalysis and childbirth

Although Freud did leave evidence of an academic interest in childbirth, it was greatest earliest in his career, before he developed his theories of penis envy and the oedipal complex (Balsam, 2012). He contended that pregnancy forces a woman to confront her own mother (Freud, 1931/1961). Winnicott noted in his classic paper on hate in the countertransference (1949) that a mother's hate for her baby is, among other things, fueled by the fact that the baby poses a danger to her in pregnancy and birth. This attentiveness to maternal ambivalence particularly in relation to childbirth is unique coming from a male analyst at this time.

A new feminist psychoanalytic understanding that parts with Freud's ideas about the female has developed. It acknowledges the biological challenges of reproduction and appreciates them as potential sources of pleasure and pride, but it also recognizes them as inherently terrifying and anxiety-producing. The pleasurable and painful aspects of birth are clearly intertwined. Contemporary writers like Balsam (2012) and Holmes (2008) base their work on the assumption that the female body and female psychological development are inseparable and synergistically related. Female development is approached from a life cycle perspective in which bodily changes in the course of a woman's life are integral to an understanding of her emotional life (Balsam, 2012). They have established and expanded the area of inquiry into female corporeality and its intrinsic interplay with psychic life. These writers have had to break several theoretical taboos of classic Freudian thinking in order to open up the examination of the interplay between female physicality and psychic life, or what I will call "feminist-embodiment psychoanalysis."

Childbirth, particularly in the female mind, is surrounded with fantasies, desires, and concerns. Balsam (2012) notes that a female body event like childbirth is prepared for developmentally and worked over in the minds of girls and women "years *before*, and in women, years *after* the events themselves" (p. 76). It is through the witnessing of older pregnant relatives or friends, and what follows of fantasies and concerns about their own potentials for reproduction, that girls develop their body image. Balsam (2012) identifies three topics that are central to understanding the psychoanalytic material on childbirth: female genital anxiety, female exhibitionism, and female body pleasure.

Holmes (2008) builds her thesis on the psychology of childbirth on the idea that it can potentially be very helpful to psychological growth and maturation because of its tendency to "thrust a woman's inner world into the object field where it can be dealt with in terms of reality" (p. 30). Pregnancy forces a reworking of the relationships to the internalized parental objects, particularly the infantile aspects of them (Holmes, 2008). In this way, pregnancy and childbirth in particular can facilitate a restructuring of the psychic triangle of internalized maternal and paternal objects and self. The maturational effect lies in the new authority the self can gain in relationship to the internalized parental objects. Holmes theorizes that this "internal triangle" of maternal and paternal objects and self is confronted in the three major events of female development: the menarche, childbirth, and menopause. The crisis of childbirth is particularly ripe with potentials for reconfiguration of the internal triangle and thereby integration of mental functioning. Holmes (2008) arrives at this particular importance of childbirth on the basis of her understanding that "pregnancy and childbirth function as equivalents of the phallus. Like the penis, the fetus is self and non-self, both subject and object; this double role gives woman the self-containment and self-reliance that the penis gives man" (2008, p. 36). During pregnancy, the woman can project feelings and anxieties about parental objects and self onto the fetus and thereby separate from them. Consequently, the act of pushing out the self-object/fetus signifies a potentially drastic restructuring of the relationship between internalized parental objects and the self. What makes the psychological stakes so high in birth is its symbolic and also viscerally concretized confrontation with the inner parental objects. Experiences of losing control, not succeeding in actively taking charge of the task, and feeling violated by interventions, whether medicalized or not, are likely experienced as major defeats of the self. It is plausible that childbirth in this way triggers unconscious oedipal traumatic material, and this could explain some of the intense feelings of failure that Balsam (2012) notes many women report after childbirth.

Balsam (2012) is in line with Holmes (2008) on the potential for psychic restructuring in childbirth: "It seems that the experience of childbirth may be so potent that the regression mobilized in the service of the ego may even make room for an internalization of an alternative mothering experience for a birthing woman" (Balsam, 2012, p. 91). During pregnancy, the mother experiences a bifurcated identification with both her own mother and the fetus (Bibring, 1959). Childbirth marks the abrupt termination of this symbiotic identification. The identifications and the regressive pressure they exert on the woman are often frightening (Holmes, 2008), even though they are often also accompanied by longings. Primitive longings for symbiosis coupled with the fear of the engulfing pre-oedipal mother can produce the intense ambivalence that Parker (1995) described as an inevitable and important part of maternal development. Furthermore, childbirth marks the point of expulsion of the self-object that the fetus represents, which has carried important projections throughout the pregnancy (Holmes, 2008). The termination of the symbiosis is therefore potentially both threatening and rewarding. Holmes notes that the symbiosis in pregnancy reflects a paradox: "It requires identification with mother for the unconscious to permit pregnancy, but by identifying with mother enough to get pregnant, a woman can finally, in childbirth, achieve true individuation and psychic separation from mother" (2008, p. 31).

We see acknowledgements of the sexual and orgasmic aspects of childbirth throughout the psychoanalytic literature on motherhood. Balsam (2012) describes the intimate relationship between the development of the little girl's body pleasures and her mother's private sexuality, linking the maternal object and a woman's sexuality from an embodied perspective. The fetal movements are understood as evoking pleasure, and the milk coming in is a central sexual event. The baby is a "natural sex object" for the mother. What is radically different in feminist-embodiment psychoanalysis from the philosophy of Orgasmic Birth is the focus on the pain and hatred as equally important in the motherhood transition and in childbirth as the pleasure. For example, birth can be seen as a loss of the sexual pleasure of the fetal movement. This understanding is seen in Holmes' thesis (2008), where childbirth is a massive loss in the sense of the very concrete way the delivery of the baby parallels the psychological detachment from a self-object that is saturated with projections. The pain and loss of childbirth is just as important as the sexual pleasure, and the tension and ambivalence that follows is central. The plasticity and fluidity of the female body, however natural and developmentally important, is also cause for anxieties around childbirth. Balsam (2012) confirms that flux is the normative for a woman's physicality, stating that "females mentally register a rhythm of dimensional corporeal oscillation" (p. 84). She also contends that many likely experience these shifts with anxiety.

This brings up an issue in female and maternal development that I call the boundary problem. Reproduction exerts tremendous pressure on all thinkable boundaries for a woman—physically, mentally, emotionally, spiritually, and socially—and there is no way out of this pressure in the maternal transformation (Vissing, 2015). Because it is largely driven by body processes, the unique pressure of motherhood will be reacted to from the body rather than mentally. A woman who wishes to have a baby will therefore be confronted with the problem of how to maintain and assert her boundaries so she is not taken over by the transition, while still accepting the boundary instability and fluidity as necessary and gratifying. The fluidity of boundaries imbedded in female life holds powerful creative and destructive forces; they accumulate with intensity throughout pregnancy and culminate in childbirth. Balsam (2012) suggests a plausible dynamic of female anxieties about childbirth:

> The basal state of the constant flux of the mature female body is peaked by pregnancy and childbirth. Could it be that hidden anxieties about this major personal confrontation with this body flux, accompanied as it is by serious matters of life and death, is a kind of black hole that lurks in many, many female psyches?
>
> (p. 85)

With this feminist-embodiment psychoanalytic understanding, we can appreciate the anxieties of childbirth without understanding them as symptoms of cultural and obstetric oppression. Rather, they are imbedded in the female unconscious as primitive reactions to the inescapable corporeality of female life. Zeavin (2011) has aptly described the destructive and horrifying aspects of birth:

> No matter how thrilling the birth of a baby . . . it is always in a sense traumatic. Giving birth inevitably evokes our most primitive fears and fantasies:

many women describe the fear of coming undone, of violence to the inside of their bodies, a fear of being unseemly and even grotesque.

(p. 63)

Conclusion

In the idealization of birth, the negative aspects are split off and understood explicitly as the result of an unhealthy and/or abusive obstetric system and implicitly as a woman's failure to assert and empower herself. In the Orgasmic Birth narrative, we are offered the fantasy that childbirth and motherhood without any boundary pressure is possible. From feminist psychoanalytic perspectives, this has dire consequences for maternal subjectivity. A woman will have a hard time expressing ambivalence and anxieties in a philosophy that understands negative feelings as symptoms of an oppressing system that should be resisted. A childbirth philosophy that places responsibility on the mother, whether directly or indirectly, as in the exaggerated focus on a woman's potential control over the birth, is concerning. A perfect birth is certainly a central and needed fantasy in the female psyche, but it must be reconciled with reality, similar to the maternal task of reconciling the fantasy baby with the real. The fantasy that one can conquer the powers of childbirth through the right mindset and enough resistance to control health care authorities is tempting. Reproductive capacities and birthing skills are understandably heavily coupled with femininity in our unconscious, but we must be cautious of any philosophy that promotes a "living out" of these fantasies because it sets women up for failure and makes it hard to reconcile fantasy with reality. If a woman believes her femininity rests solely or primarily on her birthing capacities, she is at a loss in her struggles toward her intertwined but not synonymous identities as a female and as a mother.

The Birth Rights Movement is one of the few forces in the world that sincerely and actively attempts to embrace, honor, and protect female reproductive life. However, the glorification of the birthing process has a caveat in that it may perpetuate splitting, idealization, and anxiety and, in so doing, dilute the maternal subjective experience. I find it likely that it also harbors the unconscious rage against the female body and the mother that is so deeply imbedded in our psyche and drives us to control her.

In childbirth, a woman will be confronted with her personal history of genital anxiety and body pride and the intertwined relationship between the two. There is a potential for experiencing intense body pride, the joy of finally feeling the pinnacle of one's body's awesome abilities, and the realization of pleasurable fantasies about the satisfaction of delivery. However, these aspects are then contested against the woman's history of genital anxiety, fears of penetration or damage to the genitals, fears of failing in one's femininity, and general fear of death. A woman will likely wish for the former aspects to dominate and win, and she may, consciously or unconsciously, be fearful of the latter. I find it plausible that victorious and idealized fantasies are developed as defenses against these primal anxieties. I do not consider such defenses to be a priori pathological; they are on the contrary protective and helpful. The crucial difference is whether a woman can make use of them with increasing consciousness in her development of her maternal identity, or if they become collective unconscious and rigid projections in an ideological fight.

Note

1 Pascali-Bonaro and Gaskin are advisory board members of Human Rights in Childbirth (http://www.humanrightsinchildbirth.org/advisory-board/).

References

The Association for Pre and Perinatal Psychology and Health. (2015, March 7). *Birth psychology*. Retrieved from http://birthpsychology.com

Balsam, R.H. (2012). *Women's bodies in psychoanalysis*. New York, NY: Routledge.

Baraitser, L., Spigel, S., Betterton, R., Curk, R., Hollway, W., Jensen, T., . . . Tyler, I. (2009). Editorial: Mapping maternal subjectivities, identities and ethics. *Studies in the Maternal, 1*(1). Retrieved from http://www.mamsie.bbk.ac.uk/back_issues/issue_one/editorial. html

Benjamin, J. (1988). *The bonds of love: Psychoanalysis, feminism, and the problem of domination*. New York, NY: Pantheon.

Bibring, G.L. (1959). Some considerations of the psychological processes in pregnancy. *Psychoanalytic Study of the Child, 14*, 113–121.

Chard, T., & Richards, M.P.M. (Eds.). (1992). *Obstetrics in the 1990s: Current controversies*. New York, NY: Cambridge University Press.

Chodorow, N. (1978). *The reproduction of mothering: Psychoanalysis and the sociology of gender*. Berkeley, CA: University of California Press.

Datta, S. (2001). *Childbirth and pain relief: An anesthesiologist explains your options*. Chester, NJ: Next Decade.

Davis, E., & Pascali-Bonaro, D. (2010). *Orgasmic birth. Your guide to a safe, satisfying, and pleasurable birth experience*. New York, NY: Rodale.

Dick-Read, G. (1933). *Natural childbirth*. London: Heinemann.

Dick-Read, G. (1942). *Childbirth without fear: The principles and practice of natural childbirth*. London: Heinemann.

Drapkin-Lyerly, A. (2012). Ethics and "normal birth." *Birth, 39*(4), 315–317.

Epstein, A. (Director). (2008). *The business of being born*. [Motion picture]. United States: New Line Home Entertainment.

Freud, S. (1961). Female sexuality. In J. Strachey (Ed. & Trans.), *The standard edition of the complete psychological works of Sigmund Freud* (Vol. 21, pp. 223–246). London: Hogarth. (Original work published 1931)

Gaskin, I.M. (2002). *Spiritual midwifery* (4th ed.). Summertown, TN: Book Publishing Company. (Original work published 1975)

Gaskin, I.M. (2011). *Birth matters. A midwife's manifesta*. New York, NY: Seven Stories Press.

Haydock, S. (2014). *Unhindered childbirth: Wisdom for the passage of unassisted birth*. Publisher: Author. Printed by CreateSpace Independent Publishing Platform, USA.

Holmes, L. (2008). *The internal triangle. New theories of female development*. New York, NY: Jason Aronson.

Jones, J.C. (2012). Idealized and industrialized labor: Anatomy of a feminist controversy. *Hypatia, 27*(1), 99–117.

Kitzinger, S. (1981). *The experience of childbirth*. New York, NY: Penguin Books.

Karmel, M. (1959). *Thank you, Dr. Lamaze*. Philadelphia, PA: Lippincott.

Malacrida, C., & Boulton, T. (2014). The best laid plans? Women's choices, expectations and experiences in childbirth. *Health, 18*(1), 41–59.

Parker, R. (1995). *Mother love/Mother hate.* New York, NY: Basic Books.

Pascali-Bonaro, D. (Director). (2008). *Orgasmic birth: The best-kept secret.* [Motion picture]. United States: SG Entertainment.

Tew, M. (1990). *Safer childbirth? A critical history of maternity care.* London: Chapman & Hall.

Tritten, J. (2010). Birth is a human rights issue: A movement. *Midwifery Today, 96*, 5–36.

Universal rights. (2015, December 16). *Human Rights in Childbirth.* Retrieved from http://www.humanrightsinchildbirth.org/universal-rights/

Vissing, H. (2014). The ideal mother fantasy and its protective function. In L. Ennis (Ed.), *Intensive mothering: The cultural contradictions of modern motherhood* (pp. 104–114). Toronto: Demeter Press.

Vissing, H. (2015). Triumphing over the body: Body fantasies and their protective functions. *Journal of the Motherhood Initiative for Research and Community Involvement, 6*(1), 168–175.

Winnicott, D. (1949). Hate in the counter-transference. *International Journal of Psycho-Analysis, 30*, 69–74.

Zeavin, L. (2011). "What about the episiotomy?" A response to Katie Gentile's article "What about the baby?" *Studies in Gender and Sexuality, 12*, 59–64.

9

FROM INFERTILITY AND EMPTY WOMB TO MATERNAL FULFILLMENT

The psychological birth of the adoptive mother

JoAnn Ponder

For prospective parents unable to conceive a child, the adopted child becomes a replacement for the biological child who previously existed only in hopes and fantasies. There are similarities between biological and adoptive motherhood, but also some significant differences and special challenges for the adoptive mother. Under the best of circumstances, the adoption does not result in an instantaneous identity and fulfillment as a parent, which involves a more gradual process of coming into being. The available literature offers few insights into this process, in that it focuses more on the adopted child than the adoptive mother. I have chosen to term the mother's journey as a "psychological birth" in order to denote a process such as *The Psychological Birth of the Human Infant* (Mahler *et al.*, 1975). The following chapter explores the available psychoanalytic and developmental literature, along with insights from my clinical practice with adoptive families and my own journey to becoming an adoptive mother after years of infertility.

Infertility and the decision to adopt

Adoption is seldom a heterosexual couple's first choice for creating a family, and often occurs following infertility. Individuals may experience strong emotional reactions to infertility, including shock, disbelief, frustration, and blame (Burns, 2005; Rosen, 2005). Medical treatment is costly, intrusive, and time-consuming, interfering with sexual functioning and spontaneity, straining relationships, and taxing emotions. Each menstrual period, unsuccessful treatment, and failed pregnancy is experienced as a profound loss, rekindling earlier losses. Over time, this can engender feelings of bereavement, helplessness, and pessimism. The individuals may get angry, as if cheated of something that should be theirs. Infertility thus activates castration anxiety and narcissistic injury (Blum, 1983). In self-psychological terms, infertility threatens a sense of self-cohesion, giving rise to anxiety and fragmentation.

From an interpersonal view, it leads to the emergence of dissociated aspects of the self, earlier modes of organizing experiences, and altered perceptions of relationships (Rosen, 2005).

Though the decision to adopt may nurture hope, prospective parents can feel entitled to compensation for losses and difficulties sustained during infertility (Malave, 2005). They may feel the right to choose their child's sex, age, or source country, choices possibly influenced by narcissistic motives, unconscious fantasies, and cultural or gender stereotypes. After years of infertility treatment, those who want a baby fast may be resentful of the screening process to adopt, frustrated by bureaucratic obstacles, and disappointed by the limited availability of infants, especially Caucasians (Miles, 2000). Factors such as the child's age and race may also complicate the bonding process.

Bonding with the adopted child

Children adopted after infancy often have histories of neglect, abuse, institutionalization, or multiple changes in caregivers. These issues can lead to anaclitic depression (e.g. Spitz, 1946), attachment disorders (e.g. Main, 1991), or other emotional problems (e.g. Downey, 2000). Even with newborns, there are differences in nurturing biological and adopted children. Bonding begins during pregnancy when hormones such as oxytocin are released (Schechter, 2000). Psychologically, the mother makes the child a part of her body, prenatally and postnatally, especially in breastfeeding (Furman, 1993). In contrast to the wanted biological child with hormonal and genetic advantages for bonding, the adopted child may begin life in an ambivalent intrauterine environment (Schechter, 2000). For adoptive parents, there is "instant and disorderly gestation through adoption" (Waterman, 2003, p. 177) rather than a gradual unfolding of the psychological state of parenthood (Sherick, 1983). Adoptive parent and child are strangers at first, and parents faced with the fact that the child came from someone else's seed and womb, especially if the child is dissimilar in appearance (Etezady et al., 2000).

Based on prior experience with Black and Korean children adopted by White parents, color-blindness is unrealistic in parenting (Miles, 2000; Waterman, 2003). For transracial adoptions to succeed, parents must be willing to relinquish their identity as a "White family" (Reed, 2000). They must confront their own racism and recognize their tendency to idealize or devalue their child's race, consciously or unconsciously, as negative stereotypes can emerge during crises, conflicts, and the child's adolescence (Miles, 2000). While they are encouraged to foster an association with the child's race and culture, the child may view too much or too little association as a subtle rejection (Miles, 2000).

Despite the challenging beginnings for adoptive families, the difficulties can be managed. Bonding and attachment are complex processes arising not only from parents' and child's biological characteristics, but also from the parents' past experiences, psychological make-up, fantasies, and expectations, in combination with the child's temperament and parent–child temperamental compatibility (Etezady *et al.*, 2000). Clearly, self-awareness and compassion are important characteristics for the adoptive mother. According to Waterman (2003), adoptive mothers are capable of a primary maternal preoccupation (Winnicott, 1956). With a "good enough bond" (Miles, 2000), processes like emotional containment (Bion, 1962), mirroring (Kohut, 1977), the mutual regulation of infant–mother social interactions (Tronick, 2007), and mutually attuned attachment (Schore, 1994) foster the child's mental and social development. This led Siegel and Hartzell (2003, p. 34) to state that "adoptive parents should in fact be called biological parents because the family experiences they create shape the biological structure of their child's brain." This is reassuring in that my husband and I met our child literally as a stranger in a foreign country, yet we managed to form a family.

My own process of becoming an adoptive mother

I myself was one of those women who wanted it all—an advanced degree, successful career, financial security, husband, and child, more or less in that order. Like many other women over the last few decades, I postponed childbearing until it was too late. I went through years of treatments for infertility, but never became pregnant. After the failure of in vitro fertilization, my husband, Carl, and I decided to adopt. Nonetheless, I occasionally thought about how some women miraculously became pregnant after adopting a child. Hope can be both relentless and unrealistic, and my fantasies of pregnancy did not fully disappear until menopause.

The decision to adopt a child provided tangible hope, but also prompted new concerns about where to adopt. Carl and I soon ruled out the United States due to the limited number of infants available, the extremely long waiting periods, and the increased prevalence of open adoptions in this country. Open adoptions have become the norm for a variety of reasons, such as decreasing the child's sense of abandonment and maintaining his/her ties to family and cultural heritage. However, I was unsure about how to navigate a relationship with another mother, especially if she had drug/alcohol issues, exerted a negative influence on the child, became unreliable in keeping promises, or abandoned the child again. Conversely, I worried that an adopted child entering the turbulent teenage years might prefer to live with the birth mother. This is probably rare, but I nonetheless felt insecure as a prospective parent, my confidence likely shaken by my inability to conceive. Carl and I did not consider adopting an older child from the foster system with a history of neglect, abuse, or other trauma. I intended to continue working as a psychologist and did not think that I had enough inner resources to knowingly take on a child with special needs.

Carl and I decided on an international adoption, luckily before this window started to close due to policy changes in various countries (Koch, 2008). We ruled out Eastern Europe due to the prevalence of alcoholism there, which was a concern both in terms of genetic predisposition and prenatal exposure. Moreover, the overcrowded orphanages there resulted in fairly high rates of attachment problems. Hence, Carl and I decided on China, especially given that we preferred a girl. I also recall Carl laughingly making comments that Asians are intelligent. While he and I did not really expect a "trophy child," we wanted a healthy baby who was likely to develop typically.

After more than a year of evaluations, paperwork, and delays, Carl and I received the exciting news that the Chinese child placing agency had assigned a 10-month-old girl to us. We were informed that she was abandoned within a day after birth. She spent several weeks in an orphanage, where she was assessed as normal, and then placed in a foster home. She was moved to a different foster home after an accident that burned and scarred her legs, though records are inconsistent about when that happened. The adoption agency emailed photos of the baby girl to Carl and me. I was drawn to look at the photo, yet also fearful of doing so, afraid to become attached lest something happen again to spoil my good fortune. I stared at the photo of the baby girl with brown skin, black hair, a round face, almond-shaped eyes. She was cute, but was she really mine?

It was three more months before Carl and I were approved to travel to China to bring our daughter home. Finally, the adoption staff brought the baby from her foster home and handed her over to us in a hotel hallway. Her clothing was odd to us, and she bore the unfamiliar scent of a stranger's home. I gazed at her, trying to take in a permanent mental picture as I told myself, "This is my *baby*. This is *my* baby now." Intellectually, I knew that she was my child, but I did not feel like a parent yet. Similarly, she did not know that Carl and I were her forever parents or even her new caregivers. She cried inconsolably for hours until she fell asleep, then awoke periodically and cried softly through the night. All three of us were exhausted the next morning when we met with adoption officials. We changed the name that the orphanage assigned, translated as "Island Facing the Sunshine," to the Western name of Caitlin. She did not cry much those next two weeks, but seldom smiled and often glanced around as if seeking her foster mother. Caitlin tolerated physical care, but did not allow me to comfort her. Intellectually, I knew that it was a positive sign that she missed her foster mother rather than immediately attaching to me. Though I had read about infant mourning and knew what was happening, it was gut-wrenching to see.

Carl, Caitlin, and I had a meeting with her foster parents in order to ask questions and say goodbye. Caitlin obviously recognized them, yet seemed subdued, likely due to feelings of confusion. Through an interpreter, I told her foster mother about Caitlin's apparent sadness and asked if the baby smiled much. The foster mother reassured me that Caitlin was a happy, easygoing baby, and informed me how well she ate. When I started crying, the foster mother reassured me that everything would be fine—though she and her husband, too, started crying when it was time to say goodbye. Despite my sadness for Caitlin's current distress, I felt relieved that she was placed with a couple who clearly loved her.

I was exhilarated to arrive home after two weeks in China, when Caitlin reached out to me for the first time and said "Mama." Perhaps I needed a sign from her to feel like a mother and not just a caregiver. As Caitlin's grief subsided and my mothering capacities unfolded, a bond developed. I fell madly in love with Caitlin, thinking that she was a dream too good to be true—yes, *too* good to be true. Separation anxiety was palpable on her part, more subtle on mine. My favorite lullaby to sing to her was *You Are My Sunshine*, which was a reference to her previous name. Initially, I gave little thought to the ending lyrics, which ask for the sunshine not to be taken away. In retrospect, I always feared the loss of my child somehow, for example, declining an open adoption due to fears that the birth parents would emotionally kidnap or actually reclaim the child.

My fears and insecurities gradually decreased as my natural parenting instincts took hold, I experienced success in caring for Caitlin, and she responded positively to my love and care. As I began to feel like a real mother, I was awestruck by the immensity of this transition. While women can divorce, change jobs, and so forth, a mother is *always* a mother. This was forever. It was as if Caitlin and I developed a natural rhythm, a give-and-take flow in our interactions, and it was this dance that made me feel fully like a mother. This rhythm might be similar to what researchers such as Beebe, Tronick, and others (summarized in Beebe & Lachmann, 2013, and Tronick, 2007) have identified as the dyadic regulation of affect between infant and mother. The mutual regulation was identified through microanalyses of videotaped infant–parent interactions, and occurs largely outside of the participants' conscious awareness. However, I recall a more macro-level experience that suggested that subtle, intuitive regulation was occurring. One night at the dinner table when Caitlin was about 18 months old, I noticed that she was staring at me with her head slightly cocked, her mouth closed, her eyes squinting, her eyebrows knit, one arched higher that the other. I said to Carl, "Look at Caitlin! I wonder why she's looking at me like that . . . where did she learn to make *that* expression?" Carl replied, "Well, she certainly didn't learn it from me!" It was then that I realized that the facial expression was the way that my mother had looked at me with disapproval when she did not like what I was doing, a sort of nonverbal censure. We have not spent much time around my mother, so I figured out that I must be doing the same thing to Caitlin. So there it was, the intergenerational transmission of "the evil eye!" My look of surprise caused Caitlin to burst into laughter, whereupon I sensed that she was teasing me. The whole family laughed uproariously that night at the dinner table, though I felt weird that I had been channeling my mother without being aware of it.

As Caitlin and I perfected our mother–daughter dance, my professional views and perceptions shifted as well. Whereas my psychological reports about others previously referred to clients as "mothers" or "adoptive mothers," I now began referring to "birth mothers" or "mothers." In other words, the "mother" was the person rearing the child, whether the mother was biological or adoptive. Initially, this was not a conscious change in perspective, but an evolution based on my own experiences and internal perceptions. My coming into being as a mother was based mostly on my experiences with Caitlin, but also aided by individual psychotherapy. I received therapy from the time I was awaiting a child until she was a toddler. The therapy helped me to grieve my infertility, recognize ambivalence as normal, modify idealistic expectations, and develop self-compassion. Nonetheless, there were still blind spots . . . as there probably always are in parenting.

When Caitlin began biting people during her toddler years, it never occurred to me that she had a speech problem, so I was surprised when daycare staff recommended an evaluation. Whereas I thought that Caitlin was saying single words in English and still babbling a lot, the results indicated that she was talking in sentences, but had a severe articulation disorder that rendered her speech unintelligible. I felt awful when I realized the many times that I failed to respond to her, and how frustrating this was for her. Immediately after the evaluation, I told her that we would get help so that she could learn to speak clearly. Her biting stopped that very day, her articulation improved slowly over years of speech therapy, and her enhanced communication revealed a sharp, creative mind. Ever since then, I have come to view biting as an important sign that the child is trying to communicate something.

When Caitlin did not learn her numbers and letters as quickly as most preschoolers, I told myself that children learn at different rates. When she came home from kindergarten crying that she was stupid, I reassured her otherwise. Despite my experience in evaluating learning disabilities, I felt blindsided when the teacher recommended special educational services. Leery that resource placement would further hurt Caitlin's self-esteem, I arranged for services from the private sector: a neuropsychological evaluation, academic therapy, and tutoring. I remain convinced that if Caitlin was placed in special education classes, she might still be there. With intensive intervention from the private sector, her academic skills were on grade level within a year, and exceeded grade level by the following year. As her achievement soared, her confidence blossomed, though I still wonder if my desire for a typical or smart child made me slow to recognize her developmental challenges. Was I only seeing what I wanted to see? In retrospect, I do not think that I was less sensitive or attuned than most other parents might have been under the circumstances. Nonetheless, it was a painful process of self-examination that led to my conceptualization of the adopted child as a replacement child.

The concept of the replacement child

I believe that infertility results in object loss much like bereavement, except that the loss is a fantasy of what might have been, rather than an actual child. Hence, I believe that the adopted child can be a replacement for a fantasy, much like a replacement child takes the place of a deceased child. In a classic paper by Cain and Cain published in 1964, the replacement child was defined as one conceived to take the place of a child who died. Well-known examples are artists Vincent van Gogh (Nagera, 1967) and Salvador Dali (Dali & Parinaud, 1973), each of whom was given the same name as his deceased brother. Conceiving a new child and then giving him the name of a deceased sibling was more common in the past, when there were high birthrates and infant mortality. However, problems ensued when the bereaved parents remained apathetic, grief-stricken, and withdrawn, with a narcissistic overinvestment in the deceased child (Cain & Cain, 1964). They avoided mourning by projecting idealized expectations for the dead child onto the substitute (Legg & Sherick, 1976). Since replacement children were treated more as embodiments of a memory than persons in their own right, they often developed identity disturbances.

In 2000, Anisfeld and Richards extended the replacement concept to adoption and other situations, but did not explore the dynamics specific to adoption. I suggest that when fertility treatments fail and prospective parents rush to adopt, their unresolved emotional issues can impair the capacity to be emotionally present for the child. If the parents project idealized fantasies onto the child, this might impede the parents' ability to see the child for who he or she really is. When narcissistic vulnerabilities are activated, the parents may project problems onto the child or birth parent.

Infertility, anxiety, and the insecure parent

The adopted child is born to parents who did not want the pregnancy, or mistreated the child (Cohen, 1996). However, the child may attribute the relinquishment to his or her defectiveness, resulting in a sense of not fitting in first with family and later with others (Frankel, 1991). The child then is reared by individuals with parallel experiences of anxiety and insecurity (Cohen, 1996). I believe that infertile individuals who have not worked through their feelings of inadequacy are prone to feel unsure of their parenting skills, insecure about the parent–child relationship, and threatened by contact with birth parents. Adoptive parents who project their insecurities may show defensive hypervigilance to potential problems in the adoption (Hushion, 2006). In most cases, such insecurities dissipate with time and experience, though a few families require therapeutic intervention. Mutual successes in mastering doubts and anxieties about the adoption may strengthen parent and child, resulting in a uniquely affirmative bond (Frankel, 1991).

Infertility, object loss, and the depressed parent

Adopted child and parent experience parallel losses, as the child often is cut off from former biological generations, the infertile adult from future generations (Landerholm-EK, 2001). For the child adopted in infancy and the infertile adult, there was little or no real experience with the lost object, so the inner representations are based mostly on fantasy (Bonovitz, 2006). Infertile adults must relinquish the idealized image of the biological child that might have been (Reed, 2000), much as bereaved parents must mourn the deceased child before attaching to a replacement. Mourning the loss of the wished-for biological child permits more acceptance of the adopted child, and fosters psychic integration that allows both representations to coexist in the same person. This reduces parental projective identification, enabling parents to tolerate the child's sense of loss and establishing the child's sense of continuity between birth mother and adoptive parents (Bonovitz, 2006). Unresolved mourning can result in preoccupation, withdrawal, and depression (Malave, 2005), interfering with the parents' empathy, reflective function, and attunement (Etezady et al., 2000).

Depressed mothers show differences in both the quality and content of their speech to infants, as compared with non-depressed mothers. Depressed mothers tend to speak in a flat, monotonous manner rather than using "motherese" (Marwick & Murray, 2008), and their speech focuses on maternal concerns rather than being centered on the infant (Murray *et al.*, 1993). In addition, depressed mothers are prone to express hostility to their sons in particular (Morrell & Murray, 2003). Depression also affects the mother's behavioral responsiveness in one of two ways: either she becomes withdrawn and lost in her own thoughts, or she behaves in a hostile, intrusive manner (Murray *et al.*, 2009).

In a laboratory paradigm simulating the withdrawn form of maternal depression, Tronick and colleagues (1978) found that infants had distressing responses to even short periods of maternal unresponsiveness. Mothers were instructed to stare at their babies in an expressionless, still-face manner for just a few moments. The infants typically showed progressive reactions in which they first appeared startled, then made gestures and other bids for their mothers' attention, cried or otherwise protested, and then withdrew or even slumped over. When depressed mothers responded to their infants' distress, they often did so in a rejecting or unsympathetic manner (Murray *et al.*, 1996). With chronic maternal misattunement, there is a failure to form dyadic states of consciousness needed for the infant's social and cognitive growth (Tronick & Weinberg, 1997) and an increased risk for insecure attachment (Murray *et al.*, 1996). In extreme cases, the child may internalize the image of a deadened mother (Green, 1983), and the trauma may be transmitted intergenerationally like a "ghost in the nursery" (Fraiberg *et al.*, 1973).

Adoption usually is a compromise rather than a first choice after infertility left the prospective parents feeling damaged. For parents unable to conceive, the adopted child may be a reminder of their inadequacy (Hushion, 2006). To add insult to injury, society relegates a lower status to adoptive parenthood, inherent in common terms such as referring to birth parents as the "real parents." Adoptive parents must stop devaluing adoption to enjoy caring for the child (Etezady *et al.*, 2000) and manage the transformation from unwanted to wanted for the child and in their own minds (Brinich, 1995). Adoption thus is born of loss, but this implies both risk and opportunity for the family's development (Landerholm-EK, 2001). Provided that adoptive parents accept ambivalence as normal, adoption can rekindle senses of hope, empowerment, and connection (Malave, 2005).

Infertility and narcissistic defenses in parenting

Prospective parents may feel entitled to compensation for infertility, and narcissism may affect choices about adoption. In seeking the perfect adoption, they might search for a child similar to them, wanting to minimize or deny biological differences (Malave, 2005). During infertility treatment, they often had years to embellish their fantasies and idealized expectations. While all parents have ideals that are modified over time, the expectations for the replacement child originally were intended for someone else, either the deceased or non-existent biological child.

Given that the fantasies often consist of idealized aspects of the parents (Burns, 2005), I strongly believe that the gap between fantasy and reality may be wider for a biologically unrelated child.

Infertility thus can activate narcissistic vulnerabilities and defenses. These defenses are poignantly portrayed in several plays by Edward Albee (Glenn, 1974; Siegel & Siegel, 2001). The best example is "The American Dream" (Albee, 1960), a story of a wealthy couple who adopted because they could not conceive. However, the baby was a disappointment, the parent–child relationship antagonistic. When the baby cried and looked only to father, the mother gouged out baby's eyes. When the child shouted an obscenity at her, the parents cut out his tongue; when he masturbated, they cut off his penis and hands. When there was virtually nothing left of him, they returned him to the adoption agency. Soon afterward, a knock at the door revealed the boy's twin—another unfortunate replacement child. Albee clearly spoke from personal experience in that he was adopted in infancy by a fairly affluent couple, but found his mother critical and unsupportive. When he was 18 years old, she demanded that he become the son that *she* wanted or else leave home. He chose to go, subsequently channeling his painful issues into creative expression.

In contemporary relational terms, a "child's core self becomes internally bonded to the early parental objects through interactions that reinforce who the parent perceives the child to be and who the parent denies the child to be" (Bromberg, 2006, p. 6). In order to preserve the early attachment patterns on which the core self rests, the child begins to dissociate those aspects that the parent denied. According to Bromberg (2006), parental disconfirmation constitutes a developmental trauma, typically cumulative, in that we all want and need to be seen for who we are.

Adoptive parents may view themselves as altruistic rescuers, yet envy others' fertility. After trying so hard to conceive, they may disparage the birth parent, given the negative circumstances leading to the relinquishment of the child (Malave, 2005). While some adoptive mothers vicariously live out fantasies of fertility through daughters, other mothers react with fear and disapproval of sexuality, possibly fueled by the daughter's "illegitimate" birth (Gilmore, 1995). Birth parents also may be blamed for the child's unacceptable aggressive drives (Viola, 2000). Narcissistic parents may attribute the child's "good" aspects to the parenting and environment that they provided, and the "bad" aspects to genetics. They may project problems onto the child and/or birth parents.

Infant observations were integrated with Kleinian theory to describe how the child complies with preverbal relational scripts projected by the parent (Seligman, 1999; Stern, 1995). In addition, the child's temperament, cognitions, and inner world influence interactions with the parent. Thus, the family members' inner representations interpenetrate each other through projective and introjective identification (Bonovitz, 2006). If parents have not mentalized their own losses and trauma, this undermines the ability to see the child as his or her own person (Fonagy *et al.*, 2002). In extreme cases, the parents' unresolved trauma and fear lead to disorganized attachment in the infant (Main & Hesse, 1990). For these reasons, child psychoanalytic psychotherapy utilizes play to access unconscious parent–child communication (Bonovitz, 2006). Concurrent work with parents explores how their history affects the child (Novick & Novick, 2005). The following case illustrates my treatment of a young boy with impaired affect regulation and his adoptive mother who was depressed and prone to project particularly malevolent traits onto him.

Clinical example and discussion

Several years ago, a concerned mother contacted me for help with her 5-year-old son, "Sam." She was worried about his noncompliance, anger, and aggression. After doing some research and reading, she had become convinced that these problems were symptomatic of oppositional defiant disorder. She further believed that Sam had a poor prognosis and was headed for a life of crime. She described herself and her husband as educated professionals, active in their church and devoted to family. Almost as an afterthought, she mentioned that Sam and his younger brother were adopted, whereas her third son was biological. She thought that adoption had no bearing on Sam's problems, however, because she loved all three children equally. The clear implication was that something was wrong with Sam.

I met with Ms. X for an initial consultation to gather some background history. I learned that she was a full-time homemaker since adopting Sam, and previously employed as a preschool teacher. Mr. X was a professional soccer coach, also experienced in working with children. He and Ms. X got Sam at birth in an open domestic adoption. When I asked if they experienced fertility problems, she snapped, "Isn't that why most people adopt?" I saw that I had trodden on a sensitive topic, so I attempted to repair the wound. Though I do not typically self-disclose much to clients, I thought that it might help to reduce her defensiveness if I took a more open and collaborative approach with her. I quietly affirmed her, "Yes, I know. I'm an adoptive mother, too." Ms. X seemed surprised, but her anger gradually dissipated. I learned that Sam's biological father was unknown, his birth mother an unwed teen who dropped out of high school. Sam's birth mother was now married and living in another state. She telephoned Sam occasionally, but had not visited him for about 2 years.

According to Ms. X, Sam was colicky, irritable, and difficult to soothe as a baby. I thought about infant observational studies, which have found that boys are more affectively reactive and less able to self-regulate their affective states than girls, thereby requiring more assistance from their caregivers (Weinberg, 1992; Weinberg & Tronick, 1992). Boys remain more demanding and emotionally reactive as they grow up (Weinberg, 1992). According to Tronick (2007), the boys' problems in regulating their affective states render them prone to frustration and anger, which may give rise to aggression. Sam was a sensitive baby, possibly with a particularly reactive temperament. His mother said that he had speech problems and became increasingly temperamental at age 2 years, when his parents adopted his next younger brother. Sam's speech problems subsided, but his aggression escalated when Sam started kindergarten. Ms. X said that he had one or more temper tantrums daily upon arriving home from school. He excelled academically, however, and had no major behavioral problems at school. When I hear of children who have angry outbursts at home, but not at school, I consider a number of hypotheses: (1) there are family problems, (2) there is inadequate structure at home, and/or (3) the child has struggled to manage his emotions all day at school and has little energy and few internal resources left to cope with problems after school. Sam's mother also was bothered by his fidgeting at church, which she considered to be another sign of his unruliness.

When I asked what was happening at home when Sam started kindergarten, his mother said that she became pregnant as he finished preschool. It was a high-risk pregnancy, so she was confined to bed most of the summer. Obviously, she was less available to help him as he started school. Three months after Sam entered kindergarten, she gave birth. It turned out to be another boy, though she was wishing for a girl. Moreover, Ms. X was unable to breastfeed. After years of trying to become pregnant, I imagined that her pregnancy and early maternal experiences were disappointing, possibly reinforcing her feelings of inadequacy as a woman and a mother. Coincidentally, Sam's birth mother telephoned often that summer and fall. Mr. and Ms. X disapproved of her prior lifestyle and feared that she might have a negative influence on Sam. Therefore, Mr. and Ms. X asked Sam's birth mother to stop calling so often, whereupon she virtually discontinued contact with Sam.

During my first meeting with Sam, his mother sat in the waiting room with his infant brother. She had a faraway gaze, seemingly oblivious to her surroundings and eerily staring into space even while the baby screamed. I was concerned about her lack of attunement to the infant, but a little hopeful about the baby's continued bids for attention. Sam readily separated from his mother to accompany me into my office. He was polite and seemed eager to please me. Though he flitted from activity to activity, he was easily redirected if necessary. After the session, I accompanied him back to the waiting room. When I told his mother that I found him charming, she retorted that he was conning me. Indeed, he showed a pronounced change when reunited with her, becoming agitated and hyperactive. He ran around the room, kissed the baby repeatedly, and started poking him despite his mother's frustrated directives to stop. It was almost as if Sam could not hear or restrain himself, as if he were somehow in another world.

The next few weeks, I administered some psychological tests, including projective tests that Sam completed, and symptom checklists and behavioral rating scales that his parents and teachers completed. The results suggested the presence of impaired affect regulation and underlying depression. Based on Sam's behavior and test responses, I also wondered about the possibility of disorganized attachment. Sam identified one of the Rorschach inkblots as a monster with broken, dangling arms, and other figures had transparencies that revealed their hearts. I interpreted that Sam felt helpless, damaged, and brokenhearted, with poor object relations. I told his parents that sometimes children become aggressive to take control when they feel powerless. A child who anticipates rejection may unconsciously provoke it rather than passively waiting for it to happen. When Ms. X asked if my child had emotional problems, I replied that she became frustrated and aggressive when I failed to notice her speech problems. I told Ms. X that, even for us trained professionals, our biggest blind spots are with our own children. My acknowledgement of my imperfections in parenting possibly made it easier for her to begin to consider hers.

With regard to a psychodynamic formulation, I believe that Ms. X currently was resentful, disappointed, and depressed due to her fertility problems. Although I do not know for certain if she was depressed at the time of Sam's adoption, I cannot help but wonder, given that she was still depressed even after bearing a biological child. Her depression likely contributed to poor or inconsistent attunement to Sam, a boy who had a particularly reactive temperament as an infant. Hence, Ms. X was ineffective in helping to emotionally regulate him. When his parents adopted his next younger brother, Sam experienced sibling rivalry. At the same time, Sam was frustrated due to his speech problems. These issues compounded the opposi-tional behavior that 2-year-olds present to establish their autonomy. When Sam was 5 years old, his mother gave birth after months of bed rest, and his birth mother stopped telephoning. He likely perceived these as rejections, intensifying earlier feelings of loss and abandonment from his relinquishment. Sam experienced little emotional support with separation anxiety upon entering kindergarten, in that his mother was bedridden, then busy caring for his newborn and 3-year-old brothers. She projected her inadequacies onto him, finding his aggressive drives unacceptable, giving undue significance to his fidgeting at church, and attributing badness even to his desires to please me. It was as if she considered him a bad seed from troubled birth parents, malevolent projections that contributed to his damaged self-image.

I believed that Sam would benefit from treatment, though he might require fairly long-term intervention. I recommended individual psychotherapy using a play modality, and parent consultation to address the negative projections and assist in developing improved strategies for dealing with his emotions and behavior. This case example will focus on the parent consultation rather than the therapy with the child. The parent consultation used a combination of psychodynamic, educa-tional, and family systems approaches. Though I believe that Ms. X could benefit from individual psychotherapy, I did not think that she was ready, given that she denied any significant depression on her part. I also would have recommended infant–parent intervention, but she denied any problems or risk on the part of the baby. Therefore, I retained Sam as the identified patient and designed interventions to address the parenting problems without labeling them as depressive symptoms.

I reviewed developmental norms and basic behavioral principles with the par-ents, emphasizing their competencies in working with children. I suggested brief time-outs from stimulating activities if Sam required calming. I recommended that he remain in their presence due to his fears of abandonment, however, and that they actively assist him with self-soothing strategies. When Ms. X announced that she had begun keeping a log of his angry outbursts, I asked that she also record what was happening prior to the outburst in order to determine what triggered it. As it became obvious that Sam reacted with anger when feeling slighted or ignored, his parents became more adept at heading off his tantrums.

Whereas Ms. X initially dwelt on Sam's problems, his father minimized them. I helped them explore Sam's strengths and weaknesses, in order to develop more integrated object representations. I encouraged them to talk to Sam, get to know his feelings and opinions, and see how he viewed the world, in hopes of improving their mentalization skills (Fonagy *et al.*, 2002). When the parents described an incident, I facilitated their reflective functioning (Slade, 2006) by asking how Sam might have perceived the event. I recommended Siegel and Hartzell's (2003) book, *Parenting From the Inside Out*. I especially like its emphasis on reparation following emotional ruptures, which helped in my own parenting.

Based on my experience in working with adoptive parents, they are given little guidance about the amount and kind of contact with birth mothers appropriate to their child's developmental level, nor are they "given permission" to consider their own readiness for contact. I suggested regular, predictable contact with Sam's birth mother, in order to minimize unwanted surprises or repetitions of perceived rejection. I initially suggested infrequent contact, however, because Mr. and Ms. X's discomfort with Sam's birth mother hampered their ability to contain Sam's emotions about her. I secretly felt grateful that I did not have to deal with Caitlin's birth mother due to my own fantasies that the birth mother could have a negative influence or, conversely, that Caitlin might prefer her to me.

A few months into treatment, Sam began asking more questions about his birth mother as his birthday approached. Although birthdays are bittersweet for the adopted child, his adoptive mother told him that he was lucky to have two mothers. If he was so lucky, I asked her, then why did his birth mother relinquish him? Ms. X said that she always told him that his birth mother was too young to properly care for a child. That was true, I said, and perhaps someday he would understand. In the eyes of a young child, however, there is *no* reason to justify giving away a baby. Ms. X appeared startled and sad, as if she had never considered the depth of his loss. This awareness might have helped her to begin forging an emotional connection with him over their mutual losses. I encouraged the parents to reassure Sam that he was not relinquished because something was wrong with him. They also should tell him that they are his "forever parents" who love him even when they disapprove of his behavior.

Within a few months of starting treatment, Sam was calmer and more focused. He began carrying a teddy bear almost everywhere—a bear with a visible heart sewn on its chest. Sam gave his own middle name to the bear. I considered the bear to be Sam's transitional object, a mother-substitute used for self-soothing (Winnicott, 1953). As Sam's angry outbursts decreased, his mother stopped logging them and began focusing on his positive qualities. In addition, she smiled and interacted with the children more often. Within a year, Sam was having only one outburst per week.

Fifteen months into treatment, Mr. X found a better job in another city and the parents announced plans to move the next month. Ms. X said, "This will be better for the family in the long run, but I know it will be hard for Sam to leave you and his friends. Can you help me find a good therapist? And how can we help Sam with deal with the disruption?" I used my professional contacts to find a therapist with a similar theoretical orientation to mine. As I terminated my work with Sam, I helped his parents plan a smooth transition to a new home and school. Mother and son had come so far, Sam with increased self-soothing, and mother with sensitivity to how parental issues impacted him.

During my last session with Sam, I gave him a stuffed penguin with a baby penguin attached to its belly. I suggested that Sam and his parents see the documentary movie, *The March of the Penguins* (2005, directed by Luc Jacquet), a beautiful study of animal bonding and resilience. One month after the final session, I received a note from Sam's mother. The new therapist was not me, but they were adjusting. Six months later, Ms. X left a frantic voice mail. She said that Sam had cut the baby penguin off the adult, then brought the baby bird everywhere—to school, bed, and so forth. He had just lost the baby, and now his mother wanted to buy another one like it. I let her know about an online source. What a sad metaphor, the baby penguin lost from its mother, but what a nice ending, the adoptive mother replacing the lost object.

Summary

In summary, infertility engenders feelings of sadness, inadequacy, and resentment. Infertile adults who lose hope for a biological child need to mourn, much like parents who lost an actual child. When prospective parents rush to fill the void by conceiving or adopting, their unresolved grief can impair their capacity to be emotionally present and attuned to the replacement child. If narcissistic defenses are mobilized, parents have difficulty modifying idealized expectations originally intended for the deceased or non-existent biological child. Some adoptive parents compensate for insecurities by projecting problems onto the child or birth parent. I came to these conclusions not only from a literature review and clinical experience, but also from my own psychological birth as an adoptive mother.

I remember a lunch date with Caitlin the summer that she was 7 years old. I felt warm inside as we sipped our hot and sour soup and spoke of our shared love of spicy food. Then she announced another reason that she liked this soup: "My birth mother owns a famous soup kitchen in Nanchang where she makes hot and sour soup." This claim prompted feelings of competition and envy on my part, because hot and sour soup is not in my cooking repertoire. For an instant, I was annoyed that this other mother intruded on my reverie with my daughter. After all, I went all the way to China to adopt Caitlin so that I would not have to share time with her birth mother. I quickly caught hold of myself, realizing that Caitlin spent less than 24 hours with her mother and undoubtedly has no verbal memories of her. Thus, the soup kitchen was just a fantasy, or Caitlin's version of the family romance (Freud, 1909/1959).

Perhaps Caitlin needed to idealize her birth mother in order to deal with difficult emotions that inevitably will arise later. Perhaps I needed to idealize this mother, too, because her sacrifice enabled me to become a mother when my own biological clock ran down. She might have whetted Caitlin's appetite for soup, in a manner of speaking, but I am lucky to be present to nourish the child. And so Caitlin and I continued a lively conversation in which she embellished her story of her birth mother, the soup kitchen, the busy market street in Nanchang, and the Great Wall of China. The warm glow returned, but this time we were more like a triad than a dyad: an adoptive mother, a child, and the invisible birth mother known to both of us only in imagination.

Caitlin made her birth mother's presence known again the following Christmas Eve as we savored our traditional pork tamales. When Carl raved about finding the best tamales ever, Caitlin corrected him, "No, my birth mother makes the best tamales." I gently challenged Caitlin by asking how her mother in China learned to make tamales. Unperturbed, Caitlin replied, "Well, her niece comes from Mexico." By the following summer when Caitlin was 8 years old, she told me that the stories of her birth mother's culinary accomplishments were just "tall tales." I consider them part and parcel of Caitlin's adoption journey, specifically, her attempt to integrate her Chinese heritage with our Tex-Mex customs to form a multicultural identity.

Despite the fading of Caitlin's family romance, the time has come to make a permanent place at our family table for the birth mother who always will be part of our lives, despite her unknown identity. We all have enough on our plates, so to speak, including a shared sense of loss. I want to develop more compassion for this other mother and for myself. Even if my narcissism slowed my attunement to Caitlin's special needs as a toddler, what parent is perfectly attuned? Now that I made mental space for the lost birth mother alongside my non-existent biological child, I am more capable of seeing Caitlin for who she is.

The "shadow of adoption recedes" (Siskind, 2006, p. 9) as adoption becomes one of the significant events in the family history, but not its sole identity. Whatever the risks in adoption, parents who mourn their losses, accept ambivalence as normal, and temper their idealism are better equipped to help the child negotiate loss and achieve the depressive position. While nobody is perfect, parental empathy, attunement, and a good-enough bond help to transform the adopted child from unwanted to wanted (Miles, 2000). Concurrently, the adoptive parent's self-image may evolve from damaged goods to real parent. Through this ongoing developmental process, adopted child and adoptive parent both can become satisfactory replacements for the lost objects.

References

Albee, E. (1960). The American dream. In *Two plays by Edward Albee*. New York, NY: New American Library.

Anisfeld, L., & Richards, A. (2000). The replacement child: Variations on a theme in history and psychoanalysis. *The Psychoanalytic Study of the Child*, 55: 301–318.

Beebe, B., & Lachmann, F. (2013). *The origins of attachment: Infant research and adult treatment*. New York, NY: Routledge.

Bion, W. (1962). *Learning from experience*. London: Maresfield Library.

Blum, H. (1983). Adoptive parents—generative conflict and generational continuity. *The Psychoanalytic Study of the Child, 38*: 141–163.

Bonovitz, C. (2006). Unconscious communication and the transmission of loss. In K. Hushion, S. Sherman, & D. Siskind (Eds.), *Understanding adoption: Clinical work with adults, children, and parents.* Lanham, MD: Jason Aronson, pp. 11–34.

Brinich, P. (1995). Psychoanalytic perspectives on adoption and ambivalence. *Psychoanalytic Psychology, 12*: 181–199.

Bromberg, P. (2006). *Awakening the dreamer: Clinical journeys.* Mahwah, NJ: Analytic Press.

Burns, L. (2005). Psychological changes in infertility patients. In A. Rosen & J. Rosen (Eds.), *Frozen dreams: Psychodynamic dimensions of infertility and assisted reproduction.* Hillsdale, NJ: Analytic Press, pp. 3–29.

Cain, A., & Cain, B. (1964). On replacing a child. *Journal of the American Academy of Child Psychiatry, 3*: 443–456.

Cohen, S. (1996). Trauma and the developmental process: Excerpts from an analysis of an adopted child. *The Psychoanalytic Study of the Child, 51*: 287–302.

Dali, S., & Parinaud, A. (1973). *The unspeakable confessions of Salvador Dali.* London: Allen.

Downey, W. (2000). Little orphan Anastasia: The analysis of an adopted Russian girl. *The Psychoanalytic Study of the Child, 55*: 145–179.

Etezady, M., Akhtar, S., & Kramer, S. (2000). The multifaceted psychosocial impact of adoption. In S. Akhtar & S. Kramer (Eds.), *Thicker than blood: Bonds of fantasy and reality in adoption.* Lanham, MD: Jason Aronson, pp. 1–17.

Fonagy, P., Target, M., Gergely, G., & Jurist, E. (2002). *Affect regulation, mentalization and the development of the self.* New York, NY: Other Press.

Fraiberg, S., Adelson, E., & Shapiro, V. (1973). Ghosts in the nursery: A psychoanalytic approach to the problems of impaired infant-mother relationships. *Journal of the American Academy of Child Psychiatry, 14*: 387–421.

Frankel, S. (1991). Pathogenic factors in the experiences of early and late adopted children. *The Psychoanalytic Study of the Child, 46*: 91–108.

Freud, S. (1959). Family romances. In J. Strachey (Ed. & Trans.), *The standard edition of the complete psychological works of Sigmund Freud* (Vol. 9, pp. 237–241). London: Hogarth. (Original work published 1909)

Furman, E. (1993). *Toddlers and their mothers: Abridged version for parents and educators.* Madison, CT: International Universities Press.

Gilmore, K. (1995). Gender identity disorder in a girl: Insights from adoption. *Journal of the American Psychoanalytic Association, 43*: 39–59.

Glenn, J. (1974). The adoption theme in Edward Albee's Tiny Alice and the American Dream. *The Psychoanalytic Study of the Child, 29*: 413–429.

Green, A. (1983). The dead mother. In A. Green, *On private madness.* Madison, CT: International Universities Press, 1986.

Hushion, K. (2006). International adoption: Projection and externalization in the treatment of a four-year-old girl and her parents. In K. Hushion, S. Sherman, & D. Siskind (Eds.), *Understanding adoption: Clinical work with adults, children, and parents.* Lanham, MD: Jason Aronson, pp. 35–46.

Koch, W. (2008). Fewer foreign children adopted. *USA Today,* Feb. 10.

Kohut, H. (1977). *The restoration of the self.* New York, NY: International Universities Press.

Landerholm-EK, L. (2001). The experience of abandonment and adoption, as a child and as a parent, in a psychological motivational perspective. *International Forum of Psychoanalysis, 10*: 12–25.

Legg, C., & Sherick, I. (1976). The replacement child—A developmental tragedy: Some preliminary comments. *Child Psychiatry and Human Development, 7*: 79–97.

Mahler, M., Pine, F., & Bergman, A. (1975). *The psychological birth of the human infant: Symbiosis and individuation.* New York, NY: Basic Books.

Main, M. (1991). Metacognitive knowledge, metacognitive monitoring, and singular (coherent) versus multiple (incoherent) model of attachment: Findings and directions for future research. In C. Parks, J. Stevenson-Hinde & P. Morris (Eds.), *Attachment across the life cycle.* New York, NY: Tavistock/Routledge, pp. 127–159.

Main, M., & Hesse, E. (1990). Parents' unresolved traumatic experiences are related to infants' disorganized attachment status: Is frightened and/or frightening parental behavior the linking mechanism? In M. Greenberg, D. Cicchetti, & E. Cummings (Eds.), *Attachment in the preschool years: Theory, research, and intervention.* Chicago, IL: University of Chicago Press, pp. 161–182.

Malave, A. (2005). From infertility to adoption. In A. Rosen & J. Rosen (Eds.), *Frozen dreams: Psychodynamic dimensions of infertility and assisted reproduction.* Hillsdale, NJ: Analytic Press, pp. 128–164.

Marwick, H., & Murray, L. (2008). The effects of maternal depression on the "musicality" of infant directed speech and conversational engagement. In S. Malloch & C. Trevarthen (Eds.), *Communicative musicality: Narratives of expressed gesture and being human.* Oxford: Oxford University Press. Referenced in Murray, L. (2009). The development of children of postnatally depressed mothers: Evidence from the Cambridge longitudinal study. *Psychoanalytic Psychotherapy, 23:* 185–199.

Miles, C. (2000). Bonding across difference. In S. Akhtar & S. Kramer (Eds.), *Thicker than blood: Bonds of fantasy and reality in adoption.* Lanham, MD: Jason Aronson, pp. 19–59.

Morrell, J., & Murray, L. (2003). Parenting and the development of conduct disorder and hyperactive symptoms in childhood: A prospective longitudinal study from 2 months to 8 years. *Journal of Child Psychology and Psychiatry, 44:* 489–508.

Murray, L., Kempton, C., Woolgar, M., & Hooper, R. (1993). Depressed mothers' speech to their infants and its relation to infant gender and cognitive development. *Journal of Child Psychology and Psychiatry, 34:* 1083–1101.

Murray, L., Fiori-Cowley, A., Hooper, R., & Cooper, P. (1996). The impact of postnatal depression and associated adversity on early mother-infant interactions and later infant outcome. *Child Development, 67:* 2512–2526.

Murray, L., Halligan, S., & Cooper, P. (2009). Effects of postnatal depression on mother-infant interactions and child development. In T. Wachs & G. Bremner (Eds.), *Handbook of infant development* (pp. 192–220). New York, NY: Wiley-Blackwell.

Nagera, H. (1967). *Vincent van Gogh: A psychological study.* London: George, Allen & Unwin.

Novick, J., & Novick, K. (2005). *Working with parents makes therapy work.* Lanham, MD: Jason Aronson.

Reed, K. (2000). Separation-individuation theory and interracial adoption. In S. Akhtar & S. Kramer (Eds.), *Thicker than blood: Bonds of fantasy and reality in adoption.* Lanham, MD: Jason Aronson, pp. 61–89.

Rosen, A. (2005). Facts and fantasies about infertility. In S. Brown (Ed.), *What do mothers want? Developmental perspectives, clinical challenges.* Hillsdale, NJ: Analytic Press, pp. 171–191.

Schechter, M. (2000). Attachment theory in light of the adoption research. In S. Akhtar & S. Kramer (Eds.), *Thicker than blood: Bonds of fantasy and reality in adoption.* Lanham, MD: Jason Aronson, pp. 139–152.

Schore, A. (1994). *Affect regulation and the origin of the self: The neurobiology of emotional development.* Hillsdale, NJ: Lawrence Erlbaum.

Seligman, S. (1999). Integrating Kleinian theory and intersubjective infant research observing projective identification. *Psychoanalytic Dialogues, 9:* 129–159.

Sherick, I. (1983). Adoption and disturbed narcissism: A case illustration of a latency boy. *Journal of the American Psychoanalytic Association, 31*: 487–513.

Siegel, A., & Siegel, R. (2001). Adoption and the enduring fantasy of an idealized other. *Progress in Self Psychology, 17*: 129–147.

Siegel, D., & Hartzell, M. (2003). *Parenting from the inside out: How a deeper self-understanding can help you raise children who thrive.* New York, NY: Jeremy P. Tarcher/Putnam.

Siskind, D. (2006). The world of adoption: An introduction. In K. Hushion, S. Sherman, & D. Siskind (Eds.), *Understanding adoption: Clinical work with adults, children, and parents.* Lanham, MD: Jason Aronson, pp. 3–10.

Slade, A. (2006). Reflective parenting programs: Theory and development. *Psychoanalytic Inquiry, 26*: 640–657.

Spitz, R. (1946). Anaclitic depression: An inquiry into the genesis of psychiatric conditions in early childhood. *The Psychoanalytic Study of the Child, 2*: 313–342.

Stern, D. (1995). *The motherhood constellation.* New York, NY: Basic Books.

Tronick, E. (2007). *The neurobehavioral and social-emotional development of infants and children.* New York, NY: Norton.

Tronick, E., Als, H., Adamson, L., Wise, S., & Brazelton, T. (1978). The infant's response to entrapment between contradictory messages in face-to-face interaction. *Journal of the American Academy of Child and Adolescent Psychiatry, 17*: 1–13.

Tronick, E., & Weinberg, M. (1997). Depressed mothers and infants: Failure to form dyadic states of consciousness. In L. Murray & P. Cooper (Eds.), *Postpartum depression and child development.* New York, NY: Guilford, pp. 54–81.

Viola, P. (2000). The pain of broken bonds. In S. Akhtar & S. Kramer (Eds.), *Thicker than blood: Bonds of fantasy and reality in adoption.* Lanham, MD: Jason Aronson, pp. 199–210.

Waterman, B. (2003). *The birth of an adoptive, foster or stepmother: Beyond biological mothering attachments.* London: Jessica Kingsley.

Weinberg, M. (1992). Sex differences in 6-month-old infants' affect and behavior: Impact on maternal caregiving. Unpublished manuscript referenced in Tronick, E. (2007). *The neurobehavioral and social-emotional development of infants and children.* New York, NY: Norton.

Weinberg, M., & Tronick, E. (1992). Sex differences in emotional expression and affective regulation in 6-month-old infants (Abstract). *Society for Pediatric Research, 31*: 15A. Referenced in Tronick, E. (2007). *The neurobehavioral and social-emotional development of infants and children.* New York, NY: Norton.

Winnicott, D. (1953). Transitional objects and transitional phenomena. In D. Winnicott, *Playing and reality.* New York, NY: Routledge, pp. 1–34.

_____ (1956). Primary maternal preoccupation. In D. Winnicott, *Through paediatrics to psycho-analysis: Collected papers.* New York, NY: Brunner/Mazel (1992).

Mother as therapist / therapist as mother

COMMENTARY ON SECTION IV

Mother as therapist / therapist as mother

Ellen L. K. Toronto

Truth be told women's reproductive issues affect all of our lives. A difficult birth, numerous miscarriages, an unwanted pregnancy—all significantly impact a mother's relationship to her child and our unwillingness to address and assimilate these issues remains a cloud that only obstructs our vision. My understanding of my own life would have been greatly diminished if I had never been able to process my mother's reproductive history. She was married at 30 and tried unsuccessfully to get pregnant for several years. She became pregnant at 35 but gave birth to a still-born full-term child. We were told that the cord was wrapped around the baby's neck, cutting off her air supply, but in retrospect it was likely a strangulated umbilical cord. My mother had my sister a year later, a subsequent miscarriage, and then me when she was almost 41.

The still-born baby, named Elizabeth Lynn, was a very active presence in our lives. We often heard that she would have been a perfect child and that we—my sister and I—fell far short with our pranks and antics. "If Elizabeth had lived . . . " my mother would say and then follow with a commentary on what we had done wrong. The results for me were consequential. I played the replacement child—the "dead baby"—until a gifted analyst was able to help me bring this adaptation into consciousness. But my mother suffered as well. She had no one to talk to about it because at that time no one even recognized the tragedy of losing a baby. Women might have whispered about it, but it certainly never reached public consciousness. Erik Erikson (1968) stated that "everyday miracle, pregnancy and childbirth, have disquieted every man through childhood, youth and beyond. In his accounts and historical periods, man acknowledges this as a probably necessary sideshow" (p. 264).

The last two chapters cast a blazing light on the "sideshow" and illuminate the very real suffering that accompanies pregnancy and birthing as well as its unpredictable aftermath. Both authors are also psychodynamic therapists and both have addressed the ways in which their pregnancies and subsequent births became a

palpable presence in the consulting room. Darcy explores the impact of her pregnancy on a very difficult patient. She quite accurately points to her psychically and
culturally determined role as the too-good mother being a factor in the patient's
inability to express her rage at her displacement by the new-born child. Darcy illustrates the tenacity of our image of the nurturing mother as it constricts her—both
the woman herself and the woman as therapist—in her ability to tolerate the full
range of emotion in her patients.

On the other hand, I believe that Darcy overlooks the excellent work that she
did with this challenging patient before her maternity leave. She was able to connect emotionally with this woman in a way that was undoubtedly beneficial. Perhaps the therapist's own experience of shame clouded her capacity to see her good
work. As her pregnancy progressed, however, she encountered a "perfect storm" of
emotion—her own and her patient's as they both dealt with their lack of attuned
mothering.

I am reminded of a case which Darcy mentioned in my personal communication with her. My patient, whom I will call Fran, was a woman in her mid-fifties
while I was a young mother. She had come into treatment following an auto
accident in which she was severely injured and suffering a lot of pain. We initially
had a very positive connection, stemming in part, I believe, from her resemblance
to my own mother. She was petite in stature with the same high cheekbones and
sculpted features of my mother. As treatment progressed she was better able to
manage her pain as well as her relationships with her children who found her difficult to deal with. This difficulty was due in part to her driven manner of speech
and propensity for telling events in excruciating detail, characteristics that I found
challenging as well.

As we probed more deeply into Fran's background she related that although she
had four adult children, she had had numerous miscarriages which had been very
painful and disappointing to her. She came from a religion that valued fecundity
in women. Around this time, I became pregnant with my fourth child. My patient
worked in the neonatal unit of the hospital where I gave birth. She was present
when my pediatrician announced that my baby was "the fourth son in this family." After a Caesarean Section I returned to my part-time practice within 10 days.
The treatment devolved after that for reasons that remain unclear although Darcy's
paper has been very helpful in this regard. Looking back, I believe that it was also
"a perfect storm" of unmet needs and raw emotion that I can only now begin to
untangle.

An incident around that time captured the infinite convolution of the treatment with Fran. I had recently returned from my C Section. Fran wore a neck
brace due to her injuries and was unable to drive, so her daughter had dropped
her off. For some reason her daughter then parked directly behind another car in
our parking lot and walked off with the keys. A few minutes later there was a frantic knock at my office door. There stood a large woman in a hot pink bridesmaid
dress. She was a tenant in the building and she told us that we had to move the
car because she was late to a wedding. We had no keys and no way to move the

car. With the help of the large woman, we contemplated moving the car by pushing it out of the way, but my patient was disabled and so was I. To this day I can't remember what we did but the incident has stayed in my mind as representative of this treatment.

There is no doubt that a pregnant therapist complicates the treatment. We can ignore that fact or we can address questions such as the following: Is the pregnancy of either patient or therapist an enactment? What can be done if a patient works at the hospital where the therapist gives birth? Just who is the mother then? Who is the baby? Who carries the pain of miscarriages and difficult births? Should therapists be forbidden from getting pregnant because it complicates the treatment too much? To that last question I will answer a resounding "No." Complications are the stuff of life and our commitment in this volume is to speak about them as openly and clearly as possible.

The final chapter includes a "gripping" account of the birth experience itself and the ways in which it can effect changes in the emotional makeup of the birthing woman. Reale describes in vivid detail her descent into a psychic hell that she felt as a life-altering encounter with her own limits. She found that in returning to work she was pushed again to those limits and required all of her emotional reserves to survive. I venture to say that for many, if not most women, their pregnancies and birthing experiences are also life-altering—shaping and influencing their existence in ways we are only beginning to explore.

For me the most striking aspect of Reale's account was that she could *remember* in great detail the birthing experience. I wrote accounts of all four of my birth experiences as we were encouraged to do at the time. But even though I attempted to recall the unbearable pain which I knew I had felt, I could not, *even the next day*, remember what it was like. It was known to me, but unformulated, outside the realm of language or identifiable feeling. Reale describes it as follows:

> It was at this moment I went very far—too far—within myself. Like sub-level far. One may relate it to "sleeping" during labor, but it felt much more dissociative than sleep . . . I would "come to" every minute or so and feel panicked that I WAS STILL THERE, STUCK. I knew I was losing my grip.
>
> *(p. 230)*

I know that I also kept falling asleep during my first delivery of twenty-four hours, but in retrospect it is likely that I was in a dissociative state that I had never identified until now.

Two of my deliveries, like Reale's, were traumatic—the first, a breach birth and the last, an emergency C Section. But until reading this paper I have never considered the idea that a woman can suffer PTSD from traumatic births. Women have, as Reale points out, been told that birthing it something you endure and then forget when the beautiful baby is placed on your belly. But this paper points out that traumatic birthing affects the mother—sometimes changing forever, for good or ill, her ability to manage her life or care for a child or return to her profession. Reale has alerted us to the knowledge that pregnancy, birthing, and the aftermath are from a psychological perspective an "undiscovered country."

I feel hopeful in reading these papers from young professionals. They have clearly extended my thinking and my understanding about my own experiences as a pregnant/birthing therapist and woman who is forever altered in ways that we are only starting to comprehend.

Reference

Erikson, E.H. (1968). *Identity youth and crisis.* New York, NY: Norton.

10

TOO WARM, TOO SOFT, TOO MATERNAL

What is good enough?

Meredith Darcy

As a therapist becomes a mother, calling the experience "emotionally difficult" can be a serious understatement. The major transformation of one's self and identity, and managing these momentous changes, can be more challenging than ever expected. My personal accommodation to this understatement personally can be taken as the background "music" for the words you will read as I explore the question in the title.

Background

In the following chapter, I will review a 5-year treatment of a woman that ended abruptly upon my return from a maternity leave. I will discuss this idea of the maternal ideal and how it affected both women and ultimately the treatment.

What started out initially as a dyad became a therapist, a patient, and an infant, thus bringing to mind Winnicott's (1960) much quoted, "There is no such thing as an infant, meaning that whenever one finds an infant, one finds maternal care, and without maternal care there would be no infant" (p. 587). Both therapist and patient's individual ideas of an imagined or fantasized mother, as well as our past and imagined experiences of being mothered, came to powerfully affect us in the room. I will call this the maternal ideal—an idealized notion of what it means to be a mother.

Literature review

Benedek (1970) describes psychological striving for motherhood as a core feminine wish, and she emphasizes the importance and influence of the maternal ego ideal as it influences maternal wishes and attitudes. More than an id wish, a narcissistic gratification, motherhood is a most coveted aspiration of the maternal ego ideal (p. 139). More than the desire for motherhood, the vital capacity for *motherliness* depends upon the psychosexual maturity of the total personality, but especially upon the maternal identifications. Identification (Benedek, 1976), an unconscious process, begins in the oral, symbiotic phase of development. During this phase, infants of both sexes will introject the image of their mother and incorporate their capacity for empathy and tenderness. With this primary object relationship, the infant will organize the nascent superego, and it is generally assumed that the developmental changes in gender characteristics evolve from this primary identification with the mother (p. 158).

Wishful fantasies of being a mother as distinct from being mothered are organized and integrated at later developmental levels (Benedek, 1970). In latency, the over-determined maternal attributes are secured in the maternal ego ideal. In adult life, the child reproduces the old self and objects, while also representing the bond between the parents and the realization of a mature maternal ego ideal. Maternal ideals and aspirations are deeply rooted in the unconscious feminine superego and contribute to humanitarian concerns and caring responsibility, and the development of discipline and ethics in the succeeding generation. Internalization of the ideal mother is linked to wishes for an ideal family (p. 139).

On the concept of the wish or wishful phantasy (Sandler, 2003), it can be said that every wish involves a self-representation, an object representation, and an interaction between the two. There is a role for both self and object. Thus the child who has a wish to cling has, as part of this wish, a mental representation of clinging to someone else; but she also has, in her wish, a representation of the object responding to her clinging in a particular way (p.19). Pines (1982) writes about the woman's relationship to her body, to herself, to her own mother as an object, and to her experience of being physically and emotionally mothered. The mother is to her child both the symbol of the maturational environment and of motherliness itself. Her physical presence and emotional attitudes towards her child and its body are integrated with the child's experience and her conscious and unconscious fantasies. The representation of an internal mother created in this way is a lifelong model for her daughter to identify with and also to differentiate herself from (p. 312).

Entering motherhood promotes deep psychological changes in a woman during pregnancy—a woman confronts psychological and physical transformations and prepares herself to become a mother in order to take care of a helpless and immature baby, in need of protection (Ammaniti & Trentini, 2009). This process is strictly connected with the development of maternal representations of herself as a mother and of the future baby as a result of maternal projections, dreams, attributions, and conscious and unconscious fantasies. These maternal representations are rooted in the personal history of every woman from infancy to adolescence, specifically mirroring the actual life and the relationship with her own mother (p. 543).

Grete Bibring *et al.* (1961) wrote:

> Pregnancy is a crisis that affects all expectant mothers, no matter what their state of psychic health. Crises, as we see it, are turning points in the life of the

individual, leading to acute disequilibria which under favorable conditions result in specific maturational steps toward new functions. We find them as developmental phenomena at points of no return between one phase and the next when decisive changes deprive former central needs and modes of living of their significance, forcing the acceptance of highly charged new goals and functions. Pregnancy as a major turning point in the life of the woman represents one of these normal crises, especially for the primigravida who faces the impact of this event for the first time. We believe that all women show what looks like remarkable, far-reaching psychological changes while they are pregnant.

(pp. 25–26)

The pregnancy of the analyst is a major event in the life of both analyst and patient. Patients have "real" reactions to the pregnancy, reactions that are relatively transference free, genuine, and realistic (Fenster *et al.*, 1986). Working with a pregnant therapist, and the changes happening within the confines of the analytic space, is real, and is happening in present time, and is affecting both therapist and patient. Shifts occur in affective state, perspective, identity, and role—the therapist is going through a significant life-changing event intrapersonally and interpersonally, in front of, and ultimately with, her patient. Fenster *et al.* (1986) stressed the significance of a facilitating change in the "real" relationship as a result of the therapist's pregnancy. She believes that the analyst's pregnancy can enhance the therapeutic relationship in an important way: that pregnancy provides a valuable opportunity for a mutually caring "real" relationship while enlivening the transference between patient and therapist.

The patient, traditionally "the one" going through the major life change while entering the treatment space, is now confronted with another person embarking on a life-changing transition. The image of two people together in a life raft (Joseph Newirth, personal communication), managing the dangerous tumult of sea, while also surviving each other—these are the risks of a dynamic treatment while living a real life. Attempting to work through conflicts that arise during pregnancy may provide helpful and effective therapeutic experience for some patients, while for others, the reality of what is happening within the room may prove too difficult or painful to bear.

Beginning treatment

Abbot was one of my first patients in private practice, referred to me as part of a post-graduate training program specializing in eating disorders. I was 34 when I started working with Abbot. For 3 years prior, I had been working exclusively with children and adolescents, doing play therapy with foster kids. While being both eager and excited to begin working with adults and to build my private practice, I was also attempting to build my family; my husband and I had been trying for several years to conceive a child. Working with these children had begun to take its toll on me—I had wanted them all, and my anger at the parents and the foster care system had become too intense for me. My private practice was the much-needed respite (or so I thought) from the toils and torments of working with the unlucky, and sometimes uncared for, foster children I had been devoting my time and energy to.

Abbot, called Abby, was a prickly middle-aged woman. Upon our first meeting she questioned my age and youthful appearance ("you look like a baby"), my training, and whether I could in fact help her. She was reluctantly seeking individual psychotherapy—an overeating support group at a local treatment center required conjunctive individual therapy. Abby immediately remarked on my unfortunate choice of office décor. When she commented that my expensive, modern, leather therapist chair, a coveted piece I was quite happy with, was "the ugliest piece of furniture that she had ever laid eyes on," I found myself unexpectedly laughing aloud, being both caught off guard and entertained by her "honesty" and lack of decorum. Usually upon entering my office, she would adjust the venetian blinds to her liking. This would never bother me.

I found her brashness disarming, and, although well aware she was working quite hard to keep me at a safe distance, she intrigued me. Abby tried to be cold and would intellectualize her feelings, but she had a charm, spirit, and boldness (often called *chutzpah*) that I truly enjoyed and even admired. I found her challenging, off-putting manner to be very familiar.

I come from a loud, intrusive, competitive, hypercritical Eastern European-Jewish family. Having been in psychoanalytic psychotherapy for over a decade at this point, I had learned a certain way to emotionally manage these loved, yet off-putting cast of characters, and it was a relief to finally not take their insults and criticisms personally. It was liberating to understand that the pain a person may be consciously or unconsciously attempting to inflict was coming from his or her own discomforts and not (only) from me. Eventually, I could spend time with a difficult great-aunt, who could never understand the "rats nest of hair" upon my head and my aversion to a hairbrush. I understood this was her (unfortunate as it may be) way of connecting, with the world and me. And I accepted it, and her, and would "enjoy" (in retrospect, tolerate) her company nonetheless.

Abby had difficulties relating to others and would use food to self-soothe and regulate affect. As with many people with eating disorders, Abby would concretize her emotional experience; she was not able to think symbolically. She experienced her feelings as literally being in her body. Therefore, if her problem was experienced in her body, she would do something to the body to relieve this discomfort (e.g. compulsive overeating). She felt "bad" and therefore she was bad—ashamed of herself and needs. Concretizing neediness in the body makes it more possible to actually manage and control such needs (Sands, 2003), because the body can be used in a way that purely affective experience cannot: eating disorders provide a concrete, doable solution to the experience of intolerable, overwhelming affect and need.

Abby would often state matter-of-factly that she was obese, a "fact" I would question. She had a big presence, and at times I would find her intimidating—to me she seemed strong, athletic, somewhat overweight, yes—but the term "obese" had never crossed my mind to describe her build or frame. At times, I would point out this discrepancy between our points of view. I felt I was seeing her body in a *"positive"* way, but to her, I was actually **NOT** *seeing her*, and she would become indignant, questioning my judgment and authenticity. This was a common struggle Abby and I would have over the next 5 years; her need to be seen as bad, ugly, and fat and my need to see her in a kinder, more accepting light. Abby's body hate, her concrete experience of self-hatred felt in her body and about her body, was palpably felt in the room. Moments like these were vivid testimony to the oft-stated observation that the body is where the self lives.

Abby described her parents as being preoccupied with their appearance, especially about their weight and size. She claims to have inherited her father's body; he was always dissatisfied with his weight, trying to lose that extra 20 pounds, and was very critical of himself and others. He viewed "fat" as a weakness: ugly and self-indulgent. Abby describes her mother as being tiny and eating like a bird—well practiced at being self-denying. I still remember a story Abby told me: One evening after dinner, while talking to her mother about something, Abby spontaneously and uncharacteristically started to cry. After several minutes of talking about what was upsetting her—Abby looked around to find that her mother had left the room. Abby defended her mother's actions, "We don't talk about real things—she was uncomfortable, so she left." This present-time story reminded me of other childhood interactions Abby had described—her mother being either uninterested or unable to listen, take her in, or soothe her. Abby's stories illustrated a remoteness that seemed abundantly clear to me, yet Abby would protect her mother. Her idealized notion of her mother was fiercely protected. Unable to assign her blame, Abby took full responsibility for her un-lovability, acquiring decades' worth of self-hate and self-blame for the ugliness of her "neediness"—an experienced ugliness, manifestly residing in the subjugation of her hated body. Sands (2003) writes that "the subjugation of the body" is an attempt to dominate one's needy self-experience rather than the maternal object. Abby's attempts to destroy her early experience of dependence on, and need for, the chronically misattuned and unresponsive other, has brought with it unbearable feelings of rage, helplessness, and shame.

The foundations of the self and the distinction between self and object are shaped by an integration of bodily experience with mental representation (Pines, 1982). If the child was satisfied by her mother's body, she rightly felt that her own body satisfied her mother (Balint, 1973, p. 200). If the child has not felt satisfied by her mother at the pre-oedipal stage, not felt that she herself has satisfied her, she can never make up for this basic loss of a primary stable sense of well-being in her body and with her body image unless she sacrifices her normal drive towards a positive oedipal outcome (Pines, 1980). Narcissistic injury, giving rise to narcissistic rage, envy of the mother and lack of self-esteem, will add to the difficulties of separation from her (Pines, 1982, p. 312).

The therapy

Abby hated coming to therapy—she would tell me this often. She explained that our time together was her most difficult time spent each week. Abby much preferred her group therapy experience and often reminded me that she was only coming to individual treatment because it was "mandatory". She valued her interactions with this group—it was her primary social contact during the week. I would speak with her group therapy leader several times throughout the year regarding Abby. This therapist would often complain that Abby's authoritative, directive, and critical style of communicating was alienating others in the group. She would often threaten, "If Abby doesn't get with the program . . !" Abby would frequently discuss this therapist with me. She often would remark upon her physique: her fit figure and toned arms.

Despite her palpable discomfort with individual psychotherapy, Abby began coming twice weekly about 3 years into her psychotherapy treatment. Another change occurring this third year of Abby's treatment was that after several years of trying unsuccessfully to conceive a child, I began a series of IVF treatments. I was hopeful that this reproductive technology could finally make me the mother I had wanted to be. I had always known I wanted to become a mother, and like many women my age in metropolitan areas, I had put my education and career first, assuming that conceiving children in my mid-thirties would be a viable option.

Over the next 2-year period, I went through five IVF cycles. Out of those cycles, I became pregnant three times, and from those pregnancies, I had two early-term miscarriages and one full-term pregnancy. During this personally challenging time, Abby was regularly coming to her two sessions weekly. She seemed more committed to her treatment, willing to introspect, trusting the process and me. Our connection seemed to be strengthening and growing. Also during this time, Abby began to experience even greater anxiety and discomfort due to my changing body. My breasts had grown considerably and I was looking much more like a woman and less like a "baby." As expected with the fertility treatment, and the requisite medications, I gained about 10 pounds.

"You're gaining weight," she confronted me, accusingly, after my second miscarriage. We discussed her fantasies of my out of control eating, marital troubles, and depression. She voiced her anger and anxiety about working with me—how could she trust me, come to me for help, knowing that I was so "out of control"? I never told her explicitly about either miscarriage. However, after repeatedly asking me, quite pointedly, "**Why are you gaining weight?**" and extensive exploration about her fantasies, I asked her if she _really_ wanted to _know_ *why* I had gained weight. But she purposely changed topics. Would I have told her? I might have.

I told Abby about my third pregnancy at about 22 weeks, after blood tests and anatomy scan revealed a healthy baby boy. She was relieved at first, having noticed **more** weight gain, but didn't want to mention it (which seemed so unlike her!). She expressed feeling hurt that I had not shared my news earlier, as "friends usually tell each other after three months." Although aware this label of "friend" was not an accurate depiction of our relationship, I chose not to interpret her need to keep me on equal (safe and comfortable) footing and see where it would take us. All of my years of play therapy had taught me to "play" and accept—I wanted to encourage an openness, not derail what was being created in the room. Staying in the affective frame (Slochower, 2013) that a patient needs can protect and positively impact those whose emotional experience was chronically obliterated (p. 609). When we would discuss my growing belly and subsequent leave, she would assure me it was fine for me to bring my baby boy into the office and she would hold him for me during her session. She thought I should name him Ozzy. I would smile and happily explore her fantasies with Momma, Abby, and Ozzy; she would bounce him on her knee and take him to the park while I saw other patients. She was part of our lives, and we were all together.

With our increased discussion regarding my growing body and exploration of her fantasies about our relationship, she had begun to have greater awareness and ability to articulate more feelings. Abby began to describe the loneliness she would experience at night, triggering her binge eating. She began discussing her feelings regarding her parents more honestly and would detail their interactions with greater depth and texture. She began to experience and articulate feeling unloved and lonely. I felt I was making headway, but was also insufficiently aware that our progress was perforating Abby's carefully constructed armor.

Abby started to become increasingly more angry and frightened. "You're huge!" she would regularly gasp, physically recoiling when I opened my office door to greet her. She seemed to hate my growing body, much in the same way she hated her own, and seemed to see my new "woman's" body as soft and "bad" and my vulnerability as weakness. Abby was having a hard time with my changing role, with seeing me as "mother." Here I was her "friend," and now I was becoming a "mother." Abby's criticisms of me were strikingly at odds with my own image of myself. We were having such different emotional reactions—I felt like super mom, so maternal—loving my growing pregnant body, as well as Abby.

She started complaining about "knowing" too much about me, and began lashing out at my "emotional openness." She became critical and accusatory of my "warmth" and "softness", blaming me for not being "a good enough therapist." She claimed that I had not maintained my professional boundaries: I had allowed her to "see me" and to "know me." This was now personal, *too* personal: *not* professional any longer. She seemed scared and frightened. She said she could not imagine a male patient working with me, as I was too gentle, supportive and kind—not tough enough. My maternity and these images of "loving" qualities were simultaneously triggering both longing and fear, causing her attack.

I was there in the room: being and growing. I was vulnerable: excited, but also anxious about the pregnancy itself. Did she "know" or could she sense these intensifying feelings within me?

Abby was angry: she was experiencing real feelings towards me and was confused and scared about what that meant. Now I was pregnant and becoming a mother—Abby began to feel hurt. She claimed to feel tricked, that I had "allowed" her to connect with me, knowing full well that I was trying to conceive a child and would be leaving her. Her feelings of loss and abandonment were great; she felt angry, hurt and rejected by me. Understandably, there is intrinsic loss in any break in treatment, but she was also mourning my changing identity—she would cry, calling me "little Meredith." She would sob, **"Little Meredith is having a baby!"** Evidence of Abby's early disruptions in care—parental unavailability, early rejection and emotional misattunement and neglect (Slade, 2000)—was now being triggered by feelings of abandonment and grief in response to our work together and my impending leave.

Was there room for us both, Little Meredith **and** Little Abby?

My dream

I had a dream around this time (I was 6 months pregnant): I was in a cafe in NYC—I saw an unidentified woman whose name began with A. I was very angry with her—she was acting petty and immature. I was frustrated and yelled at her, "leave me alone!" Suddenly, A became my waitress, and she would not bring me my lunch. I waited an hour, and then complained to the manager. I was furious and embarrassed. In the dream I thought, why had I not complained, spoken up earlier?! Why do I feel I am always so angry and why do I feel bad things are always happening to me? I felt like an outsider: isolated and alone.

This dream seems to express my feelings of intense powerlessness, regarding my infertility, my family, and my unexpressed anger towards Abby—why had I not spoken up? Did I want Abby to be more "helpful" or more accepting of my maternity? More generous and less self-serving? There was a dynamic being played out between Abby and me similar to those between my mother and me. Both women were "needy" with a similar age gap between us. It might have been too much at the time for me to be able to pull back, see her objectively, and identify her neediness. In the countertransference, I am once again the "child" to the in-need and attacking mother. And now pregnant, the question is: who is really taking care of whom? (E. Toronto, personal communication).

My reactions

Working with Abby, I had begun to feel ashamed of my humanity, my warmth and my softness, and was unaware of the depth of my anger towards her. Like in my dream, I felt ashamed by my anger and frustration. I couldn't tolerate my hatred of Abby, triggered by her attacks, which flooded me with shame. Joseph Newirth aptly explains how difficult it can be for therapists to deal with their own sense of shame: "It's a very powerful thing that inhibits us, to enter into our own feelings of 'I hate this person.' In countertransferential situations we are identified with a patient's unconscious, but we are often bringing up our own shameful experience. It's a very powerful experience for most of us, because we'd rather control it. So we learn how to be *good*" (italics added, 2009, p. 15).

I believe that my way of dealing (or actually **not** dealing) with Abby's aggression and my lack of awareness of the anger I felt towards her, veiled in the "mother ideal," stood in the way of a genuine connection. Abby may have been managing her own feelings of vulnerability, by attacking or withdrawing, presumably feeling hopeless to ever have her needs met. But I was lost in the depth of my unmanaged hate, of my anger, so an honest exploration of what was really happening in the room was impossible. Impossible because unless I recognized my *own* hate, I could not recognize the existence of the part of Abby I was hating—so the rage felt by that part of Abby would increase in proportion to the extent I was invalidating her right to exist. One could surely see this as an enactment of Abby's relational trauma with her mother. It would have been wonderful if I had recognized it at the time, but I did not. I was too wounded, blinded by shame and self-doubt. I was injured and reeling from Abby's words: I felt I **was** too feminine, too passive, not tough enough, too inexperienced and supportive. Was I a "good" therapist? Do "good" therapists **hate** their patients? Could I actually be a good mother? Was I selfish to want both a substantive career AND motherhood? I was so ashamed of all my ill-perceived mistakes of practice ("was I too warm, too soft, too maternal?") and fertility ("had I waited too long to have a child?")! The therapist is in a terrible bind when bearings and boundaries are unwittingly lost, and, in the end, gets caught in the patient's intense shame dynamic (Bromberg, 2006).

An unbearable shame spiral was overtaking us both—causing the pain and experiencing the pain had merged. Abby was overwhelmed by her intense feelings of need and shame; she was feeling misunderstood, angry, adrift and alone—reminiscent of how she had felt during childhood. Bromberg describes how (2006, p. 140) the child's own need for loving recognition becomes despised and shame ridden. This need becomes dissociated, and when triggered, releases not only the unmet hunger for authentic responsiveness, but a flood of shame. Someone feeling guilt is saying "I <u>did</u> something bad" while someone feeling shame is saying, "I <u>am</u> bad." There is a big difference.

In retrospect, I believe that my longing to create a loving family was very strong, but this longing to love, this mothering fantasy, was hobbling me. My "all-generous, all-giving" maternal ideal was an unrealistic expectation of myself—I was acting like the fantasized mother I wanted to be and wish I'd had. This blanket, overt "acceptance," this idealized form of empathy, on one hand may have helped Abby to connect with me and express her own rageful and unacceptable feelings. But on the other hand, the abundance of contempt and her intense negative affect created an avalanche of shame and need within her, with no safe, containing function. Her feelings were accepted, but were they "held" and **felt** by me?

When a therapist cannot tolerate a patient's pain, by not having enough distance from it to notice its magnitude, the patient will experience this as further emotional abandonment—this will trigger shame rather than provide recognition. In this dynamic of failure each person feels shame: the patient feels that her pain is unbearable and toxic and the analyst feels that her "help" is toxic to the patient (Benjamin, 2007). Historically, all attempts by analysis to cure patients through the technical stance of trying to be good objects have failed. A patient needs a human being as a partner, a human being who can accept her own limitations and failings (Bromberg, 2006). Beneath the quilt of Abby's assailments were cries of, "See me—my hate, rage, need, self-hatred—feel that!" I was NOT. I had left the room.

For Abby, her only protection against losing genuine mothering was to never experience herself as the baby who needed it. I had not been paying attention to the part of her that protected her against the betrayal that was "sure" to follow any hope or trust that I was different from her own mother. I was not acknowledging the existence of the part of her dissociative mental structure that I didn't want to see—her protective use of mistrust that would forever keep alive the trauma of the past as if it was a here-and-now inevitability.

At the time, I believed that I was trying to "hold" her—hold her hurt about feeling close to me, threatened by my changing self, and fearful of my imminent leave—her rage and her contempt for my "femininity" and separateness. I felt I was *accepting*, rather than *interpreting*, her emotional state and perception of me. Slochower (2014) writes that holding a hostile denigrating patient means trying to accept her dismissiveness and belief in one's incompetence, without challenging it. At the time I felt I was communicating my resilience, that her need and rage would not destroy or obliterate me, that I could survive her attacks without retaliation. *But I was not holding.* Slochower states it is not only essential that the analyst be in touch with her own hate towards the patient, but also "use it" in a partial way via tone and background affect with which she communicates. "Holding hate" means being alive and forceful in a way that enacts one's latent hate, rather than interprets (personal communication).

I believe that my acting out this preconceived mother ideal was devoid of depth, allowing me to dissociate my rage, hate, and aggression. This "therapeutic stance"— this idealized maternal ideal—was failing. I was not connecting with my own authentic hate or anger—or with the part of Abby that was the object of it. I would gloss over and minimize Abby's panic and hostility, much in the same way I would ignore my family's aggression. I was embodying an idealized and dissociated version of *myself-as-mother*—impenetrable and unreal.

My maternity leave

To ease my guilt and discomfort regarding leaving Abby, I suggested she see her group therapist for individual treatment during my leave. In retrospect, this was an attempt to "manage" the relationship, as a substitute for participating in it. My managerial efforts, trying to restabilize the relationship and find a "solution," only escalated the enactment (Bromberg, 2006). This was the group therapist that Abby greatly admired (she often spoke of her muscular, fit body and her "professional" therapeutic stance). Abby agreed, and worked individually with this therapist during my 16-week leave.

In retrospect, my suggestion of a covering therapist seems more like an expression of my hostility, although at the time I felt I was actually "helping" Abby. Like in my dream, I wanted Abby to "leave me alone!" and have this other therapist deal with her— a dissociated expression of the anger that I would have to face if that part of Abby was truly in the room with me. Why hadn't I expected Abby to wait for me, both of us capable of managing her intense feelings of abandonment? Was the idea of my new baby, my actual baby, causing me to question my desire to continue working with her? Was Ozzy in fact Abby, her infant self that I would care for and nurture? Was there actually room inside me to hold, love, and feed them both? Did I *want* to?

My return

Upon my return from maternity leave, Abby seemed still in a state of utter despair. Her first session back in my office, Abby stated that she didn't want to work with me any longer. She cried, mournfully, stating that she felt more comfortable with the other therapist, who maintained a more professional distance and sense of anonymity. She wanted to continue working with her. Abby ran from my office, mid-session, crying. Her exit felt like someone was breaking up with me, and like I had been punched in the stomach.

I called her several times and wrote her a detailed letter, but I never saw or spoke with Abby again. I can now begin to understand her intense feelings triggered by my transformation into a mother. This was not what she had signed up for—I was the "baby" who couldn't help her when she started seeing me. Now I was the mother who wouldn't see her—I had left the room, emotionally and literally. My maternity leave, and Abby's grief and abandonment she must have experienced during this period, was simply too painful for her to bear reconnection.

Inherent in any maternity leave is loss, a destabilizing time for both patient and therapist. Abby was experiencing "affective overload" from a variety of sources converging simultaneously—one of which was the abandonment she felt regarding my maternity leave, and another being the non-negotiable changes in my identity and role. I had rapidly changed, physically and otherwise, right in front of Abby's eyes. I was different, older, motherly, craving maternity. My maternal ideal, this all-generous, loving, accepting *terra mater*, was clashing with Abby's "safe" and familiar internalized idealized mother: one who was cold, distanced, unsupportive and unavailable.

In the end, Abby felt rejected by my all-accepting, faux-empathically attuned maternal ideal. This maternal idealization had blinded me to the power of her rage, fear, and hate—and to my own. Leonard Friedman writes (1986): If a patient is mean, envious, degrading, competitive, angry, or seductive, the analyst must feel the act as mean envious, competing, degrading, etc. in order to feel it as such. In Hate and the Countertransference, Winnicott (1949, p. 72) writes

> The analyst is under greater strain to keep his hate latent, and he can only do this by being thoroughly aware of it. . . . In . . . certain analyses the analyst's hate is actually sought by the patient, and what is then needed is hate that is

objective. If the patient seeks objective or justified hate he must be able to reach it, else he cannot feel he can reach objective love.

My inability to feel and express my own anger, and respond honestly to hers, left Abby on her own, burdened by intense need and confusion.

Having a baby is a tumultuous time. A woman's life is turned upside down in every way. Becoming a mother is overwhelming—her previous identity is shed and a new one emerges. This new, unknown self can be a confounding mystery. Idealized images of the mother we want to be or the mother we think we **should** be flood our minds and inundate our consciousness. Repairing the childhood we wish we had and becoming the mother of our dreams is a seductive and powerful urge. But an idealized, unreal, sense of ourselves will only be destructive, and attempts to fulfill a maternal ideal will reveal its futility. The greatest gift a mother can give to her child is for her to be herself, by simply allowing her child to get to know her and to be seen "without make-up" (Winnicott, 1993). This honest and simple state proves to be a difficult challenge. When the mother is also the therapist, the challenge of being authentic—"and not made-up"—can be more difficult than she ever dreamed.

References

Ammaniti, Massimo, & Trentini, Cristina (2009). How New Knowledge About Parenting Reveals the Neurobiological Implications of Intersubjectivity: A Conceptual Synthesis of Recent Research. *Psychoanalytic Dialogues, 19*: 537–555.

Balint, Enid (1973). Technical Problems Found in the Analysis of Women by a Woman Analyst: A Contribution to the Question "What Does a Woman Want?" *International Journal of Psycho-Analysis, 54*: 195–201.

Benedek, Therese (1970). The Family as a Psychological Field. In E.J. Anthony & T. Benedek (Eds.), *Parenthood* (pp. 109–136). Boston, MA: Little, Brown.

Benedek, Therese (1976). On the Psychobiology of Gender Identity. *The Annual of Psychoanalysis, 4*: 117–162.

Benjamin, Jessica (2007). A Review of Awakening the Dreamer: Clinical Journeys by Philip M. Bromberg. *Contemporary Psychoanalysis, 43*: 666–680.

Bibring, Grete L., Dwyer, Thomas F., Huntington, Dorothy S., & Valenstein, Arthur F. (1961). A Study of the Psychological Processes in Pregnancy and of the Earliest Mother-Child Relationship—II. Methodological Considerations. *Psychoanalytic Study of the Child, 16*: 25–72.

Bromberg, Philip (2006). *Awakening the Dreamer.* Mahwah, NJ: The Analytic Press.

Fenster, Sheri, Phillips, Suzanne B., & Rapoport, Estelle R.G. (1986). *The Therapist's Pregnancy. Intrusion in the Analytic Space.* Hillsdale, NJ: The Analytic Press.

Friedman, Lawrence (1986). Kohut's Testament. *Psychoanalytic Inquiry, 6*: 321–347.

Newirth, Joseph (2009). Violence and Aggression in the Consulting Room. *Psychoanalytic Perspectives, 6*: 1–21.

Pines, Dinora (1980). Skin Communication: Early Skin Disorders and their Effect on Transference and Countertransference. *International Journal of Psycho-Analysis, 61*: 315–323.

Pines, Dinora (1982). The Relevance of Early Psychic Development to Pregnancy and Abortion. *International Journal of Psycho-Analysis, 63*: 311–319.

Sandler, Joseph (2003). On Attachment to Internal Objects. *Psychoanalytic Inquiry*, *23*: 12–26.

Sands, Susan (2003). The Subjugation of the Body in Eating Disorders: A Particularly Female Solution. *Psychoanalytic Psychology*, *20*: 103–116.

Slade, Arietta (2000). The Development and Organization of Attachment: Implications for Psychoanalysis. *Journal of the American Psychoanalytic Association*, *48*: 1147–1174.

Slochower, Joyce (2013). Psychoanalytic Mommies and Psychoanalytic Babies: A Long View. *Contemporary Psychoanalysis*, *49*: 606–628.

Slochower, Joyce (2014). *Holding and Psychoanalysis*. New York, NY: Routledge.

Winnicott, Donald W. (1949). Hate and the counter-transference. *International Journal of Psycho-Analysis*, *30*: 69–74.

Winnicott, Donald W. (1960). The Theory of the Parent-Infant Relationship. *International Journal of Psycho-Analysis*, *41*: 585–595.

Winnicott, Donald W. (1993). *Talking to Parents*. Reading, MA: Addison-Wesley.

11

GET A GRIP

How a psychotherapist's postpartum
depression disrupted the illusion of the
idealized mother and changed forever what
it means to "hold"

Kristin A. Reale

As all crises are, being struck by postpartum depression was an incredible life-changing experience. It was a turning point not only in my personal life, but also professionally as a clinician. The Greek root of the word crisis means "to sift." And sifting I have done. To come eye to eye with your own insanity is both completely terrifying and a true gift as a clinician. What we do not yet know about ourselves, what we have not yet experienced and processed in our own psychology, is where our biggest clinical blocks lie. These are the possible pitfalls of being in clinical practice and mistakenly feeling settled in yourself. I feel honored and humbled—and no small measure of trepidation—to share my experience. But I truly believe it is vitally important as clinicians to honor our experience as vulnerable and visceral as it can be. We owe it to ourselves, our patients, our profession to stay authentic and low to the ground, avoiding the hazards of grandiosity as we practice. We can all drift into feeling like we are protected from things our patients experience: confusing painful relationships, anger and rage, the difficulties of parenting, divorce, violent acts, trauma, and mental illness. We have an illusion that we are somehow much more prepared for life's difficulties, or will somehow be able to take a pass and avoid them; that because we have "done our work" and may intellectually and emotionally understand more about the mental sphere than a non-clinician, that we then are more in control of our lives, our psyches. We, of course, *are not aware* when we are in this protected *illusion*, and so whenever we sense that we have entered an illusion, what a useful time to stop and look inward!

A few facts . . postpartum mood disorders will affect 25 percent of new mothers. That is one in four (Stone, 2014). It is thought that women will get "depressed" within the first few weeks after giving birth, but the *truth* is a woman can be affected by postpartum mood disorders for the entire first year after giving birth, possibly 2 years. Postpartum mood disorders go quite far beyond postpartum depression.

In fact, most women do not feel depressed, but instead feel overwhelming anxiety, panic, agoraphobic and obsessive compulsive symptoms, and psychosis. They may look to be over achieving at motherhood—not lying in bed. They may be so anxious about motherhood and *relating* to the infant and the world that they present as perfectionistic, not removed. They may be overcompensating with control, not avoiding responsibility. This is not to say that there are not many women that experience crippling depressive symptoms, including a lack of desire to attach and care for their infants (Stone, 2014).

Of approximately 4.3 million live births, *about 1.3 million women will suffer from postpartum depression and postpartum mood disorders every year*. What do these numbers mean? Let me put some perspective on those statistics: each year roughly 300,000 women suffer a stroke, 800,000 are diagnosed with diabetes, 230,000 women are diagnosed with breast cancer; 1.3 *million* women suffered postpartum mood disorders. In fact, more women will suffer from postpartum depression and related mood disorders this year than the number of new cases for both men and women of tuberculosis, leukemia, multiple sclerosis, Parkinson's disease and epilepsy—*combined* (Stone, 2014). Yet, there is an overwhelming shroud of shame that still blankets women in society about seeking help, being wholly honest, and talking through their painful experience postpartum.

I have to think that this secrecy is due in large part to the well-worn idealization of the good mother. Good mothers *do not* lose their mind. And to talk of a therapist having postpartum depression? This feels *even more* secret. Good therapists *do not* lose their mind. It feels sinful to talk about. This is due of course, I believe, to the link between the idealization of good mothers and the good therapist. There is an overwhelming expectation of selflessness from a mother—and a "good therapist"— and not much room for the acceptance of the full force of one's own complicated emotional response. How do we then come to understand the real experience of motherhood when we look to the affective responses provoked in us in the face of overwhelming demands? How do we reconcile the idealization of being selfless with the reality of one's own subjective experience of holding?

There are lot of discussions, papers, and supervision around the *pregnant* therapist, the *unseen* baby in the room, the altered relationship between patient and therapist due to the added fantasized member in the mix. But what about *after* the baby arrives and the months and couple years after? How does motherhood change the psychotherapist and her feelings of being a therapist? What is she experiencing behind the curtain? How has her own tangible experience of motherhood transformed her ideas of what it means *to mother*, and *be a mother*, and *to hold*? As I address these questions I hope to further our thoughts about the medical and psychological epidemic that is postpartum depression. I will explore these issues using my own postpartum experience in conjunction with a long-term clinical case of mine, including Winnicott's reflections in his seminal paper "Hate in the Counter-transference" (Winnicott, 1958). In so doing, I want to challenge the ideas of the idealized mother, and in turn, the idealized image of the good therapist.

Review of the literature

Before relating my own experience I want to briefly explore the relevant literature. First, there has been a vast amount of psychiatric/medical research on postpartum depression focusing on the biological/hormonal factors for women. However, surprisingly, it has come to my knowledge through my own research that there has been astonishingly little published psychoanalytically about postpartum depression and the root causes. Furthermore, I have found *nothing* published on the intersection between the development of PTSD and postpartum depression after a woman experiences a difficult and traumatic birth experience. After hearing countless harrowing birth stories personally and professionally, I find this just as surprising. If upwards of one in four women experience postpartum depression, how can it be that a minuscule amount of literature exists investigating the psychoanalytic underpinnings of postpartum depression? As a woman and as a clinician, I find this very concerning. I can only imagine the neglect of the subject matter is due to an unconscious patriarchal need to repress the sometimes dark experience of the new mother in order to preserve the historically idealized mother for deep-seated cultural and psychodynamic reasons.

We know that the image of the idealized mother has an entrenched colluded role in our shared historical reality (Winnicott, 1958; Dally, 1983), and this idealization unfortunately has not served women well with regard to their adaptation and emotional needs postpartum. As reviewed by Nadelson (1984), Dally (1983) has written an excellent piece on the established historical forces regarding the creation of the idealized mother. Dally focuses on a very important turning point in the conception of the mother—the post-World War II shift—which she attributes to the impact of John Bowlby's work on attachment and bonding. She states that Bowlby's work resulted in an idealization or over-idealization of motherhood and influenced a movement toward the intense sole dyadic relationship of mother and baby. Nadelson (1984) notes that Dally emphasizes that the majority of women began to raise their children without the help and engagement of fathers, family, or community for the first time in history (Dally, 1983). Dally observes that the result has not only confined women to their homes and increased their feelings of guilt but has also not raised a cohort of healthy individuals.

Following Dally's premise based on her historical research of the idealized mother, it seems that she is one that is isolated and pressured to be perfect: two major factors in the risk of postpartum depression (Blum, 2007).

Furthering this view and pointing to more current literature, Blum (2007) comments that women feel incredibly isolated due to the pressure coming from years of infant-focused research that the infant and growing child's mental health rests squarely on the idealized mother's shoulders. The need for women to perform as the idealized mother has minimized the role of the father, as well as the need for extended family, social community, and cultural institutions which also play a huge and dynamic role in a child's development. To feel this immense pressure to be the "*everything*" to and for their children can trigger women to become depressed, especially those who were already at risk (Placksin, 2000).

The withstanding unaltered popular belief of the mother ideal has left very little room for women to truly experience their true selves as "good enough" mothers (Winnicott, 1965). It has induced more guilt and repressed anger, and has created a disapproving environment, both societally and within families, making it very difficult for women to seek and receive help (Placksin, 2000). Women may find themselves very much in physical need, having endured a long labor birthing a baby, or a major abdominal surgery having a C-section—both serious somatic undertakings—leaving the new mother *in need of being mothered herself.* Placksin (2000) comments on this experience of birth, in that most often mothers are told that *whatever* outcome birth took, no matter how traumatic, or seemingly violent toward their bodies (noting long excruciating labors, extensive episiotomies, or emergency C-sections) that the mother should automatically be pleased that the baby was "healthy" and "we needed to do what was needed to be done." This, unfortunately, as noted by Placksin (2000) and others in postpartum literature, leaves zero room for the mother's experiences and negates the importance of her birth story. Here, within the mother's *very first* experiences of *becoming a mother*, we experience the first glimpse of the need to idealize motherhood with the narrative being "selfless."

It has been widely accepted and disseminated in many psychiatric and medical circles that the majority of PPD is caused by the major hormonal shifts that occur during pregnancy and especially with birth. And as the image of the idealized mother persists, I have found, after reviewing the current literature, that the traumatic intergenerational histories of motherhood have been neglected in favor of the more culturally palatable biological side of motherhood. Focusing on the biological foundations of mental illness seems to be an enduring and appealing place for the American culture when considering mental illness, regrettably overlooking the deep and complex psychological keystones. But while a portion of this biological research may be applicable, Blum (2007) calls for the need to focus more psychodynamically, stating that

> numerous studies have examined the potential roles of estrogen, progesterone, testosterone, prolactin, oxytocin, cortisol, biogenic amines, and other physiological agents in relation to postpartum depression and despite extensive investigations, there has been no major study demonstrating a direct association between these [hormonal] changes and subsequent major depression.
>
> *(2007, p. 50)*

Interestingly Blum (2007) goes on to state that studies of the presence of neurotransmitter systems and neuro-regulators have not been able to distinguish women with postpartum depression from those without postpartum depression (Llewellyn *et al.*, 1997). After further investigation it seems that the strongest evidence of a biological cause of postpartum depression is what the literature refers to as "mood reactivity," meaning that women who have had premenstrual dysphoric disorder (PMDD) may be predisposed to postpartum depression (Bloch *et al.*, 2005). However, this view sees women in a biological vacuum, and begs the question as to what other psychoanalytic forces could also exist in conjunction with PMDD.

While we know that there are certain external and psychosocial factors that have been concretely stated that predispose a woman to be at risk of PPD including: prior depression, prior postpartum depression, an unwanted pregnancy, depression or anxiety during pregnancy, low levels of social support (especially in the marriage), lack of sleep, and the experience of stressful life events during pregnancy or the early postpartum period (Robertson *et al.*, 2004), these factors have unfortunately not been researched through the lens of *maternal psychology*. Noting that there has been an incidence of *adoptive* mothers who have also suffered from postpartum depression—as well as documented cases of fathers—we must call into question the focus of PPD having been framed as a mostly biological or only psychosocial causation (Blum, 2007).

Furthermore, while a great amount of research has been done on the psychological needs and ideal mental outcomes of the *baby* (Bowlby, 1978; Beebe *et al.*; Beebe & Lachmann, 2002; Schore, 2000, 2010), very little attention has been focused on the new mother's intricate maternal *psychological* needs while in the face of this incredible physical and emotional demand of the infant. Through the well-branded notion of the idealized mother, and arguably even through the lens of the much lowered bar of the "good enough mother," it has been assumed that women can "naturally" and "instinctually" fulfill the immense needs of an infant 24 hours, 7 days a week—as if the new mother has been in some kind of training for this new role for years. In reality, the new mother has had zero training, except perhaps how *she was taken care of as an infant herself.* The literature of Schore *et al.* only takes into consideration the absolute needs of the baby while neglecting the immense demand these research findings put on mothers.

Thankfully, although on a minimal basis, there does exist some psychodynamically driven postpartum literature such as Blum (2007). He investigates a far more psychoanalytically minded view of postpartum depression and calls for the biological framework to be challenged. Blum (2007) notes that there is a kind of "trifecta" psycho-dynamically that leads to postpartum depression. This causal "trifecta" includes women who have difficulties in expressing their own anger, unmet dependency wishes and needs, and a very conflictual relationship with their own mother (Blum, 2007). The dependency conflicts typically take on a unique counter-dependent form: over-compensatory ways of being may have been adaptive for the mother's life and survival *pre-baby*, but she finds herself *un*defended against and *exposed* to her overwhelming *own* needs to be taken care of in the face of a newborn. Interestingly, counter-dependence is noted to be a common trait found in health and *mental health professionals* who are consciously and subconsciously accustomed to taking care of others and sidelining their own needs (Blum, 2007). This brings me to my own story and how I am a wonderful example of the counter-dependent new mother who suffered in the midst of the misunderstood postpartum experience, crumbling under the pressure of the idealized mother and the pressure to perfectly hold.

The pregnancy: Planning and preparation

It was the summer of 2009. It had been raining in Brooklyn, New York, for a record number of days, 18 to be exact. I loved it—I was entering my 10th month of pregnancy and didn't feel like being out and about in the world—especially if it was a hot summer day. The cool weather and rain felt just right for my mood and need to hibernate. My swollen ankles looked as wide as the feet of an elephant, my belly like a bursting balloon, and my interest in the world minimal. I was turning very inward, preparing to give birth. As Winnicott (1989) would say, the maternal preoccupation was at a fever pitch intensifying. I had taken maternity leave from my thriving private practice where I treat adults, couples and children, and also my teaching post, two weeks prior. I had decided to exit a bit earlier than expected. I was finding it hard to concentrate and allow myself to be emotionally affected by my patients, let alone trek on the subway and around New York City each day. I had done my best to take care of everyone's needs to prepare for my planned four-month leave and I was ... done. I was looking forward to beaching myself on my couch, shopping for my last nesting materials online, and waiting; waiting for the signs of labor and the beginning of what I did not realize was the shocking journey into birth and motherhood. I thought I was prepared.

I had planned to give birth at home in my Brooklyn apartment: birth pool, shower curtain on the bed, husband, doula and midwife in place. I felt ready. I was excited to take on this experience. I was more curious than scared and trusted the support I had in place. As I reflect, I realize how naively prepared I felt for the emotional experience of new motherhood and my launch into being a working mother. Not only had I always wanted children, and felt "naturally maternal," I had spent my entire career thus far dedicated to understanding attachment, parenting and mothering, primal needs, and human development. I was teaching in the Master's Social Work program at New York University and loved talking and teaching about Winnicott, Bowlby, Fonagy, holding and containing. I *understood* so much and felt a mirage of control over my future experience as a mother.

No matter how much one tells you about the pain in childbirth, or what it is "like," or that "you just don't know until you go through it," a first-time pregnant woman cannot truly *hear* them. I thought I had an idea, true to my desire to always be one step ahead, an over-compensator, wanting to feel a bit in control. It was uncomfortable for me to imagine that there was no way of knowing unless I went through it. I had already been through so much. You mean I can't just *learn about it, prepare for it* and *know*? This thought made me feel insecure, and so I think pushed away my fear of the unknown, and fear of being out of control. I had read as much as I could about natural childbirth, the process of labor, and had attended a thorough 6-week home birth "class," which had also turned into a wonderful support group of smart and enlightened women outside of class. I was as *intellectually* prepared as possible.

Before going to bed most nights, I would read a few birth stories from a book written by midwives on a famous Virginia commune, "The Farm," and marvel at the knowledge I was obtaining. Reading inspirational story upon story, I was captivated by the women's reports of learning to trust their own bodies, believe in the power and process of labor, and how they let themselves *experience* birth without technological intervention. The mind–body connection was paramount in the births on "the farm" and I related to this notion wholly, and so desired to be not numb but in the physical experience of birth. It was enlightening to learn about the process of un-medicalized birth: every woman in my family had an epidural and hospital birth, one of which I was present at, so there were no natural birth stories passed down in my family. The hospital birth I attended seemed traumatic: too much of epidurals, suction, and forceps used; little to no attunement to the mother. No one had given birth and *felt* it. I was learning more *by reading* what women actually go through if they are given the opportunity and time to give birth. While helpful, I felt a sadness that a book of strangers felt closer to what I was about to go through than people I actually knew and loved. I was entering uncharted territory. These stories from midwives and women would prove crucial for me in finding comfort while in the midst of my own labor.

Labor: Sinking into hell

My body was preparing for about ten days before I went into actual labor; each night I would think "this *has* to be it." Although, it turns out, my body was just *"practicing"* as they say. My actual labor would not start until the eve of my due date. And when it started, it was like an "ooohhh, *this* is it." My contractions started painful and steady, and then ramped up to a full-force roar . . . and then stayed there, and *stayed*, and *stayed* for hours on end. I did not experience a plateau per se; what I experienced was a climb of the steepest cliff. About 17 hours in, after a grueling day of swaying, moaning, and intensely vocalizing my labor, I began to feel very frightened. The pain was only amplifying and I knew that I was not in transition yet, which was, as I had heard and read, the holy grail of labor where you were sure to feel that you were going to die, be split in two, break apart and not make it. I was completely exhausted hanging in the arms of my husband and doula. I was beginning to feel trapped, and so very alone. I couldn't imagine at the time surviving and going deeper into labor. My midwife had been staying in close contact with my doula by phone and was in the area but not yet at my home. This separation from her proved to be something I would process in the months and years after.

At some point my mind shifted from feeling like I was hanging off the side of a cliff from my fingertips, and instead, to a vision of barely standing in a rough rocky ocean, my feet sinking in the soupy sand, knees buckling, body swaying and being slammed by waves of contractions. Each time I would think I had my feet planted again to prepare for the next wave, *BAM!* I would be pushed over again by a mountainous wave. My breath would be sucked from me as I felt like my head was being pushed underwater. Soon a very strange, quiet, calm came into my body, and my conscious experience. At this point, I laid my head down on the side of the soft birth pool, which I had been wading in for a few hours now, finding zero relief in the water. The calm provided a break from my relentless contractions, but I knew that this was the not a *comforting* calm, but instead the calm before a major, major storm of hurricane-like power. It was at this moment, I went very far—too far—within myself. Like *sub-level* far. One may relate it to "sleeping" during labor, but it felt much more dissociative than sleep. Sleep sounds too pleasant, too restful for what this was. I would "come to" every minute or so and feel panicked that I WAS STILL THERE, *STUCK*. I knew I was losing my grip. After several bouts of my waking panic, I felt some surge of energy coming back. And *all at once*, I began to feel like I was tumbling down a mountainside again. At that point I began to throw up, my water broke, and I became even more of a naked primal animal. Although I may have been still, internally I felt as though I was thrashing about. I felt like I was going to DIE, right there in my living room, in a pool of my own blood.

About 22 hours into my labor, I returned to a more present consciousness, and felt completely taken over again by the force. I thought of three or four different stories I had read at that point from the farm commune—"throwing up is a good sign." Check. "It is completely normal to feel like you are going to die." Check. "This all means you are getting close to the end." *Really?* Okay. I knew now, on a very deep vulnerable level, I needed my midwife HERE NOW. She arrived moments later, and when she did I felt an *unimaginable* relief. I felt a soothing presence, a complete reassurance, a pure safety: my knowing she was there was like my *own* baby self being scooped up and "held." What I know now, is that this was the very closest—and only thing—I had ever felt to unbreakable love.

About 3 *hours* later, I pushed my baby out and felt more relief than I ever thought possible. In that moment of relief—as many women experience—I went from an unbelievable state of suffering, primal screaming, and need, to . . . some version of myself again. It was like breaking through some thick opening back into fresh air, like pushing up from the ocean floor. I literally said hello again to everyone present in the room: like I had been away on some nightmare trip and just returned. They all marveled and giggled at this. It was amazing how all at once I was "back." I felt like introducing myself again as the "new me." My baby was of course perfect in every way, and snuggled into my arms as I laid in the birth pool for a time afterward.

The dark dawn

In the weeks after my baby was born, I was invaded with such waves of anxiety that I had never experienced before. I felt de-realized and had an overpowering fear of losing control. I was terrified that my mind and body were separating, splitting. I had a very difficult time feeling who I was any longer. I would say, "It's like I can't find myself!" I felt my identity was very hard to access, knowing that some or all of me was absolutely changed by giving birth and that a new identity hadn't formed yet. I felt in no (wo)man's land. And my husband, scared and confused, would just stare back at me. My autobiographical history felt very fuzzy, distant, unreal to me.

Memory felt fleeting, and the fear of not holding on to memory itself was tortur-
ous. I felt painfully in the present, almost no concept or trust in time: this was
absolute undiluted anxiety. I had experienced panic in the past and also a dysthymic
depression in my late teens into my early twenties, but never this. I had, all at once,
an unfortunate but better view into what some of my patients had described feeling. For the first time in my life, I felt truly "mentally ill," and I was so terrified
I would never find my way back.

One of the most difficult symptoms I experienced was of obsessive thoughts of
being harmed. These would desperately frighten and confuse me. I began fearing
jumping out the window, fearing objects in my kitchen or on the street . . . knives,
forks, broken glass. I felt unprotected and exposed to the world's ways. Traumatic
news stories affected me like never before. I felt an awful merger with the possibility of tragedy, as if I finally understood how scary life could be. Where I had once
been—for the most part—defended against life's sometimes tragic ways, I was now
defenseless at its doorstep. I *begged* to go back to my old way of feeling. I began to
really understand why our defenses are there and how they function. For the first
time in my life, I felt scared of existing. Totally unintegrated. I was *falling, unheld.*

Soon thereafter I sought treatment knowing this was beyond "the baby blues"
and that I was not feeling more stable on my own. Through remarkable psychiatric
and psychotherapeutic support, in conjunction with a new mothers' group, I found
stability and could breathe into new motherhood. It took weeks to feel better and
those days and nights were some of the longest of my life.

Returning to practice and my Self

I returned to my practice in the early fall, about 4 months after having parted from
patients for the time being. I did not know what to expect, from me or from them.
I felt wobbly on my feet, emotional and unsure about leaving my 3-month-old
while I went to work to attune to others. While I was feeling much more stable
than in the weeks prior, I was overcome by how I used to think how simple this
would all be: women who work and who are mothers are *all over* New York City.
My neighborhood was *teeming* with new moms, many of whom returned to work
at three months postpartum. How do they do this? Before I had given birth I had
looked at returning to my practice as a concrete necessity, a simple equation: drop
the baby off at that sweet organic daycare. Separate. Go to work. Be the responsible
good therapist. Then return home to be mama through the night. I did not realize that *not only* would the separation from my baby feel "off" but shifting into my
professional identity of "therapist" would also feel off: neither identity confident.
What did it mean to me now to "hold" and "contain" my patients? What would it
feel like for my patients to need to look at me as someone *together* when I now felt
like I was *just forming*?

My patients were excited to know I was returning, to schedule their hour and
settle back into treatment. As I would commute on the train those first weeks,
I would think, "Okay, I have walked into the face of death and survived, I have lost

my mind, AND I have come back to the living to tell the tale." I was not the same person, and I questioned if I could be the same therapist anymore. I was a bit afraid of what I would find.

I had begun seeing a patient named Sarah about 2 years before going on maternity leave. In her late 30s, married and a mother of two young girls, she felt a constant nagging depression and suffocating emptiness, lack of meaning and identity. She was an accountant by trade, working part-time at a very successful firm, making a very lucrative salary. But she was very unhappy and I wasn't sure she had the capacity to feel any pleasure. She felt she had never achieved any sense of adulthood or her own identity, and her life felt like a rehearsal. Sarah came from a very successful academic family, the youngest herself of two children. Beyond her defensiveness of her parents "doing their best," I sensed she had lived her childhood never being soothed, truly related to, or understood. Her older sister was a recovering heroin addict, who I gathered had soothed her own hopelessness and desperate psychological pain in her life with her drug of choice: an opiate closest to mother love.

Filled with nothing but envy for others' lives and others' sense of purpose and meaning, Sarah would describe the complete lack of pleasure she felt in friendships, sexuality, and in her own mothering; *she was evacuated*. Coming from two successful parents who were also narcissistic, Sarah herself had a very narcissistic personality, one that had taken me months to grasp. While committed to coming to treatment each week, she would often show up with "nothing to talk about," give me a sly look, and joke about how she wanted me to tell her what to "do," to "fix" her. There was an intense pressure I felt from her. I found myself often frustrated with her lack of ability to think, to symbolize, or "use" our work. Although she presented with little material, she was needy of me, asking me if I could just "live her life for her." I would vacillate, sometimes enjoying my work with her and other times feeling very overwhelmed by her outright and unconscious parasitic dependence on me, sucking me dry. It was clear she was envious of my own "good" that I held inside; there was a sense she wanted to destroy me. This, to no surprise, was very difficult and virtually impossible to broach and process with her clinically.

Through the months of treatment and with the help of my supervision group, I was beginning to see and understand her pathology: how much she remained in the paranoid schizoid position, concrete and unsymbolized in her thinking; how much containment she needed and how slow and painstaking our work needed to be to have her form her *own* thoughts and feelings and how devoid she was of an internal world. Unable to understand her own anxiety or feelings, she had to remain locked in a symbiotic state, always reaching for merger. I was only *vaguely* aware of how incredibly burdensome it must have been for me all this time to stay present with her overwhelming dependence. I think I must have "disappeared" during some previous sessions with her and presented myself as the "good helpful therapist," not accessing my anger and my annoyance with her provocative, challenging, dependent ways.

I felt concerned about how Sarah had coped during the months of my leave. A year earlier, she had been the first patient I told I was pregnant, not necessarily all by choice. And not surprisingly, she had a very visceral reaction to my news. I was only about 6 weeks pregnant at the time, thrilled to have learned I was going to have a baby, and already surging with hormones and feeling "fuller." I had not planned on telling my clients until at least twelve weeks into my pregnancy, sure of its viability. But Sarah had sat down for her weekly session, just a few days after my learning my own big news, and she began to cry, to sob. She said she was "all of sudden" finding herself feeling very upset and worried that I was going to have a baby. She was very concerned about me leaving and having my own family. What if I decided to not come back? What if my family and I decided to move? What would she do without me? I was literally shocked that THIS could be—and was probably going to be—my first conversation with a patient about my pregnancy?

I felt unprepared. It wasn't supposed to go like this. I felt exposed. How should I respond? Should I tell her? How could I just "explore" what the idea of me having a baby meant to her? I needed to acknowledge the truth she felt that a baby was indeed in the room. I was convinced that due to her intense need for me to be attuned to her, she was unconsciously hyper-attuned to me. She was in a symbiotic relationship with me. I am still not certain what she "picked up" on other than a possible unconscious connection to my own thoughts of being pregnant, but I decided to validate her reality in that same session and share this very personal news with her. I was pleased that I chose this route, and at the time, she appreciated my honesty with her. I think she was proud of herself. It was as if she had actually taken my mind, devoured me, and stolen my news. Over the next months, we grappled with the meaning of it all, how she was pained with the future loss of me, her fear of "floating" out there alone and her feeling that my priorities would change.

I was uncertain about how I felt returning from my leave to work with her. I knew it would be intense, and I had an obscure fantasy of needing some kind of armor so that she didn't completely invade me. The morning we met, a week into my return, I was feeling calmer and what I thought was a sense of preparedness to accept her level of dependence, ready for what she was to toss onto my lap. Looking back, as with my newborn, I think I was more intellectually than emotionally prepared for the sheer intensity it would bring. As I sat with her those first moments, I was immediately struck by how much hostility she had toward me. All in one instance it felt that she wanted to take my mind from me once again. I listened, I joined, I quietly nodded, I responded, and I tried my best to empathize with her experience. But I felt trapped and that nothing I said or did made space for us to relate. There was no transitional space.

All at once, I felt the waves of anxiety. The fear came charging into me. I was terrified I was going to jump out the window. *Literally.* I did not *want to* jump out the window, but I wasn't completely certain my body wouldn't hurl *itself* out the window without my choosing. I was becoming unintegrated. This feeling, difficult to articulate, was absolutely tormenting. I was depersonalizing, dissociating. There I sat *on the 26th floor* of a skyscraper, a foot from an open window on a gorgeous crisp fall day, feeling this paralyzing separation from myself. I looked down at my hands and forced them to cling to the leather arms of my chair. "Hold on, Kristin, you have to *get a grip*." I was very aware all at once that Sarah's spilling of her mind needed desperate containment. I needed to begin to give *my self* space to think, to symbolize for her, for us, her anger, my anger, my fear, her hate of me and my motherhood, my hate of her needing me so and driving me crazy. I had to conjure my own transitional space. My desire to literally escape, jump out the window, was a concrete manifestation, like those first weeks with my newborn, who also, like Sarah, couldn't think yet, couldn't symbolize. Sarah was just parts coming at me, needing integration. Knowing that I could indeed "do" something with this all in *my* mind partially soothed my anxiety and the need to flee. As difficult as it was, inch by inch, I pulled my mind away from the window, away from escape, back into time, to relating. Over the course of the next few months in my practice, I would experience a similar reaction of wanting to jump out the window while sitting with several of my more disturbed patients. Finding my grip became a new familiar part of my practice.

Discussion

My journey into pregnancy and motherhood was life-changing both personally and professionally beginning with the labor and delivery. I had not realized, for instance, how tied I was to my midwife. While my husband and doula were "great" and doing everything they could to support me, what I did not realize was how psychologically connected I felt to my midwife as my protector, my eye-to-eye support, my mother-substitute, and how much I needed her there with me as my labor experience intensified. My own attachment system was being deeply triggered. My complicated psychological history and current needs were calling out: the matrix of a difficult maternal relationship with my own mother, a complicated and trauma-filled individuation process earlier in my life, and a need to develop an ever more varied emotional world that made space for ambivalence, anger, and need came together to form my very own postpartum depression. What I now understand was that my craving for an attuned mother my entire life would come to a head during labor and the first months of motherhood, exposing me to the deep fissures that had occurred as a result of being psychologically dropped *again and again* as a baby and child. I was *never* quite "held" due to my own mother's inter-generational trauma and those fractures were to be revisited again and again in the most painful and unexpected ways. No matter how much "work" I had done on myself psychologically in the decade and a half prior, I now believe that the surge into new motherhood provoked my concealed wounds like nothing before could reach. My being the independent, "parentified," well-trained therapist I was, I was unaware of some of the hidden needs that lurked within me until they were hem-orrhaging. Feeling frightened without that moment-to-moment attuned care from my midwife, I believe, was the first "break" in my mind in which I experienced a lost, un-held, devastating aloneness that mimicked trauma from my childhood. I was not conscious that I would need her to such a degree to protect me from sinking into my abandoned dark well.

My introduction to motherhood was not soft or sweet, or "natural feeling." There was nothing *touching* about the physical process of becoming a mother. It was violent, out of control, agonizing, exhausting, so raw, unending. This, too, I later learned, is how I would also describe breastfeeding and the emotions of new motherhood the first months after birth. Breastfeeding was unbelievably painful and unending. My baby would sometimes feed non-stop for hours in what most new mothers learn to be "cluster feeding." The ways in which my baby would attach to the breast I never expected: his tiny mouth was so strong, the suction so deep, there was no question he was wired for survival. I was completely exhausted, yet every 3–4 hours I was on duty feeding him around the clock, in pain or not. As much as I would describe it, I think my husband had such a hard time imagining that the idealized notion of breastfeeding wasn't as it seemed—that I must be exaggerating. To get my point across, I one day joked that he should imagine that breastfeeding could be likened to a rabid squirrel grabbing hold of his testicles with his mouth every couple hours—and chewing on them. He never doubted the pain I was describing again! Oh how I was so surprised by the demolished image of idealized notion of breastfeeding, just one part of motherhood among many that I have had to re-conceptualize through my own personal experience.

I now wonder if the shroud of the idealized mother exists to shield women from the difficult truth about motherhood, similar to how epidurals anesthetize the physical and psychological pain of birth, hiding the truth of what the physical experience is actually like. So when we face labor and birthing for what it actually is and find it grueling and complex, what do we find when we face motherhood for what it is? How does it amend how we practice? How does it reshape what and how we feel for our patients? How does it alter our own elevated expectations of holding? How does this redefine our relationship to feeling "maternal"?

When my labor was finally over, immediately I needed to talk about and process that I just survived: I think I knew on some level that I was really not the same and never would be. It was a genuine experience in crossing over. I realize now that through the experience of giving birth, my old identity had been shattered. Not only had I survived giving birth, but in that, I had birthed a new self of my own. And so the intense anxiety I was feeling was partially due to my own unconscious resistance to integrate a new sense of self—a self that would need to learn about the depths of my own psychology in ways that hadn't been asked of me before. At the same time, I would need to care for a new being that I had created, and soon after, return to my practice and learn who I was now as a clinician. I felt my own pure infancy—a new identity—and, in the weeks to come, utterly vulnerable, defenseless, unsafe, unknown, and unfamiliar . . . like a newborn.

It seems that the first weeks and months of motherhood are bound up not only in the conscious experience, but mostly the unconscious. Women speak of "not being able to think," feeling some new sense of a "purpose" or "understanding of life," or having extreme difficulty in delaying their attendance to the newborn's cries, or even allowing someone else to tend their newborn. We know that this occurs in one major non-thinking physiological sense when women's breasts begin to leak milk just at *the sound* of the babies' cries. This is a somatic not-conscious response. The merger, the level of empathy, the attuned care taking, is a very unconscious process for mothers.

We do not come to motherhood already formed as mothers. We become mothers through the long winding painful experience of birthing and mothering, feeling this intense need to attune to another. We may not have known or may have been afraid of what this intense dependent relationship can conjure up in us: love, anger, feelings of intolerance, an overwhelming desire to give, or even self-protection from all the taking. I began to question and liken this process to mine as a clinician. The absolute sheer intensity of knowing another, feeling responsible to attune to their emotional state, the feeling of being out of control of one's own emotional reactions to another, this I did not know would be a part of new motherhood. And it was revealing how feeling like an exhausted new mother reminded me of times I sat with patients not knowing *how* to contain my own overwhelming affect or response to unconscious material they were presenting and provoking. *I was looking into the eyes of what it really meant to hold*. This new identity forming as "mother"— or as I would realize also as "clinician"—did not fit nicely in a box, or in a critical theory book, or on a cover story of a parenting magazine. Holding was complicated, fulfilling, thorny, wearing, dark, and deeper than I could have ever imagined. I did not know that my new identity forming *was* the process of becoming a mother, and eventually a better clinician. I did not know it would be so painful.

While I wanted *OUT*, I also knew on some level that touring this horrid place was probably the best thing I could do to improve my skills as a clinician. My sense of "holding" my patients and being a "good" therapist was deepening and changing. Tolerating these overwhelming feelings I was having and barely holding on to myself was exhausting. I questioned if, in fact, my patients had felt "held" by me. Had I somehow been able to convey to them in words at the appropriate times that I knew and understood the deepest anxiety that was being experienced, or as Winnicott would add, "waiting to be experienced" (Winnicott, 1989)? How could I have? As I held my infant, and myself, my ideas around the depths and meaning of "holding" were stretching beyond the boundaries I once safely practiced behind.

While I do not mean to minimize in *any* way the terror and absolute discomfort I felt at these times, I feel it allowed me to become better in touch with my own more negative reactions to the needs of my patients and that I may have been protecting myself from earlier in my career. The hate that I felt may have very well been unacknowledged pre-motherhood. I became more aware postpartum of the nuanced darker feelings that stirred within me when being asked to contain someone and this knowledge, thankfully, gifted me also with more awareness of when I may have dropped *them*. Pre-motherhood I did not consciously know the hate was rumbling, did not know how to acknowledge it, feel it, and work with it.

Pre-motherhood, I believe I had a more all-accepting attitude and feeling of selflessness . . . *as long as the hour ended*. But in motherhood, *the hour doesn't end*. Motherhood opened up a whole underbelly of emotion for me that I first experienced in a dissociative state: the ambivalence toward my infant, like Sarah, was too much to bear. Wanting to jump, be taken "out," to escape, held a mirror to the sheer intensity of relationships, and what is really being asked of us as clinicians to "hold."

It turns out that holding patients, similar to holding my incredibly uncomfortable and fussy 6-week-old, was *much more slippery*. The reality of motherhood—like good treatment—is emotionally messy, complicated, contradictory, and filled with love and hate. My related identities as mother and clinician are forever forming and contrasting as corresponding parts reveal themselves. Entering each clinical experience, I am always reminded to have fewer preconceived idealized notions about my relationship to holding, the idea of being the good mother, and the intricate therapeutic process. Deep in my mind, on a very visceral level, those purely incongruous notions of love and hate are always existing, woven into all good clinical work, and providing the traction for the elusive process of psychological development and growth. As clinicians, we need not be so frightened of our more subterranean parts and experiences. Instead, we should be encouraged to welcome our vulnerability to these parts, and to see them as a crucial part of our clinical map.

References

Beebe, B., Jaffe, J., Markese, S., Buck, K., Chen, H., Cohen, P., . . . Feldstein, S. (2010). The origins of 12-month attachment: A microanalysis of 4-month mother-infant interaction. *Attachment & Human Development*, *12*(1–2), 3–138.

Beebe, B., & Lachmann, F. (2002). *Infant research and adult treatment: Co-constructing interactions*. Hillsdale, NJ: Analytic Press.

Bloch, M., Rotenberg, N., Koren, D., & Klein, E. (2005). Risk factors associated with the development of postpartum mood disorders. *Journal of Affective Disorders*, *88*, 9–18.

Blum, L.D. (2007). Psychodynamics of postpartum depression. *Psychoanalytic Psychology*, *24*(1), 45–62.

Bowlby, J. (1978). Attachment theory and its therapeutic implications. In S.C. Feinstein & P.L. Giovacchini (Eds.), *Adolescent psychiatry: Developmental and clinical studies*. Chicago, IL: University of Chicago Press.

Dally, A. (1983). *Inventing motherhood: The consequences of an ideal*. New York, NY: Schocken Books.

Llewellyn, A.M., Stowe, A.N., & Nemeroff, C.B. (1997). Depression during pregnancy and the puerperium. *Journal of Clinical Psychiatry*, *58*, 26–32.

Nadelson, C.C. (1984). Review of *Inventing motherhood, the consequences of an ideal*. *Family Systems Medicine*, *2*(1), 98–100.

Placksin, S. (2000). *Mothering the new mother: Women's feelings and needs after childbirth*. New York, NY: William Morrow Paperbacks.

Robertson, E., Grace, S., Wallington, T., & Stewart, D.E. (2004). Antenatal risk factors for postpartum depression: A synthesis of recent literature. *General Hospital Psychiatry*, *26*, 289–295.

Schore A.N. (2000). Attachment and the regulation of the right brain. *Attachment & Human Development*, *2*, 23–47.

Schore, A.N. (2010). Relational trauma and the developing right brain: The neurobiology of broken attachment bonds. In T. Baradon (Ed.), *Relational trauma in infancy* (pp. 19–47). London: Routledge.

Stone, K. (2014, June). Retrieved from http://www.postpartumprogress.com

Winnicott, D.W. (1958). Hate in the counter-transference. In *Collected papers: Through paediatrics to psychoanalysis* (pp. 194–203). London: Hogarth.

Winnicott, D.W. (1965). *Maturational Processes and the Facilitating Environment: Studies in the Theory of Emotional Development.* London: Hogarth Press.

Winnicott, D.W. (1989). Psycho-analytic explorations. In C. Winnicott, R. Shepherd & M. Davis (Eds.). Cambridge, MA: Harvard University Press.

INDEX

Page numbers in bold refer to tables. Page numbers in italics refer to figures.

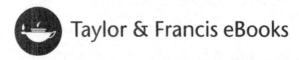

Taylor & Francis eBooks

Helping you to choose the right eBooks for your Library

Add Routledge titles to your library's digital collection today. Taylor and Francis ebooks contains over 50,000 titles in the Humanities, Social Sciences, Behavioural Sciences, Built Environment and Law.

Choose from a range of subject packages or create your own!

Benefits for you

» Free MARC records
» COUNTER-compliant usage statistics
» Flexible purchase and pricing options
» All titles DRM-free.

Benefits for your user

» Off-site, anytime access via Athens or referring URL
» Print or copy pages or chapters
» Full content search
» Bookmark, highlight and annotate text
» Access to thousands of pages of quality research at the click of a button.

REQUEST YOUR **FREE** INSTITUTIONAL TRIAL TODAY	**Free Trials Available** We offer free trials to qualifying academic, corporate and government customers.

eCollections – Choose from over 30 subject eCollections, including:

Archaeology	Language Learning
Architecture	Law
Asian Studies	Literature
Business & Management	Media & Communication
Classical Studies	Middle East Studies
Construction	Music
Creative & Media Arts	Philosophy
Criminology & Criminal Justice	Planning
Economics	Politics
Education	Psychology & Mental Health
Energy	Religion
Engineering	Security
English Language & Linguistics	Social Work
Environment & Sustainability	Sociology
Geography	Sport
Health Studies	Theatre & Performance
History	Tourism, Hospitality & Events

For more information, pricing enquiries or to order a free trial, please contact your local sales team:
www.tandfebooks.com/page/sales

 Routledge
Taylor & Francis Group

The home of
Routledge books

www.tandfebooks.com